Heaven
and the
Popular Imagination

Heaven
and the
Popular Imagination

T. M. ALLEN

☞PICKWICK *Publications* · Eugene, Oregon

HEAVEN AND THE POPULAR IMAGINATION

Copyright © 2018 T. M. Allen. All rights reserved. Except for brief quotations in critical publications or reviews, no part of this book may be reproduced in any manner without prior written permission from the publisher. Write: Permissions, Wipf and Stock Publishers, 199 W. 8th Ave., Suite 3, Eugene, OR 97401.

Pickwick Publications
An Imprint of Wipf and Stock Publishers
199 W. 8th Ave., Suite 3
Eugene, OR 97401

www.wipfandstock.com

PAPERBACK ISBN: 978-1-5326-1799-7
HARDCOVER ISBN: 978-1-4982-4315-5
EBOOK ISBN: 978-1-4982-4314-8

Cataloguing-in-Publication data:

Names: Allen, T. M., author.

Title: Heaven and the popular imagination / T. M. Allen.

Description: Eugene, OR: Pickwick Publications, 2018 | Includes bibliographical references and index.

Identifiers: ISBN 978-1-5326-1799-7 (paperback) | ISBN 978-1-4982-4315-5 (hardcover) | ISBN 978-1-4982-4314-8 (ebook)

Subjects: LCSH: Heaven—Christianity | Christianity and culture | Heaven | Death in motion pictures | Resurrection in motion pictures | Motion pictures—Religious aspects—Christianity | Future life | Eschatology | Eternity

Classification: BL540 A552 2018 (paperback) | BL540 (ebook)

Manufactured in the U.S.A.   11/09/18

For Jen
From St. Andrews
to Incline Village

Contents

Preface | ix
Acknowledgments | xi
Introduction | xiii

Part I: Theologically Engaging Popular Culture
1 Revelation, the Spirit, and Culture | 3
2 Whatever Happened to Heaven? | 28
3 What Sort of Analysis Is Most Beneficial? | 54

Part II: Imagining Identity in a Post-mortem Existence
4 Humanity's Longing for Reunion | 95
5 Will We Remember? | 123
6 Fulfillment and Bodily Continuity/Discontinuity | 156
7 Why Can't We Imagine Creation Beyond the End? | 188
   Conclusion | 200

Bibliography | 207
Index | 219

Preface

"Another book [about heaven]? Indeed, libraries exist on the subject, and yet the bigness of the subject justifies another attempt to grapple with the unknowable. As long as [humans] are aware of Beginning and End they will transcend the present."[1] In spite of Ulrich Simon's encouraging observations, the doctrine of heaven has come under considerable contestation in contemporary Christian theology, especially noticeably so within influential Protestant strands. This book argues that the theological imagining of heaven can be enriched by theological reflection on popular forms of art (with a particular, although not exclusive, focus on popular film). It shows how certain works of popular art not only keep alive dormant aspects of Christian doctrine, but also challenge contemporary assumptions regarding heaven.

Part one (chapters 1–3) lays the ground for theologically engaging popular culture. It establishes a theory of revelation that underscores the importance of the Holy Spirit's continuing action in popular culture, as well as offering a critique of particular perspectives in contemporary New Testament studies. By taking seriously the hermeneutical context for the reception of revelation throughout history, the book argues that it is of critical importance to take the wider culture seriously in theological construction.

Part two focuses on an imaginative approach to three areas of personal identity in a post-mortem existence: appearance in relation to identity-recognition in heaven (chapter 4); memory of earthly experiences (chapter 5); and bodily continuity/discontinuity and fulfillment as it pertains to imagining resurrection bodies (chapter 6). In this way, these chapters seek to offer new perspectives on, and distinctive contributions to, three areas of eschatology that have long standing trajectories within theological and philosophical studies in Western culture. Chapter 7 includes an analysis of popular films that attempt to imagine a post-apocalyptic vision of creation

---

1. Simon, *The End is Not Yet*, xiii.

after the end. The lack of contemporary films that imagine an earth-bound eschatology, it argues, is theologically significant and, indeed, a compelling reason to re-emphasize the other-worldliness of heaven.

The conclusion highlights some of the main contributions of the book; it also seeks to indicate some of the implications of this research and methodology for future studies.

Acknowledgments

The sheer expanse of literature on heaven that ornaments the Western traditions and lines bookshelves across the centuries is ever so intimidating, to say the least. The courage to take up such a topic as heaven must be inspired by a host of other fellow travellers with vision that rests on broad horizons indeed. For this, I am indebted to family, mentors, and friends without whom this project would not have been brought to fruition. To my wife and partner, Jen, you echo songs of heaven through your love, encouragement, gentleness, strength, patience, and perseverance. To you I dedicate this book. For my dad and mom, Paul and Gloria Allen, who embody the gospel of Jesus in the most profound ways, your lives point towards the reality of heaven. To my dear children Kirsten and Lucas, thank you for helping me experience the love of God every day. To David Brown, for whom I will always be thankful for giving me an opportunity to read widely, think critically, and who taught me how to turn fountains into rivers. To George Corbett, for believing in the project and seeing potential in a struggling postgraduate student. Your encouragement is marked in time and space. A big thank you to the team at Wipf and Stock, who were dedicated to moving this project forward. Thank you for giving this new author an opportunity. Of course, any remaining errors in thought or print rest with the author.

Introduction

This book suggests that the eschatological imagining of heaven can once again become enlivened by reflecting theologically on the resources provided by popular forms of art. The doctrine of heaven has come under considerable contestation in contemporary Christian theology, a tendency especially noticeable within influential Protestant strands.[2] Despite a struggle to wrestle heaven to the ground through earth-bound eschatologies that would allegedly rid the church of tradition's clutter, images for an other-worldly heaven still persist and, indeed, richly abound within contemporary culture. Popular culture, in other words, continues to furnish other-worldly narratives, and serves thereby as a reminder that "signals of transcendence" are integral to the human imagination.[3] Despite the important role that contemporary culture may have in imagining an other-worldly heaven, this has not been the subject of a full-scale theological study. This book aims, thus, to fill a major gap in the scholarship. As a study of heaven and all forms of popular culture would be too wide-ranging, my study places especial emphasis on the engagement between theology and film. Nonetheless, in the course of the book, I also make detailed reference to other genres (as, for example, in my treatment of popular music in chapter 5 and of literature in chapter 6).

By this-worldly eschatology, I refer to what has been broadly credited to Second Temple Jewish belief of a divinely provoked world-ending event, not only bringing a closure to history, but ushering in a single resurrection of the dead upon a renewed earth. According to one of the leading proponents of this type of eschatology, N. T. Wright:

---

2. See, for example, N. T. Wright's, *Surprised By Hope* (2008). Two years following Wright's publication, theologian Chris Morse of Union Theological Seminary in New York published his work contesting the relationship between heaven and life after death. See Morse, *The Difference Heaven Makes* (2010).

3. McGrath, *A Brief History of Heaven*, 111.

> In each case the referent [Resurrection] is concrete: restoration of Israel (resurrection as metaphorical, denoting socio-political events and investing them with the significance that this will be an act of new creation, of covenant restoration); [and] of human bodies (resurrection as literal, denoting actual re-embodiment).[4]

Wright has produced an extensive amount of literature to substantiate a reduced view of heaven, as will soon be made clear. I am concerned, however, with Wright's lack of attention to differing interpretations (also drawn from the scriptural texts) which lead to conclusions of participation in the life of Christ immediately upon the individual's death. By other-worldly heaven, therefore, I am referring to the more traditional Christian understanding of the place where Christ ascended (Mark 16:19 and Acts 1:11), but also to the place where the departed in Christ now dwell in the presence of God (2 Cor 5:8 and Phil 2:20).

My methodological approach to the 'doctrine' of heaven is sensitive to the ways in which practical Christian experience and the arts may contribute to the development of theology. Where doctrine can be understood in a narrow sense, "as a theoretical system of truths received by the church," my emphasis, following Anthony C. Thiselton, explores how Christian doctrine and daily living can enjoy a closer relationship.[5] In this way, I aim to cross some of the borderlands of dogma, doctrine, and belief in order to see how our understanding of heaven has a vital significance for Christian theology and practice. I am not intending to place a wedge between belief and knowledge, nor am I attempting to use hermeneutics as a way of postponing all questions asking for explanation. Rather, I advocate an imaginative approach which considers images in popular culture, both inside and outside of the church.

But why take an imaginative approach? The creative imagination, especially in relation to the arts, has often carried a less than trustworthy role in theology and philosophy. Richard Kearney has drawn especial attention to the deceptive elements associated with the imagination from the early Hellenic and Hebrew narratives onwards. He observes: "Prometheus then, no less than Adam, was portrayed as both benefactor of man and instigator of his illegitimate desire to substitute his own arbitrary creations for the original act of divine creation."[6] Paul Tillich also qualified his imaginative leanings observing:

---

4. Wright, *The Resurrection of the Son of God*, 204.

5. Thiselton, *The Hermeneutics of Doctrine*, xvi. I share Thiselton's view that a hermeneutic approach to doctrine can open up questions that impact "daily life," xvi.

6. Kearney, *The Wake of Imagination*, 81.

Such imaginative ability runs a risk of mistaking the creations of the imagination for realities, that is, of neglecting experience and rational critique, of thinking in monologues rather than dialogues, and of isolating itself from cooperative scientific effort.[7]

Even in light of such cautionary admissions, Tillich could not resist sharing how much his "love for the arts ha[d] been of great importance in [his] theological and philosophical work."[8] Kearney, in a similar way, begins one of his major works by declaring: "It is true that the imagination lies at the very heart of our existence. So much so that we would not be human without it."[9] For Tillich, "art is the highest form of play and the genuinely creative realm of the imagination."[10] Robert Roth reminds us that "theology deals with non-empirical subjects and therefore needs another kind of explanation."[11]

Popular culture continues to search the depths of the poetic imagination concerning heaven, especially in the area of film. Barbara Walters, for instance, documented a number of cultural developments concerning heaven in her 2006 documentary, *Heaven: Where Is It? and How Do We Get There?* If heaven is one of the most dominant narratives in Western religious thought, especially in the tradition of North American Christianity, Walters' statistics solidify the notion: nine out of ten Americans interviewed believed that heaven exists. Even more tellingly, "most assume they are going there at the end of their lives."[12] Walters explores a wide range of popular music, including Eric Clapton's "Tears In Heaven," Mariah Carey's "One Sweet Day," Belinda Carlisle's "Heaven Is a Place on Earth," and Bob Dylan's "Knockin' On Heaven's Door."[13] Her examples all creatively discover ways to express what McDannell and Lang call the majority tradition view or the "anthropocentric heaven" with lyrics that leave hope for love and reunion in the afterlife.[14] Walters goes so far as to call heaven a "staple" of popular culture in which television commercials use heaven for consumer motives and where the "sacredness" of heaven invades all space from films such as

---

7. Tillich, *On the Boundary*, 25.
8. Ibid., 26.
9. Kearney, *Poetics of Imagining*, 1.
10. Tillich, *On the Boundary*, 26.
11. Roth, *The Theater of God*, 78.
12. Paul, *Heaven*, DVD, (2005–6).
13. Ibid.
14. Lang, *Heaven*, xiii–xiv.

Bruce Almighty to cartoons, such as *The Simpsons*, to television shows such as *Desperate Housewives*.[15]

In Walters' interview with Alan Segal of Barnard College, Columbia University, Segal commented, "The film industry has sort of become our collective imaginations—a way to discuss what is important in life."[16] Theology is also a way of discussing what is important and asks how God is related to every aspect of our lives, including aspects of our collective imaginings regarding heaven. In a moment of reflection, C. S. Lewis observed: "there have been times when I think we do not desire heaven but more often I find myself wondering whether, in our heart of hearts, we have ever desired anything else."[17]

In developing a critical approach to popular imaginings of heaven, I have been particularly influenced by the work of Austin Farrer, Richard Kearney, David Brown, and Douglas Hedley, all of whom have made major contributions to contemporary discussions regarding the role of the imagination in human understanding.[18] Jürgen Moltmann, Paul Fiddes, and Walter Hollenweger have influenced my developing pneumatology in relation to culture, as well as James K. A. Smith, Anthony Thiselton, Ormond Rush, and Jaroslav Pelikan in highlighting the vital role of hermeneutics, especially in areas of reception and interpretation.[19] Patrick Sherry, Richard Viladesau, and Frank Burch Brown have influenced my thinking on the relationship between aesthetics and theology.[20] For example, Viladesau provides three points of interconnectedness, or "distinct centers of interest within 'aesthetics'":

---

15. Paul, *Heaven*, DVD, (2005–6).

16. Ibid.

17. Lewis, *Problem of Pain*, 130.

18. Farrer, *The Glass of Vision*. Kearney, *The Wake of Imagination* and *Poetics of Imagining*. Brown, *Discipleship & Imagination* and *Tradition & Imagination*. Hedley, *Living Forms of the Imagination*.

19. Moltmann, *The Source of Life* and *The Spirit of Life*. Fiddes, *The Promised End*, as well as his essay, "Concept, Image and Story in Systematic Theology." Also see Fiddes' *Participating in God*. Hollenweger, Pentecostalism and his essay, "All Creatures Great and Small." James K.A. Smith, *The Fall of Interpretation* and *Imagining the Kingdom*. See Thiselton, *Hermeneutics*, as well as, *The Hermeneutics of Doctrine*, and *Life after Death*. Also see Thiselton, *New Horizons in Hermeneutics*. Rush, *Still Interpreting Vatican II*. Pelikan, *The Vindication of Tradition*.

20. Sherry, *Spirit and Beauty* and *Spirit, Saints, and Immortality*. Viladesau, *Theological Aesthetics*. Brown, *Good Taste, Bad Taste, & Christian Taste* and *Religious Aesthetics*.

1. The general study of sensation and imagination and/or of 'feeling' in the wider sense of nonconceptual or nondiscursive (but nevertheless 'intellectual') knowledge.

2. The study of beauty and/or of 'taste.'

3. The study of art in general and/or of the fine arts in particular."[21]

Viladesau insightfully draws attention to the way in which the different uses of *aesthetics* "will coincide or diverge to varying degrees."[22] For my purposes (especially in chapter 5), I will be referring to *aesthetics* in how Viladesau describes his first point of clarification, as the "study of sensation and imagination and/or of 'feeling' in the wider sense . . ." with emphasis on the imaginative and emotive aspects.[23] A host of other interlocuters continue to be influential in shaping this dialogue between theology and popular culture. Of these, Clive Marsh, Chris Deacy, and Gordon Lynch have been especially relevant to my study with its, albeit non-exclusive, focus on the relationship between film and theology.[24]

The book is structured in two main parts. The first part (chapters 1–3) lays the ground for theologically engaging popular culture. Alongside presenting a critique of particular perspectives in contemporary New Testament studies, the first part seeks to establish a theory of revelation that underscores the importance of the Holy Spirit's action in culture. Also, by paying attention to the hermeneutical context for the reception of revelation through history, I seek to emphasize the importance of taking the wider culture more seriously in the development of theology.

The second part (chapters 4–7) focuses on an imaginative approach to three areas of personal identity in a post-mortem existence: appearance in relation to identity recognition in heaven (chapter 4), memory of earthly experiences (chapter 5), and bodily continuity/discontinuity and fulfillment as it pertains to the resurrection bodies (chapter 6).

Chapter 1 sets my own study of theology and popular culture within scholarship on theology and the arts more broadly; and presents the methodological foundations of, and key scholarly influences on, my work. I present an argument for the retrieval of the imagination in thinking theologically about a doctrine of revelation. Beginning with a trinitarian perspective of

21. Viladesau, *Theological Aesthetics*, 7–8.

22. Ibid., 8.

23. Ibid., "(I [Viladesau] use the word 'study' rather than 'theory' in order to include empirical, phenomenological, historical, and other such approaches besides the philosophical or systematic.)," 7.

24. Marsh, *Theology Goes to the Movies* and *Cinema & Sentiment*. Deacy, *Screening the Afterlife*. Lynch, *Understanding Theology and Popular Culture*.

God, the chapter emphasizes the importance of the Holy Spirit's continued action in our reception of revelation. A debate within modern theology concerning the Spirit's action in the world also sets the ground for later consideration of a theological hermeneutic of imagery in popular culture.

Chapter 2 traces some recent trends, particularly in contemporary New Testament studies, that pose challenges concerning the traditional Christian doctrine of heaven. N. T. Wright's work in this area has been particularly influential among Western Protestants, so I have selected to converse with Wright's contribution as a critical example of such a revisiting of Christian origins. Since the age of Reformation, it has been argued that theologians have chosen two key paths in relating theology to the world around them: they have either re-examined Christian origins in order to purify the tradition or they have tried to bridge the divide between religion and science.[25] The late Princeton historian E. Harris Harbison observed that one more primary vocational motives for theologians "may be the desire to bring faith into a more fruitful relationship with culture at some moment of crisis in the history of secular civilization."[26] Indeed, this has been my desire in an attempt to contribute to the long conversation of theologically reflecting on heaven as a potential other-worldly reality. I also consider, therefore, some recent trends in Western humanities regarding heaven that draw attention to the need for further engagement with popular culture.

Chapter 3 focuses on the question: which analyses of popular culture are most beneficial for a theological engagement? Although the selection of theological approaches to culture that I consider is not exhaustive, it does serve to show the extent to which theologians have sought to relate theology to the wider culture. By opening aspects of Christian doctrine to a hermeneutics of popular imagery, I hope that fresh insights might emerge in our collective imaginings of heaven.

Part 2 builds on the implications of Part 1. Chapter 4 highlights the importance of recognition and heavenly appearance in a post-mortem existence. Here, I suggest that a selection of popular films ranging in art forms and genre, from drama to children's animation, although not exclusively eschatological in emphasis, can creatively communicate the importance of the self in relation to others as a vital component by which we can imagine relationships in the afterlife. Accordingly, I argue that some type of appearance recognition is important, particularly in relation to the face. As the film selections suggest, moreover, appearance recognition serves as an indicator for the reality of deeper relational recognition. Near the beginning

---

25. Harbison, *The Christian Scholar In the Age of The Reformation*, 5.
26. Ibid.

of chapter 4, section two, I also include some more general reflections on the way that particular forms of film, such as animation, can challenge us in different ways, even by simply widening the range of viewership and discussion to include children through adults.

Chapter 5 emphasizes the role of our earthly memories in relation to our identities in heaven. Where a theologian such as Miroslav Volf wants to argue for the eradication of memories associated with sin in a heavenly context, I suggest that the narrative of our identities is more complex than Volf's proposal elicits. I argue that popular art, particularly popular music, and its relationship to film, re-imagines the construction of our life narratives in ways that can challenge our imagining of the continuation of those narratives in a heavenly context.[27]

Chapter 6 explores imaginative descriptions of bodily fulfillment in heaven. The historical trajectory of imagining both continuity and discontinuity between earthly and heavenly fulfillment is, for much of the Western traditions, communicated through literature. From the Bible's emphasis upon bodily resurrection and ascension, to later literary traditions, as can be observed in Dante and Milton, or even the earlier poets such as Homer and Virgil, the literary arts, as well as visual arts, play a role in bringing ancient questions forward for theological reflections of heaven. Clearly, even the mention of these names present an insurmountable area for research far too wide to explore in this book. I am merely pointing to the ways in which the literary and visual arts have a long intertextual relationship in not only providing illustrative material for Christian teaching, but also for the theological development of thinking about heaven. More recently, the popular imaginings within film have sought to convey how ancient narratives of Rome, previously considered within the literary arts, theologically engage questions of bodily continuity/discontinuity in heaven.

Chapter 7 considers film examples that imagine a post-apocalyptic portrayal of human life for the purpose of asking whether or not popular culture shows signs of difficulty imagining the type of this-worldly interpretation of eschatology as described earlier. By engaging examples of popular film, I hope to show not only how theology can be challenged by popular culture, but also how theology can learn from these popular forms of art.

---

27. See Volf, *The End of Memory*.

PART I

THEOLOGICALLY ENGAGING POPULAR CULTURE

1

Revelation, the Spirit, and Culture

In the process of unfolding a methodology, a critical first step is to offer a theology of revelation, connecting several strands, while concentrating on areas of pneumatology. Any project that includes elements of philosophical theology should ask why one must look beyond the scriptures to provide a hermeneutic of doctrine that takes seriously the Holy Spirit's continued action in the world. Considering heaven, as a reminder of God's presence in the world, where he seeks to disclose his action to finite creatures, invariably leads to the question of how one is to understand this reality.

REVELATION BEYOND SCRIPTURE

In what follows, I offer a short preface by setting forth some preliminary thoughts concerning a theology of revelation. In doing so, I hope to shed light on some of the influences on my work, as well as to contextualize my presuppositions in order to move forward in theologically engaging popular culture.

The concept of revelation has to do with the unveiling of divine truth; not just any truth, but truth that is revealed by one who is infinite, not finite. More specifically, the presupposition that underlies the current project is concerned with truth of the triune God: Father, Son, and Holy Spirit. I emphasize this trinitarian focus early on, especially for those who become anxious in theology-and-culture dialogues out of concern that one's pneumatology will become characterized by "semantic chaos."[1] Stated most aptly by Farrer:

---

1. See Jeremy Begbie's prefatory remarks in Guthrie, *Creator Spirit*, vii.

> For the truth of which I have principally to speak is not simply truth about God, it is revealed truth about God; and God himself has revealed it. So we believe: and in so believing we suppose that we exalt this truth, as something above what our faculties could reach; as something we could not know unless God himself declared it. Our intention is not to make truth as narrow as the Church which professes it, but as high as the God who proclaims it.[2]

The following scholars have made important contributions to the development of relating the imagination and revelation that are particularly pertinent for this study. First, David Brown insists that we should look at the world with the understanding that God is presently active; and that, in perceiving, one must pay close attention to "the stories and images that give religious belief its shape and vitality."[3] Secondly, Douglas Hedley has sought to develop Farrer's work on the imagination and revelation. Where "Farrer liked to speak of double agency—certain acts which are at once authentically human and yet the channels of divine influence," Hedley wants "to speak of the anagogic imagination to designate such a reciprocal relation: the human construction of symbols of God which at the same time constitute divine epiphany."[4] In a similar trajectory, this book offers a renewed interest in Farrer's and these others' attempts to "produce an account of the imagination which culminates in a theory of inspired images which is based on the doctrine that man is made in the image of God."[5]

Images are shaped within specific cultural contexts and Wolfhart Pannenberg's importance for this study emerges from his insistence that we pay closer attention to the historical drama of God's action, not just for contextual reasons, but also for understanding the public nature of revelation.[6] For Pannenberg, "the revelation of the biblical God is demonstrated before all eyes for the benefit of all people. It is not a secret knowledge available to the few."[7] He admits that his argument raises questions concerning God's self-revelation and issues of perceptibility.[8] Pannenberg shows how the biblical-historical thought is concerned with "indirect revelation on the

---

2. Farrer, *The Glass of Vision*, 1.
3. Brown, *Tradition & Imagination*, 2.
4. Hedley, *Living Forms of the Imagination*, 7.
5. Ibid.
6. Pannenberg, ed., *Revelation as History*, 150.
7. Ibid.
8. Pannenberg, *Systematic Theology*, vol. 1, 249.

basis of God's activity in history."⁹ Pannenberg is after a theology of 'word' and 'deed', seeking to refute an overly anthropomorphic understanding of revelation on the one hand, and a telepathic type of revelatory theory that bypasses the imagination on the other.¹⁰ He shows the difficulty in reconciling the variety of ways the scriptures mention revelatory experiences, and argues that indirection takes into account "an all-embracing event of self-revelation to which each of them [revelatory experiences] makes its own specific contribution. Along these lines there need be no rivalry between the OT and the NT witness to revelation."¹¹ Pannenberg is more entrenched in theological debates surrounding issues of scripture, however, and does not address sufficiently, as Farrer and Brown seek to do, how the indirection, or better yet, the mediation of revelation is part of our created situation, and the important role of imagination in the reception process. James K. A. Smith has criticized Pannenberg for his *"eschatological immediacy model"* that implies "interpretation is a state of affairs from which humanity must be redeemed."¹² Smith is correct, in my view, that "hope of overcoming and escaping human finitude" is not the most promising way forward and limits our understanding of the imagination.¹³

In a similar way, mediation does not take away from the personal relatability of God, neither does it produce a soft agnosticism communicating a theoretical availability of revelation, yet without allowing experiential access of revelation. On the contrary, "indirection" (to use Pannenberg's term) says something more about our condition as human beings and less about God's willingness to reveal. Consider the following:

> The first thing to be said of Christ's self-revelation to us is that it is by word and deed, where 'doing' is taken to embrace the action of Christ's will in his sufferings also. If we are allowed this gloss, we may be content with St. Luke's formula: "the things that Christ did and taught" are the subject-matter of the gospel.¹⁴

Therefore, reflection on the historical, redemptive act of God's incarnation in Jesus Christ is critical to one's understanding of creation, as well as of God's

---

9. Pannenberg, ed., *Revelation as History*, 150. Perhaps the term 'mediation' is more helpful in referring to revelation than Pannenberg's language of 'direct' and 'indirect.'

10. Pannenberg, *Systematic Theology*, vol. 1, 241.

11. Ibid., 244.

12. Smith, *The Fall of Interpretation*, 17.

13. Ibid., 18. Smith unpacks his criticism in chapter two, as well as pointing to Hans-Georg Gadamer and Jürgen Habermas' "philosophical ascent to the Absolute and Unconditioned" where humanity seeks to escape creational finitude.

14. Farrer, *The Glass of Vision*, 40.

ongoing action in the world taking into account both word and deeds. That being the case, there is a growing recognition among theologians of culture for the need to focus on the critical role of pneumatology. For example, in their most recent contribution, towards an incarnational approach to popular music, Clive Marsh and Vaughan Roberts show, by examining Kevin Vanhoozer's essentials for a theology of culture, how the pneumatological is the one factor running through four key doctrines, which Vanhoozer also regards as essential concerning "the issue of whether God reveals himself in and through popular culture: the incarnation, general revelation, common grace, and the *imago Dei*."[15] Marsh and Roberts' desire is to discern "how God incarnate might be revealed and the image of God be evident in traces of common grace in popular culture."[16] They contend that "the incarnation indicates who God is and the way in which God relates to the world as embodied Spirit."[17]

A further example of this pneumatological focus in theology and culture can be observed in Robert Johnston's well-written work regarding general revelation. Johnston insightfully draws on what he sees as a "cosmic pneumatology" in Elizabeth Johnson's writings, as well as "the Spirit's paradoxical presence" found in Moltmann's pneumatology.[18]

It would seem that much of the anxiety within modern Protestant theology concerning an unhealthy entanglement of anthropology and pneumatology is directly challenged by the incarnation. We must not avoid seeing a sacramental emphasis here, as well as Marsh's key observation that "pneumatology is the key doctrine in a theology *for* cultural engagement."[19] My emphasis on the role of the imagination draws both upon the sacramental approach found in Brown, as well upon the Pentecostal theological tradition that focuses on the pneumatological and intercultural aspects of theology. Marsh and Roberts articulate the discussion in these terms:

> It is essential to emphasize the universal reach of God's becoming incarnate and the extent of the doctrinal claim being made. The scandal of particularity—that God became human at a specific point in history—is, however, made too scandalously particular if the equally scandalous generosity of God's self-involvement in the created order is played down. That continuing interaction is wholly consistent with a strong doctrine of creation. It is

---

15. Marsh and Roberts, *Personal Jesus*, 130.
16. Ibid.
17. Ibid., 168.
18. Johnston, *God's Wider Presence*, 172–87.
19. Marsh, "What if David Brown Had Owned a Television?" 195.

also a direct corollary of a Trinitarian doctrine of God (the Holy Spirit continues the action of the creator God, as known in and through Christ).[20]

A hermeneutic of doctrine that foregrounds the Holy Spirit, especially concerning a doctrine of heaven, could risk missing the soteriological dimensions deeply embedded in traditional Christology, including humanity's response to Christ's reconciliation. Well aware of these concerns, as well as remaining more than sympathetic to soteriological aspects of one's relationship to Christ, the prominent emphasis on the Spirit here is that human beings experience the divine before constructing meaning or doctrine of their experience. Paul Fiddes aptly observes:

> Our experience of ourselves and in others must always be understood in the context of a God who is present in the world, offering a self-communication which springs from a boundless love. It is this self-gift of God which already shapes both our experience of being in the world and our language with which we configure our experiences. In taking a path from experience to doctrine we are retracing a journey that God has already taken towards us.[21]

Like Fiddes, I am not suggesting "setting experience or nature *against* revelation."[22] By beginning with creation, I am simply advocating a position that God is actively pursuing ways of relating to humanity, especially through the imagination. As Fiddes contends:

> I suggest that images and stories on the one hand, and concepts on the other, are all to be understood as *responses* to revelation. None are *identical* with revelation, for in revelation we are concerned with the self-disclosure of God's own being, not with the transmission of a message or even a picture. Nor is this revelation to be limited to the Bible, though Hebrew and Christian scriptures are witness to revelation in an exceptional way. Wherever God opens God's own self to draw human persons into relationship with the divine life, there will be response of varying kinds, including that of the imagination. Only this universal self-opening of God can justify the making of connections between theology and other 'writings' in our culture, of whatever kind.[23]

20. Marsh, *Personal Jesus*, 167–68.
21. Fiddes, *Participating in God*, 8.
22. Ibid.
23. Fiddes, *The Promised End*, 8. Robert Johnston also calls for a "full-orbed

Consequently, a further strand that underlies the current project is that the triune God is creator and humanity is finite. As finite creatures, we interpret our surroundings, including God's relationship to creation. Humanity is also created as rational and carries, as Dennis Danielson has described, "the longing to perceive, and to trust in, the power, wisdom, and goodness of God."[24] An important distinction, then, concerns our conditioning within culture on the one hand, and an unhealthy determinism of humanity by culture, on the other. Society does not determine a person's understanding or identity, but our understanding and identity is always conditioned by our culture. As George Marsden has argued, "since God's work appears to us in historical circumstances where imperfect humans are major agents, the actions of the Holy Spirit in the church are always intertwined with culturally conditioned factors."[25] This is not simply a matter of the fall of humanity, but part of our constitutions as social creatures that interpret and communicate in a historical context.[26]

Where I strongly affirm the role of scripture in the revelatory process, I also do not want to diminish the ongoing action of the Holy Spirit in every area of human experience, as well as the long tradition that enables human experience to interpret without somehow denying or escaping one's cultural horizon. This entails considering varying modes of doing theology. William Dyrness is right to suggest that even as "people of the book," Christians "should not play the visual against the verbal."[27] One thing important to remember is that revelation is for the culture, not for God. God does not need revelation, so God mediates in such a way that human beings can understand, because he loves his creation (John 3:16). Therefore, as God's creation, we are continually in a receptive process.

---

hermeneutic, a robust methodology that includes Scripture, tradition, and community as well as experience." See Johnston, *God's Wider Presence*, 37.

24. Danielson, "God's Other Book," 38.

25. Marsden, *Fundamentalism and American Culture*, 230. Although I disagree with Marsden for giving himself, as a historian, the option of paying attention to the "constructive enterprise, with the positive purpose of finding the gold among the dross," while limiting the theologian from the same constructive endeavors, he is correct in arguing that "God works among imperfect human beings in historical settings, 'pure' or 'perfect' Christianity can seldom if ever exist in this world. God in his grace works through our limitations; for that very reason we should ask for the grace to recognize what those limitations are. So we may—and ought to—carefully identify the cultural forces which affect the current versions of Christianity," 230.

26. Smith, *The Fall of Interpretation*, 161. Smith's challenge to immediacy theories of interpretation is a helpful corrective, as well as his emphasis on the goodness of creation, and the "situationality" of humanity.

27. Dyrness, *Visual Faith*, 156.

This historical process of receiving revelation has been described by Walter Hollenweger as "a theologically responsible syncretism."[28] Fully aware of the theologically negative connotations often associated with 'syncretisic' language, Hollenweger proposed that "the models for such a syncretism are the biblical authors."[29] His examples range from Matthew's "audaci[ty]. . .to state that the magis (not kings) found their way to the cradle of Jesus on the basis of their pagan astrology, while the Bible-reading scribes in Jerusalem tried to kill little Jesus" to Paul's use of a variety of "popular religious sayings" in 1 Corinthians 13 where Paul does not "mention Christ in the whole chapter."[30] Hollenweger states that "it becomes Christian only through its inclusion in 1 Corinthians."[31] His summary includes Aquinas' use of Aristotle in developing his theology.[32] For Hollenweger, the question is always, "how did the biblical authors deal with the religious context of their time?"[33] Again, Hollenweger turns to Paul and his letter to the Colossians. He argues that Paul quotes from the "'New Age Hynmal' of the Church at Colossae."[34] Hollenweger observes:

> *The Colossians sang:* The chaos in the cosmos must be overcome. Something must happen to this world. Paul answers: Certainly, our world is sick and must be healed; however, healing does not happen through mysterious cosmic powers, but through people who follow the one who died on a cross; that is through reconciled and reconciling people. What does Paul do here? He accepts the syncretism of the Colossians and transforms it into a theologically responsible syncretism. He socializes their syncretism, changing references to powers into references to people. The abstractions of the New Age syncretism are made concrete: Paul deals in detail with that which is under the lordship of Christ.[35]

Here, Hollenweger points to the artistic developments that were shaping the Colossian Christians. For Hollenweger, "the question is not 'syncretism yes or no,' but what kind of syncretism. Already the Bible is an example of

---

28. Hollenweger, *Pentecostalism*, 132.
29. Ibid., 136.
30. Ibid., 133.
31. Ibid.
32. Ibid., 134.
33. Ibid., 136.
34. Ibid., 137.
35. Ibid., 139.

theologically responsible syncretism."[36] Of course, Hollenweger's approach is not without limitations.[37] 'Syncretism' is a word that for some conjures up diluted images of unrecognizable theological constructions, bringing more confusion than clarity to the gospel of Jesus. Trying to rescue a word from the established theological recycle bin without getting thrown into the bin itself is often a futile effort. For some, even a 'responsible syncretism' points more away from continuity with scripture and tradition, where 'synthesis' has more connotations of continuity. On the other hand, even if the language is not as helpful in some regards, most would find Hollenweger's observations insightful and even creatively useful in an engagement with popular culture, especially in analyzing the developments within traditions. To deny theology an ability to construct from materials already shaping meaning in a culture is a limited theology that denies aspects at the core of the theological task. Hollenweger could not understand how a theology could remain non-intercultural, even simply by reading the many contexts within scripture. A further question may arise, whether or not revelation can be unmediated, and how one might avoid confusing mediation and interpretation.

For revelation to occur, mediation is essential for a finite creation. To understand, one must interpret images, including linguistic images, and human beings must utilize all available senses and place them at the disposal of the interpreter. Although views within Christianity vary greatly on this point, it may be safe to note how most scholars tend to place a high value on the historical context, even if they are using a theological hermeneutic. Scripture is an integral part of God's revelation in history. As Farrer notes, "no other writings can replace it as the channel through which the revealing events come to us."[38] Herein lies the uniqueness of the canon. Yet, Farrer is adamant that room must be left for the Spirit to work in the lives of historical figures and contexts beyond the writings of scriptures, because the Spirit goes beyond the events to help us understand what the events mean in a present context.[39] Steven Guthrie is right to point out early in his work that two prominent characteristics of the Spirit's action are that of "boundary-breaker" and that of "plan-disrupter."[40] Rather than the scriptures playing

---

36. Ibid., 132.

37. Yong describes the term, 'syncretism' as an "anathemized word," but argues that one must place the emphasis on Hollenweger's use of 'responsible' as the key term. By doing so, Pentecostal and Charismatic theologies can begin to understand many "real life" issues in a theology of religions. See Yong, *Discerning the Spirit(s)*, 210.

38. Farrer, *The Glass of Vision*, 38.

39. Ibid.

40. Guthrie, *Creator Spirit*, 9.

a merely historical role, I suggest that theology must understand the scriptures as the transcendent collection which the church has come to endorse. This is precisely the reason why I argue that systematic theologians should place any doctrine of scripture under the pneumatological category.[41] I find agreement in Ben Quash's recent comments:

> For Christian tradition it is the Holy Spirit who opens up the 'moreness' of meaning in the unfolding of history: the Spirit who, in new historical sets of circumstances, discloses the abundance of God's loving purposes; the Spirit who guides Christians from glory to glory in their assimilation to the perfect form of Christ; the Spirit who unfolds the riches that are in Christ. In opening what has been received in the past to its transformed possibilities in the future, the Spirit is therefore also the key to the way Christians read Scripture; the Spirit unlocks and sets in motion the power of Scripture to speak in each new historical motion the power of Scripture to speak in each new historical moment, and thus to reconfigure each new 'present' such that it is never simply a reproduction of the past. My suggestion here is that the grit of Scripture may be read as an intrinsic part of how this unlocking and reconfiguring is initiated; if so, it can be read as divine gift.[42]

The Holy Spirit is why and how the scripture lives in and beyond the original historical contexts. By placing scripture under the pneumatological category, one pays attention to a transcendent dimension, as well as the purely historical. Quash's observations naturally lead us to say something further regarding how a robust pneumatology is vital for a theology of culture.

PNEUMATOLOGY AND A THEOLOGY OF CULTURE

Pneumatology plays a significant role in the theology of revelation that I develop in this book. The writers of scripture give an essential place to the Spirit from creation in Genesis 1:2 to 1:27 where humans are made in the image of God to the Psalmist who gives ample evidence for the Spirit's presence throughout all creation in Psalm 139:7–10. This is, not to mention the role of the Spirit in the prophets, especially Joel 2:1ff, which will later be

---

41. An pneumatological approach to scripture can be found in Stan Grenz' treatment of biblical and spiritual authority in Grenz, *Theology for the Community of God*, 402–03.

42. Quash, *Found Theology*, 76.

interpreted by the New Testament writers in terms of presence, water, and wind, as well as Spirit baptism (John 1:32–34; Acts 2:14ff) and, transformation (2 Cor 5:1–21), all the way through the Spirit's summoning (Rev 22:17).

One may also begin to notice the influence of John Wesley's emphasis on outer and inner religious experience, which play "the most important role in Wesley's experimental understanding of religion."[43] Wesley's approach, which later percolated through the various emerging theologies of Pentecostalism in the twentieth century focused on how "experiential knowledge functioned decisively for Wesley in the entire range of religious understanding."[44] Donald Thorsen further observes: "Wesley believed that—given all the evidence available from experience, Scripture, tradition, and reason—religious belief is capable of rational assessment and rational justification (at least to the degree that any human knowledge can be rationally justified)."[45] By taking the physical seriously, one could experience the spiritual by "his [God's] grace."[46]

Within this Wesleyan trajectory, Pentecostal theologian Amos Yong has proposed a "pneumatology of quest," exploring ways of understanding the Spirit's action in other religions and the wider culture in order to develop a pneumatological imagination. According to Yong, this type of imaginative approach "embraces the tensions between pneumatology and Christology" and "gives proper place and emphasis to both Word and Spirit," "refus[ing] to allow either to be dominated by the other."[47] He concludes with the metaphor of Emmaus (Luke 24:13–35). Yong suggests, "Emmaus itself may not be locatable here on earth; nevertheless, our task as Christians is to walk along that road and to believe that the Spirit will lead us to where we should go. Should we miss the mark, he will be there to assist us back onto the path."[48]

Two theologians in particular have not hesitated to point out areas where the church has missed the mark concerning the Spirit's work in the world and have attempted to steer theology in a different direction. Both Hollenweger and Jürgen Moltmann have remained critical of pneumatologies in the West. As Hollenweger observed in the early 1980s, by "restrict[ing] its doctrine of the Holy Spirit to the realization of a Christ-centered theology

---

43. Thorsen, *The Wesleyan Quadrilateral*, 216. Also see Taves, *Fits, Trances, and Visions*, 51.

44. Thorsen, *The Wesleyan Quadrilateral*, 217.

45. Ibid., 210–11.

46. Ibid., 217.

47. Yong, *Discerning the Spirit(s)*, 319.

48. Ibid., 323–24.

and the doctrine of salvation" in firm step with the *filioque*, "the *creator spiritus*, the life-giving *ruach Yahweh* is a perplexing 'lost' entity for the west."[49] Likewise, Moltmann has been critical of the West for embracing such a one-sided pneumatology, flowing out of the *filioque*.[50] Moltmann observes:

> As *the Spirit of Christ* it is *the redemptive Spirit*. But the work of creation too is ascribed to the Father, so *the Spirit of the Father* is also *the Spirit of creation*. If redemption is placed in radical discontinuity to creation, then 'the Spirit of Christ' has no longer anything to do with Yaweh's *ruach*.[51]

Similar to Hollenweger's life-to-theology approach, Moltmann is after a "theology of life."[52] According to Moltmann: "the continual assertion that God's Spirit is bound to the church, its word and sacraments, its authority, its institutions and ministries, impoverishes the congregations. It empties the churches, while the Spirit emigrates to the spontaneous groups and personal experience."[53] Likewise, Hollenweger argued that, "'Outsiders' are needed to assist Christians in their understanding of the gospel . . . God's Spirit is at work outside the churches as well as within them."[54]

Hollenweger offers a few instances; the biblical witnesses offer many examples of the Spirit working through outsiders. For instance, Joel Green has observed the way in which Luke's account of Jesus' healing of the centurion's slave in Luke 7 shares similarities to the healing of Naaman in 2 Kings 5.[55] Among the similarities, Green mentions the fact that both are outsiders, where Jesus recognizes the "Centurion as possessing remarkable insight into the character of Jesus' mission."[56] Not to mention the story of Balaam in

---

49. Hollenweger, "All Creatures Great and Small," 44.
50. Moltmann, *The Spirit of Life*, 8.
51. Ibid., 8–9.
52. Price, *Theology out of Place*, 151. I strongly endorse Price's description of Hollenweger's approach in the following: "The 'from life to theology' method encompasses a broader spectrum of source material (contemporary, historical, biographical as well as theological and biblical) from more groups (worldwide, not just Western) and embraces other disciplines in the discussion (natural sciences, social sciences [and I would add popular culture]). In overtly engaging with the realities of life, praxis and reflection are related in an intimate and complex way. There is not 'the Truth' about the Holy Spirit which can be discovered and subsequently applied, but a continuous experience–dialogue–reflection–action process," 151. Also see Moltmann, *The Source of Life*, 10.
53. Moltmann, *The Spirit of Life*, 2.
54. Price, *Theology out of Place*, 150.
55. Green, *The Gospel of Luke*, 284.
56. Ibid., 285.

Numbers 22, as a "seer of foreign extraction."⁵⁷ Davies points out that, "later biblical tradition, however, was not so favourably disposed to Balaam (most likely referring to Revelation 2:14), presumably because the phenomenon of a heathen seer as the recipient of a genuinely divine revelation would have offended Jewish sensibilities."⁵⁸ Job, as a further example, was from the land of Uz. "Modern commentators cannot be sure of the precise location of Uz, but within the narrative, 'Job' and 'Uz' introduce the story as happening 'long ago' and 'far away.'"⁵⁹

One more example can be observed in the life of Peter and Cornelius in Acts 10. According to Pelikan:

> As was to happen throughout the narrative of Acts, a new truth was being communicated not (or at any rate not only) through a clarification and deepening of the meaning of the biblical text, as had been the case in the encounter of Philip with the Ethiopian (8:30–31), but through special visions and private revelations, one to Cornelius (10:3–6) and then one to Peter three times over (10:11–16).⁶⁰

Along these lines, Moltmann rejects modern theology's attempt to create a pneumatology that is "inexperienceable, hidden and 'other' as God himself" and finds, "it is only in the narrow concepts of modern philosophy that 'revelation' and 'experience' are antitheses."⁶¹ Karl Barth, among others, strained to keep the discontinuity between the Spirit and humanity ever apparent, "consequently the Holy Spirit reveals nothing to human beings which they could see, hear, smell or taste, and so experience through their senses . . . ."⁶² Moltmann adds, "anyone who stylizes revelation and experience into alternatives, ends up with revelations that cannot be experienced and experiences without revelations."⁶³ Once the Spirit is free to be experienced in humanity, then one can understand the broader claim that the Spirit is also able to speak outside the confines of the church in the middle of culture, where the theologian must encourage the church to venture.⁶⁴ Both Hollenweger and Moltmann have more to say about the trinitarian nature of God, thus providing defense against those who dismiss experience as a

---

57. Davies, *Numbers*, 240.
58. Ibid.
59. Janzen, *Job*, 34.
60. Pelikan, *Acts*, 128.
61. Moltmann, *The Spirit of Life*, 5–6.
62. Ibid., 7.
63. Ibid.
64. Marsh, *Personal Jesus*, 129–30.

valid body of knowledge. Moltmann for instance, finds much to appreciate in Friedrich Schleiermacher, but also indicates clearly the points at which he disagrees with the formidable thinker.[65] Nonetheless, Schleiermacher was the one who saw the hermeneutical problem and also saw the need for experience and revelation to coexist.[66]

Hollenweger insists that "it is time to acknowledge that the Spirit is the giver of all life in all cultures and religions and perhaps even the agent which holds our universe together."[67] He was willing to entertain criticism of panentheism, but he also argued that "the charge of panentheism is only justified if that is all that I have to say, restricting myself to the Old Testament pneumatology [which he observes, "has been neglected in the past]."[68] He gives ample qualifications for his remarks:

> It seems clear that a pneumatology of life must be firmly based on a new form of trinitarian doctrine which is linked up with the other tenets and traditions of Christian belief, thus demonstrating why the trinitarian doctrine is necessary in order to understand the Spirit both as a "free-floating" Spirit and an aspect of the Spirit of Christ. The "free-floating" Spirit only seems "free-floating" in our experience and perception: from a trinitarian point of view, the Spirit is "one" with the Father and Son and cannot therefore be held responsible for whatever we fancy. On the other hand, to be one with the Father and the Son does not mean that the Spirit cannot do things which are outside our understanding of the Bible and Christian tradition. But it has to be made clear how these experiences and insights (in our own and in other cultures) can be understood as expressions of the Spirit of Life. Then not every fancy and every religious exuberance will be acceptable.[69]

Hollenweger's approach is not simply a return to what Barth was so adamantly against in the work of Schleiermacher. Spending a lifetime studying global Pentecostalism, the Swiss theologian Hollenweger cannot be

---

65. Moltmann, *The Spirit of Life*, 221–25. Hollenweger also includes significant remarks on his trinitarian understanding of the Spirit in Mullen, *Strange Gifts?* 50–53.

66. See Rob Johnston's thoughtful comments on Schleiermacher in *God's Wider Presence*, 138–49.

67. Hollenweger, "All Creatures Great and Small," 50.

68. Ibid.

69. Ibid., 50–51. By panentheism, one may take Hollenweger as referring to the Spirit working through the natural, yet not identified with the natural. This is why he goes further into a more trinitarian understanding of God that he finds in the New Testament.

easily slotted into the modern generalizations of what has been described as unfruitful forms of liberalism or liberalism more generally.[70] Within intercultural theology, Hollenweger does not share forms of what has been described as liberal "minimalist systematizations of belief" nor the "neoliberal economic systems [which] are often questioned by Christian faith; neither is his a theology of "radical individualism [which] can be immensely selfish."[71] In seeking to understand how the Spirit is active in the world, Hollenweger's theology would be better described as "a theology of hospitality."[72] According to Newlands, "a theology of hospitality is inevitably a theology of risk and a theology at risk. That is also of the essence of the Christian gospel."[73] I would endorse, then, Hollenweger's and Moltmann's insistence that revelation through the ongoing action of the Spirit is not only culturally conditioned, but that aspects of popular culture can, at times, even illuminate rather than compete with the Spirit's activity.[74]

This may not convince some critics, however, who still find in theology and cultural engagement a "confusion of anthropology and pneumatology."[75] For an example of such criticism, Jessica DeCou offers a telling account of Barth's strong disagreement with what he understood as Schleiermacher's "conflation" or even "confusion" "of pneumatology and anthropology."[76] DeCou observes: "in his blending of pneumatology and anthropology, Schleiermacher remains a theologian of the spirit, but of which spirit?"[77] In quoting Barth, DeCou notes that "'Schleiermacher obviously wants to give us *more* than a theology of the Holy Spirit,' which can only be a theology of the human spirit and thus '*less* than theology could and should be.'"[78] According to DeCou, "Barth does not condemn Schleiermacher's anthropocentrism in itself, but rather the methods and motives driving this anthropocentrism."[79]

---

70. Newlands, *The Transformative Imagination*, viii.

71. Ibid.

72. Ibid.

73. Ibid.

74. Westphal, *God, Guilt, and Death*, xi. Westphal describes how methods for studying religion derived from Merleau-Ponty and Paul Ricoeur influenced his own phenomenological approach, where the methodology "seemed to illuminate the subject matter rather than compete with it."

75. Price, *Theology out of Place*, 21. Also, see DeCou, *Playful, Glad, and Free*, 33.

76. DeCou, *Playful, Glad, and Free*, 32.

77. Ibid., 34.

78. Ibid.

79. Ibid., 32.

Pannenberg, nonetheless, suggested that Barth's position brought him much closer to Schleiermacher than he would ever wish to admit.[80] Pannenberg describes part of the dilemma in the following terms:

> Individual experience can never mediate absolute, unconditional certainty. At best it can offer no more than a certainty which needs clarification and confirmation in an ongoing process of experience. This subjective certainty does indeed experience the presence of truth and its unconditionality, but only in an ongoing process. The conditionality of all subjective certainty is part of the finitude of human experience.[81]

Pannenberg does not stop here. He is after something more than faith, something historical, yet with the hope of a future eschatological infinitude for humanity, in order to combat atheistic triumphalism due to the tendency of theology to become a "hermeneutics of 'piety.'"[82] Unfortunately according to Smith, neither can Pannenberg avoid joining those who "express the confident hope of overcoming and escaping human finitude."[83] Pannenberg concedes that truth is accessible in ongoing experience as a part of the human situation, but he is more concerned with 'Truth' beyond, in back of, and in front of the subjective experience encounter.[84] Smith observes that for Pannenberg, "finitude itself is something of a fall" which in turn is "a devaluing of creation."[85]

In chapter six, I will explore certain aspects of Pannenberg's theology which help us reflect further about bodily finitude in relation to infinitude. At this point, however, his theology is less helpful in accounting for the Holy Spirit's work in all humanity, where Schleiermacher was attempting to provide openness to the Spirit's activity by "invoking the subjectivistic understanding of the inner witness of the Holy Spirit, or by appealing to the experience of faith."[86] For DeCou:

> Barth's apprehensions *do not* rule out the possibility of developing a Barthian theology of culture. His pneumatology was deliberately designed to avoid the conflation of human and holy that

---

80. Pannenberg, *Systematic Theology*, 44. Pages 44–48 provide a good summary of issues relating to Barth and Schleiermacher over the question of revelation.

81. Ibid., 47.

82. Kärkkäinen, *Christ and Reconciliation*, 6. Also, see Smith, *The Fall of Interpretation*, 66.

83. Smith, *The Fall of Interpretation*, 18.

84. Pannenberg, *Systematic Theology*, 48.

85. Smith, *The Fall of Interpretation*, 66.

86. Ibid., 46.

he found in modern discourse on the Spirit, and his profound interest in secular culture (politics, music, history, and so on) is self-evident.[87]

DeCou argues that Barth "identifies pneumatology not only as the central *problem* but as the most plausible *solution* to his struggle to understand Schleiermacher."[88] She later adds, "when asked why the Spirit did not play a larger role in his doctrine of the revealed Word," Barth points to the historical context as an explanation of why it was necessary to emphasize "the objective side of revelation: Christ."[89]

From this, it would appear that Barth was more willing to allow culture to shape his agenda than he would explicitly concede. According to DeCou, Barth's great concern was that "theology remain free from the constraints of culture, and culture remain free to be fully human secular culture—and *both* must remain free from assuming a counterfeit divinity."[90] Barth's compartmentalizing of the Spirit's activity in order to maintain the integrity of the profane and sacred may be persuasive for DeCou, but I will argue more along the lines of Hollenweger who is less concerned with the qualification and quantification of the Spirit's activity than he is with starting with the presupposition of the Spirit's work in all creation. Undoubtedly, Barth's emphasis on the objective also extended to a deep concentration on the doctrine of sin, with the purpose of bringing awareness of the evil disruption in creation. While certainly not denying such a doctrine, Hollenweger is less hampered with this focus. Contrary to some misrepresentations in theology and culture dialogue, to look for the goodness of the Spirit's activity is not a refusal to live and love in a broken world. DeCou wants to argue that through a fresh reading of Barth, "the eschatological Spirit establishes the relationship between theology and culture, while the Word provides a means for critically assessing culture without opening up theology to 'every new spirit.'"[91] Offering a corrective for those who champion Barth's theology of culture "as an extension of his doctrine of the Word" or "true words approach," DeCou suggests "abandonment" of the latter in "favor of a model guided by Barth's writings on culture and the Spirit in the context of his eschatology."[92] However, by limiting culture to a sphere of play, fellowship, and relaxation, a significant range of human experience of God seems to

---

87. DeCou, *Playful, Glad, and Free*, 45.
88. Ibid.
89. Ibid., 45–46.
90. Ibid., 46.
91. Ibid., 47.
92. Ibid., 7.

be bracketed out from possibilities proper to the imagination that DeCou wants to endorse, not to mention uncharacteristic of an approach emphasizing the Spirit and eschatology.[93]

As will be explored further in chapter five, Barth allowed himself some freedom to imagine what heavenly music could be like. At the same time, he was overly concerned that the phenomenon or signs of the Spirit would receive more attention than the Spirit.[94] This is unfortunate since signs are the materials by which the imagination is able to receive and create in order to understand where the signs are pointing, especially in relation to heaven. I think DeCou needs to go further than Barth's attempt to keep theology pure of culture and culture pure of theology. If her goal is to show how Barth's theology is helpful in constructing a theology of popular culture, it would seem more advantageous to look at the myriad ways in which theologians find the Spirit, not just as "establishing a relationship," but continuing in the relationship through involvement not, just in intending moments, but also being a part of the ongoing discernment of the revelatory impact.

This discussion concerning the relationship between the Spirit and the world is intricately connected to modern divisions over whether or not to emphasize the nearness of God (immanence) or the distance of God (transcendence).[95] I will argue in the following that an emphasis upon nearness does not necessarily minimize the transcendence of God.

(UN)HELPFUL DISTINCTIONS BETWEEN NATURAL AND SUPERNATURAL

What are we to make of the old division between natural and supernatural revelation? Paradigms focused primarily on the total depravity of creation, marked with no ability to perceive God's action in the world, are not consistent with scripture where God is revealing himself from creation onward. Marsh and Roberts show a significant movement in theologically understanding popular music by what they term, *From Sin to Sacramentality*.[96] This is not a matter of ignoring evil in the world, nor an attempt to make God in human image. Neither is this to ignore some of the unfortunate attempts found in early liberal theology to "merge the supernatural with the natural," which was a much more reductionistic approach in my mind,

93. Ibid., 155.
94. Thiselton, *The Hermeneutics of Doctrine*, 449–50.
95. For a summary of these modern distinctions see, Erickson, *Christian Theology*, 276.
96. Marsh, *Personal Jesus*, 37.

shaped more by a cultural disdain for supernatural activity, where reason left little room for the imagination.[97] Rather, God's action and continued action should remain sufficient in our natural state to leave as much room for the supernatural Spirit as we can contain in our finitude. Farrer would argue that indeed the distinction must remain, but the emphasis needs to be placed "on the adjectives," *Natural* and *Supernatural*, rather than on *Reason* and *Revelation* in order to differentiate between "two phases of God's action—his supernatural action, and his action by way of nature."[98] Lewis once argued that, "the battle is between faith and reason on one side and emotion and imagination on the other."[99] Here, Lewis was concerned with the impact of the emotions, on occasion, to "rise up and carry out a sort of blitz on his belief," while faith and reason were still very much intact.[100] Alister McGrath quotes Lewis in respect of this important distinction: "I [Lewis] am a rationalist. For me, reason is the natural organ of truth; but imagination is the organ of meaning. Imagination, producing new metaphors or revivifying old, is not the cause of truth, but its condition."[101] McGrath argues, "the world for Lewis, points to something beyond it which needs to be engaged with the imagination, rather than the intellect."[102]

Being careful not to overly minimize the difficulties between proponents of natural and/or revealed theology, one recognizes the long debates that took a toll on twentieth-century Protestant theology which, one might add, were highly conditioned by the cultural situation. In his dissertation on heaven in modern theology, Donald MacEwan traces the developments of the doctrine through the deep rupture between natural and revealed theology found in the earlier thinkers Bultmann, Barth, Bonhoeffer, Tillich, Moltmann, Pannenberg, and Jüngel, where Tillich and Pannenberg appear more sympathetic, as became clear later in the work.[103] MacEwan's project "established the crudity of the Protestants' demarcation of revealed and natural theology, and so [he] attempted to rehabilitate the understanding of theology as reflection proceeding from a nature which is revealed and a revelation which is natural."[104] Understandably, war and the horror of mass

---

97. Marsden, *Fundamentalism and American Culture*, 26.

98. Ibid., 3.

99. Lewis, *Mere Christianity*, 124.

100. Ibid.

101. McGrath, *The Open Secret*, 257.

102. Ibid.

103. MacEwan, "Missing Persons: Individual Eschatology in Twentieth-Century Protestant Theology," 16. MacEwan utilizes Pannenberg's theology of time to begin to see a new way forward, 267.

104. Ibid., 286.

destruction contributed to these theologies of 'crisis' and 'hope' that saw severe flaws in preceding positivistic theologies that wanted to minimize evil over and against human progress. Yet, by removing God so far from the world, doctrine was stretched in the direction of a soft agnosticism, which pronounced a picture of the absence of God from culture. Subsequently, McGrath has also drawn attention to the current need to understand that "nature and supernature are not to be thought of as two separate worlds, but as different expressions of the same reality."[105] McGrath provides a good summary of the friendship-ending debate between Karl Barth and Emil Brunner over this very issue.[106] An important highlight was Barth and Brunner's agreement regarding the "act of perception [in revelation]—the recognition of something for what it really is, when that reality, though publicly accessible, possesses a deeper meaning that is veiled or hidden."[107] Both understood this "act" to be one of "divine grace," but neither, especially Barth, was willing to acknowledge the extent of God's grace in the wider culture.[108] MacEwan's research on heaven points in the direction that is being pursued in the current project, as well as McGrath's open-ended conclusion to see the world, "afresh" and to "open conversations, redirect thinking, and explore new options."[109] Thus, the conversation now turns towards furthering our understanding of the relationship between the imagination and revelation.

IMAGINATION AND DIVINE REVELATION

The imagination as a conditioning factor cannot help but be in relation to truth. We must not make firm demarcations to understand the working relationship of the mind and the critical importance of the imagination. This being the case, why is the human imagination a key component for interpreting divine revelation? Farrer argues "that divine truth is supernaturally communicated to men in an act of inspired thinking which falls into the shape of certain images."[110] He continues:

> To consider a further point: how it is that the images are able to signify divine realities. The images themselves are not what

---

105. McGrath, *The Open Secret*, 15.
106. Ibid., 158–64.
107. Ibid., 163.
108. Ibid.
109. Ibid., 314.
110. Farrer, *The Glass of Vision*, 57.

is principally revealed: they are no more than instruments by which realities are to be known. The inspired man may not reflect on the instrumental function of the images, but whether he reflects on it or not, he makes an instrumental use of them. He does not think *about* the images, but about what he takes them to signify.[111]

The way in which Farrer constructs his picture is to draw attention to the Spirit's work in revealing: "we have to listen to the Spirit speaking divine things: and the way to appreciate his speech is to quicken our own minds with the life of inspired images."[112] He provides the example of the early church looking into the scriptures and interpreting the images in order to understand the Trinity.[113] Where scriptures have the power to challenge later images, later images can also challenge theological assumptions that may need addressing within a specific historical context.

Take, for example, a period in early United States history where ministers used scripture to reinforce the image of baptism as a sign of salvation for African slaves. By concentrating on baptism as a part of spiritual formation rather than a sign of physical liberation, these preachers were also concerned to "affirm they [the slaves] were not planning to use baptism as an excuse for seeking their freedom."[114] Mark Noll goes on to cite Albert Raboteau's observations concerning the "unanticipated hope": when slaves "found, for example, that the Bible had more to say about Jesus lifting burdens than slaves obeying masters, blacks discovered a secret their masters did not want them to know."[115] An important observation rests in the fact that once the doctrine was public, multiple interpretations could be extracted from the image and in the act of participation better understandings of the doctrine could emerge. The uneducated are not determined to construct the wrong interpretation, but on the contrary, popular culture often has an understanding that serves as a reminder of an interpretation within the history of Christian thought, an interpretation that may need to be applied differently in a new context. Even more significant is how experience of a doctrine often came before knowing how to read or interpret the text.[116] Noll argues, "slaves

---

111. Ibid.
112. Ibid., 44.
113. Ibid.
114. Noll, *A History of Christianity in the United States and Canada*, 79.
115. Ibid.
116. Brown, *Tradition & Imagination*, 322. Brown makes an important comment concerning the mass population throughout Christian history where illiteracy was much wider than literacy and that for "most Christians [the] primary experience of their faith will have been visual and, though probably a lesser degree, aural," 322.

made a sharp distinction between the Bible that their owners preached to them, with its emphasis on not stealing and obeying masters, and the Bible they discovered for themselves, with its message of liberation for the captive and redemption for the oppressed."[117] The use of the Old Testament narratives, Noll argues, "undergirded the powerful social dimension of the Bible among slaves," but I would go further than Noll in suggesting that placing all the weight on the Bible does not do enough justice to the cultural dimensions carried through the song traditions of the slave communities.[118] God was perhaps speaking through the images of songs within the popular culture of the slaves.[119] The hermeneutic for understanding what God was saying did not come primarily through reading the scriptures (a good portion of the population was illiterate), but through a much wider combination of popular music, often containing re-appropriations of biblical imagery, but certainly not sung in traditional congregational settings. Where illiteracy was prevalent, it would seem more appropriate to pay attention to modes of theologizing from religious experience, which incorporates a wider range of the Spirit's activity outside of Bible reading. Where "many early Americans and not a few in more recent days have regarded the United States as God's New Israel, a nation established in this New World Canaan as a land flowing with wealth and freedom," Noll is at least correct here to show where the cultural interpretation pulled in a different direction during the pre-civil war period, as well as in the twentieth century among "Christian radicals" who "reversed the typology: America is Egypt, and *escape* from American institutions is the Exodus" in order to show the evils of injustice.[120]

A second example flowing out of what Rodney Clapp named as the "Great Contradiction that is America" is found in George McKinney's article on the Azusa Street Revival in Los Angeles, California, where a number of Pentecostal leaders connected to the revival met in Hot Springs, Arkansas in 1914.[121] Between the years of 1906–14, many of these leaders, led by W. J. Seymour, a son of a slave, along with "other sons and daughters of slaves participated equally with sons and daughters of slave owners and confirmed

---

117. Noll, *A History of Christianity in the United States and Canada*, 405.

118. Ibid.

119. See Gary Scott Smith, *Heaven in the American Imagination*. Smith observes, "sermons and songs taught them [slaves] that God had liberated the Jews from Egyptian captivity and Daniel from the lion's den. As one spiritual asked, 'My Lord delivered Daniel, Why can't he deliver me?'" 91.

120. Ibid., 406.

121. McKinney, "The Azusa Street Revival Revisited," 80. I will return to Clapp's work later in chapter three, which concerns popular music and memory in heaven. See Clapp, *Johnny Cash and the Great American Contradiction*, xii.

segregationists," where they had witnessed "miracles of salvation, healing, deliverance from demon possession, and so on, as well as the 'washing away of the color line in the blood of Jesus.'"[122] McKinney argues that these leaders missed a great opportunity in Arkansas to cultivate a different reading of the situation, and by doing so, McKinney connects their "bad decision" with the following "fifty-four years of segregation and suffering that culminated in the death of Martin Luther King."[123] In this case, the church paid so much attention to racial differences of their fellow human beings that all transcendent experiences of embodied expressions, pointing towards unity, were left vacant with disastrous consequences. They had failed to recognize that they were working with a reliable hermeneutic in their experiences of the Holy Spirit. These Pentecostal experiences helped to keep alive better interpretations of the Spirit's activity. But rather than allowing for a reception of the Spirit, through shared religious experiences to shape and condition their doctrines of equality, interpretive pressure was manipulated by segregationist agendas. Whereas the revival leaders were willing to look back on the tradition to other doctrines that they were applying more freely with defamiliarizing effects, which in turn was breathing life "to affirm unity in the family of God," they were unwilling to hold the same receptive model for bridging equality.[124] In other words, where existing biblical hermeneutics produced a restrictive interpretation preventing immediate implementation, religious experience mediated through a particular cultural form helped critique existing hermeneutics.

A further illustration of the point can be found in the writing of Jaroslav Pelikan, where he offers a number of instances of this interaction in his work *Jesus through the Centuries*. Each chapter heading traces some type of historical development in the life of the church and society that illustrates where emphasis was added, challenged, or simply changed due to the cultural situation. Rather than suggesting that culture enjoys all the leverage in applying interpretive pressure on the church, a more effective and positive way of understanding the human situation is to look at the dissonance in relation to revelation in all areas of culture, including the church, and see where the Spirit is working beyond the reductionism, cynicism, fundamentalism, nihilism, and other closed systems that argue for context, yet pay no attention to what the Spirit is doing in the here and now. As Smith

---

122. Ibid., 80–81.

123. Ibid.

124. Ibid. Only recently have classical Pentecostal groups such as the Assemblies of God and Church of God in Christ begun reconciling dialogue after decades of separation historically scarred by racial tension. See Dan Van Veen, "AG and COGIC Leaders Gather in Historic Meeting," (AG.org News & Information, 2013).

comments, "Christian worship resists two sorts of reductionism: a dualistic, supernaturalistic gnosticism, on the one hand, and a materialistic, flattened naturalism, on the other."[125] He adds, "the sacramental imagination runs counter to both of these reductionistic understandings of the world."[126] Pelikan offers a telling example of how the historical development within the scriptural understanding of revelation changed from the Old Testament, where the Israelites crossed the Red Sea, which is later developed as a "'type' of Christian baptism."[127] Pelikan makes the all-important observation:

> The God who prohibited religious art as the idolatrous effort to depict the divine in visible form had now taken the initiative of depicting himself in visible form, and had done so not in metaphor or in memorial but in person and, quite literally, 'in the flesh.' The metaphysical had become historical, and the cosmic Logos who was the true image of the Father from eternity had now become a part of time and could be portrayed in an image of his divine-human person as this had carried out the events of salvation history.[128]

Farrer sees the interactionist role of images in revelation working in the following way:

> The great images interpreted the events of Christ's ministry, death and resurrection, and the events interpreted the images; the interplay of the two is revelation. Certainly the events without the images would be no revelation at all, and the images without the events would remain shadows on the clouds.[129]

This is not to assert that the imagination is beyond deviation, but rather, it needs to be just as discerning as in any other function of human understanding. Farrer is not ignorant of the common hesitancy towards images in connection with revelation among some for the sole reason that will surely arise in any critique of such a project: how does one see through the "veiledness" or limitation in order to discover the transcendent or, perhaps more commonly asked, why this image over that image? It does not follow that all images are equal in strength. Farrer's answer provides some clarity, "man reasons, and God reveals. We need not of course conclude that the

---

125. Smith, *Desiring the Kingdom*, 143.
126. Ibid.
127. Pelikan, *Jesus through the Centuries*, 91.
128. Ibid., 92.
129. Farrer, *The Glass of Vision*, 43.

proportion between the two factors is everywhere the same."[130] Farrer makes an important contribution in pointing once again back to the incarnation:

> Our supernatural act is precisely the love of a God revealed: and so the veil is done away, for we cannot love him unless we know him. Yes, but we can love a God whom we know by faith alone; and therefore the veil remains. All we have to say is that the veil, however impenetrable, is not blank. It is painted with the image of God, and God himself painted it, and made it indelible with his blood, when he was nailed to it for us men and for our salvation. We know him through the image, and by faith: our supernatural acts take their intention and form from a revealed description of the saving mysteries.[131]

I want to concede the difficulty involved in such metaphysical discussions. Farrer places this type of discussion in the framework of working with mysteries and the goal of metaphysics is never to try to break in behind the metaphor, but to constantly break the metaphor to refine and better the descriptions. "By continually breaking and bettering and breaking his descriptions the metaphysician refines his understanding of that which he tries to describe."[132]

"Description" is, nonetheless, a term to consider with great care, not least because contemporary theologians have been hesitant to provide images describing heaven, while insufficiently acknowledging the role that analogical thinking plays in the interchange of image and reality. One might be more hard pressed to find a more "descriptive" or imaginative doctrine than heaven in the history of Western culture. How, then, does this analogical refinement process work in such a way as not to draw too many fixed points, yet not completely untie the image from the truth? Farrer offers some helpful insight into how such analogical discourse is refined:

> If we want to proceed further than the last stage of refinement of analogy will bear, we can only do it by standing on the extreme tip of our tapering spit of analogical description, and pointing out to sea. We say "we are getting towards the nature of the knowing act, but still this isn't it: it is just itself, and lies beyond." Such dumb pointing is not, of course, the only resource of the metaphysician who has stretched his analogical tether to the limit. He may take up an alternative analogy for the same mystery, and work that out in a similar way; he may attempt a

---

130. Ibid., 2.
131. Ibid., 61.
132. Ibid., 63 & 68.

composite picture out of several analogies: there is no end to the things he may do. Nevertheless, in principle, the method remains what our sketch indicates: the description of natural mysteries by the criticism of analogies. And "analogies" is only another name for sober and appropriate images.[133]

Thus, there is a very long tradition of understanding how the imagination perceives the action of God in the world. Our human situation is finite, yet rationally and relationally positioned to know God's revealing love through his action in creation. As Farrer reminds us, "rational knowledge of God comes to us wholly by way of analogies: and what are analogies but sober and criticized images?"[134] In no way does this detract attention away from the supernatural revelation of God, but rather, places emphasis upon the important role of the imagination.[135]

CONCLUSION

In this initial chapter, I have sought to establish a theology of revelation that supports my understanding of the Spirit working in popular culture. By providing an account of the importance of the imagination in the reception of revelation through the historical process, I have established the importance for development and ongoing doctrinal interpretation. In chapter two, I will turn my attention to recent developments in New Testament studies and Western religious thought, and reasons why one should look towards popular culture in constructing a hermeneutics of doctrine.

---

133. Ibid., 70–71.
134. Ibid., 62.
135. Ibid., 61.

2

Whatever Happened to Heaven?

The previous chapter set forth a theological rationale for critical engagement with popular culture in this book. The second chapter has two principle purposes. First, I will argue against one of the dominant narratives in New Testament studies, which claims that the human desire for heaven, as well as the church's understanding of heaven, is misguided and that the necessary corrective is to change the emphasis away from the directional problematic of the church, from humanity going to heaven, and turn towards the biblical focus on a general bodily resurrection, where heaven comes to us at the last day.[1] I argue that this narrative deprivileges a key scriptural tradition and also does not give enough weight to the further development of the doctrine of heaven in culture. Paralleling this discussion, I will then trace some of the recent developments in Western thought concerning heaven which would seem to point us towards engaging more deeply with popular culture. In pursuing that discussion, questions pertaining to the meaning of "popular" culture will also be addressed.

NEW TESTAMENT STUDIES AND CHALLENGES TO TRADITIONAL NOTIONS OF HEAVEN

While scholars such as Colleen McDannell and Bernhard Lang observe that theologians "deplore the silly movies and angel junk that people sell and buy," this comes with debilitating implications for theology's ability to give an account of contemporary concerns with the afterlife.[2] By contrast,

---

1. See Wright's comments in Wright, *Surprised By Hope*, 148.
2. Lang, *Heaven: A History*, xiii–xiv.

a historian such as Jeffrey Russell has at least sought to regain a hearing for heaven through his multiple works exploring not only theology's disinterest but the lack of work in philosophy and other such disciplines within culture; he argues, instead, that we "need a revival of the imagination."[3] Yet theologians such as Hans Urs von Balthasar have argued that appropriate imagery for heaven ended with the incarnation of Christ; therefore, "heaven is no longer an image [or a place for that matter] but a Person."[4] Contemporary theology has in fact predominantly argued in a similar Balthasaristic vein, that immediate survival is of little consequence in the biblical traditions and the physical resurrection at the *eschaton* is what truly matters. Furthermore, biblical scholars such as N. T. Wright have argued that the traditional heaven completely misses the point of the biblical witnesses since:

> "Going to heaven when you die" is not held out in the New Testament as the main goal. The main goal is to be bodily raised into the transformed, glorious likeness of Jesus Christ. If we want to speak of "going to heaven when we die," we should be clear that this represents the first, and far less important, stage of a two-stage process.[5]

At the same time, as Anthony Thiselton reminds us, we should not be quite so quick to dismiss the observation that, "we are left with two apparently different biblical traditions."[6] He draws support from Jesus' words to the thief on the cross in Luke 23:43 and Paul's desire described in Philippians 1:23 to be with Christ, which is admittedly the "more popular" tradition.[7] The second text, following from Paul's early work to the Thessalonians in 1 Thessalonians 4:16–17 as Thiselton explains, "seems more sophisticated" and needs unpacking by interpreting more of Paul's work, as for instance in the letters to the Corinthians where Paul stresses bodily resurrection.[8] According to Wright, "sometimes the word 'resurrection' has even come to be used as a synonym for 'going to heaven,' which is about as misleading as it could be."[9] Yet, McDannell and Lang argue that "resurrection as Jesus understood it, referred to the individual's post-mortem exaltation to heaven. He challenged both the Sadducean rejection of the afterlife and the

---

3. Russell, *Paradise Mislaid*, 156.
4. Balthasar, *Prayer*, 278.
5. Wright, *For All the Saints*, 21.
6. Thiselton, *Life after Death*, 71.
7. Ibid.
8. Ibid.
9. Wright, *For All the Saints*, 2.

apocalyptic expectation of a long life on earth."[10] These historians make the case that within Luke's account of the Sadducean questioning of Jesus in Luke 20, Jesus uses the Old Testament to show how:

> The patriarchs [Abraham, Isaac, Jacob, and Moses] are dead only to us, but not to God. Rather than languishing in Sheol, Jesus asserted that the dead have risen up to God. They now live in his presence in heaven. From this conclusion it is further inferred that many men and women must also be with God in the same way.[11]

For McDannell and Lang, "Jesus imagined the new life not only as spiritual and immortal, but also as contemporaneous with this one."[12] Admittedly, these historians of thought note that Jesus "did not break with the apocalyptic hope for an end of Israel's suffering," but rather, "shared the belief in the imminent close of human history."[13] McDannell and Lang argue that for Jesus, "contemporaries surviving the dramatic end of history would have no advantage over the dead, and vice versa. The kingdom was the same for all who were received into it."[14] Here the historians follow what "seems to echo an authentic saying of Jesus" in 1 Thessalonians 4:15.[15]

Part of the concern in contemporary biblical scholarship is to cleanse tradition of misconstructed representations of heaven. In so doing, however, do such efforts risk too much? Carol Zaleski finds in Oscar Cullman, along with a host of other modern attempts, the desire

> to strip away the language of immortality in order to restore the Christian eschatological imagination to its biblical purity. The effect of this purifying critique has been to make many thoughtful Christians feel trapped in a forced choice between death as friend and death as enemy, between personal and collective forms of eschatological hope.[16]

Zaleski takes note of Simon Tugwell's work, and his argument that "the original message of Christianity was not resurrection versus immortality, but hope versus hopelessness."[17] Earlier in her work, Zaleski elaborates, "it

---

10. Lang, *Heaven: A History*, 27.
11. Ibid., 27.
12. Ibid., 26.
13. Ibid., 29.
14. Ibid.
15. Ibid., 362.
16. Zaleski, *The Life of the World to Come*, 43.
17. Ibid., 93. Also see Tugwell, *Human Immortality and the Redemption of Death*, 113.

is not a matter of arriving at a philosophic faith in immortality by reasoned steps, and then complicating this faith by adding to it the rather more extravagant claim that there will be a resurrection, to boot. Christian faith in life beyond death is revealed by faith in the resurrection and flows from it."[18]

Wright's work on the resurrection, and his refutation of heaven as the primary focus, has reached a wide audience within scholarly, as well as popular circles. For instance, Lisa Miller, in her well-written journalistic approach to heaven, cites Wright multiple times, especially regarding his insistence on securing the historical resurrection of Jesus against any connection to metaphor, including metaphors concerning heaven.[19] Wright's concern follows from his belief that metaphorical speech about the afterlife will distract public thought from the actual event of Jesus rising.[20] He insists that resurrection and heaven have nothing to do with one another when he observes:

> The resurrection narratives in the gospels never, ever say anything like, "Jesus is raised, therefore there is a life after death," let alone, "Jesus is raised, therefore we shall go to heaven when we die." Nor even, in a more authentic first-century Christian way do they say, "Jesus is raised, therefore we shall be raised from the dead after the sleep of death." No. Insofar as the event is interpreted, Easter has a very this-worldly, present-age meaning: Jesus is raised, so he is the Messiah, and therefore he is the world's true Lord; Jesus is raised, so God's new creation has begun—and we, his followers, have a job to do![21]

I disagree with Wright in three main areas. First, by dismissing what is admittedly a minority tradition in scripture, Wright does not recognize that popular culture is preserving something of this minority tradition of immediate post-mortem survival in heaven that theology should take seriously. For instance, in response to a paper by Markus Bockmuehl titled, "Did St. Paul Go to Heaven When He Died," Wright tries to suggest that he has "never rejected the traditional Christian belief that the faithful 'go to heaven' when they die'" and that he does "not regard that expectation as a 'corruption of the hope of bodily resurrection,'" as Bockmuehl accuses him.[22] He is more concerned with a vision for a new earth, instead of talking about other worlds. Nonetheless, I argue that Wright has reduced the

18. Zaleski, *The Life of the World to Come*, 42.
19. Miller, *Heaven*, xxiii.
20. Ibid.
21. Wright, *Surprised by Hope*, 56.
22. See Wright's "Response to Markus Bockmuehl," 232.

descriptive quality of human post-mortem existence that follows the tradition stemming from Luke 23:43. "παραδεισοζ" has Edenic qualities that should not be taken to be understood as Jesus saying to the thief something along the lines of, "you will be in a reduced quality of life today. We only use the term paradise to denote interim rest." Surely the thief would be not only in a better place than on a cross, but also "paradise" used in its long tradition of Persian roots depicting Eden must at the very least paint enhanced other-worldly characteristics, rather than a reduced quality of life.[23] Where Wright wants to steer us away from "*final* destination" language in describing heaven, Bockmuehl counters by observing: "the biblical Paul believes, and was understood by his early readers to believe, that to die was to go 'home' to the Lord and to enter safely—and permanently—into his heavenly kingdom (2 Cor 5:1, 8; 2 Tim 4:18)."[24]

Secondly, I argue that Wright has given insufficient attention to the positive role that culture has played in preserving important aspects of this doctrine. Wright appears to have a rather negative view of culture: culture is dismissed as the place that theologians look to perceive revelatory impact; therefore, Wright gives little if any attention to how the doctrine may, in fact, be embedded in the church due precisely to particular cultural situations. Take, for example, Cyprian's use of the metaphor of home, offering encouragement to those martyrs facing persecution. As McGrath points out, Cyprian talked of heaven as the "'native land' of Christians, from which they have been exiled during their time on earth."[25] Although Wright acknowledges the work of William Wilberforce to abolish slavery, he adds, "I do think, though, that the 'heaven-as-ultimate-home' philosophy, as developed in the nineteenth century, did eventually cut the nerve of social justice and continues to do so."[26] Wright focuses on the need to "remember especially that the use of the word 'heaven' to denote the ultimate goal of the redeemed, though hugely emphasized by medieval piety, mystery plays, and the like, and still almost universal at a popular level, is severely misleading and does not begin to do justice to the Christian hope."[27] For Wright, the many-sided interpretations of heaven in Christianity is a throw-back to late Roman antiquity where people, "found it difficult to rid its collective imagination of the many layered panoply of gods and lords, of demi-gods and heroes, that had been collecting in the culture for well over a thousand

---

23. Scott, *A Greek–English Lexicon*, 1308.
24. Bockmuehl, "Did St. Paul Go to Heaven When He Died?" 231.
25. McGrath, *A Brief History of Heaven*, 140.
26. Wright, "Response to Markus Bockmuehl," 233.
27. Wright, *For All the Saints*, 21.

years."²⁸ He expresses, then, his deep fear "that we have been simply drifting into a muddle and a mess, putting together bits and pieces of traditions, ideas and practices in the hope that they will make sense. They don't."²⁹

The dilemma that Wright faces, however, is that he wants heaven to be a place of "restful happiness," yet he also wants to postpone all resurrection life until the end of history.³⁰ He is thus neither interested nor willing to ask concrete questions about immediate survival. In critiquing his own Anglican tradition, Wright comments, "I suggest that a good deal of our current view of death and the life beyond has come from none of these [scripture, tradition, and reason] but rather from impulses in the culture that created, at best, semi-Christian informal traditions that now need to be reexamined in the clear light of scripture."³¹

At the same time, Wright instinctively knows that in order to make history intelligible, a necessary first step is painting a picture of the cultural context that enables one to understand people's values, politics, art, education, and experiences. In his massive work on the resurrection, then, Wright sets out to take account of late Roman culture.³² He recounts several examples of ancient culture from Homer to Plato but, after taking such an inventory, his conclusion is consistently negative, leaving slim probability of discovering truth through the long held practice of reinterpreting existing metaphors.³³

At this point, it is important to remember that the church has held different stances towards culture. Robert Wilken draws from the example of the early church, in that, "although Christian thinkers worked within a Greek and Roman tradition of moral philosophy that preceded them, they transformed what they received."³⁴ Although Wright is skeptical of cultural interpretations of death and what follows, in other places he is clear that the topic is of utmost importance in Western thought, as he declares:

> From Plato to Hegel and beyond, some of the greatest philosophers declared that what you think about death, and life beyond it, is the key to thinking seriously about everything else—and indeed, that it provides one of the main reasons for thinking

---

28. Ibid., 41. Johnston also argues that "Wright ends up being too tentative in his assessment of God's revelatory Presence . . ." See Johnston, *God's Wider Presence*, 36.
29. Wright, *For All the Saints*, xiv.
30. Ibid., 36.
31. Wright, *Surprised by Hope*, 27.
32. Wright, *The Resurrection of the Son of God*, 37.
33. Wilken, *The Spirit of Early Christian Thought*, xvii.
34. Ibid., xxii.

seriously about anything at all. This is something a Christian theologian should heartily endorse.[35]

Even where Wright addresses developments in literature and film in contemporary culture, his conclusion on cultural metaphors remains largely negative. In his view, "what is more worrying, this multiple ignorance seems often to be true in churches as well."[36] He adds, "when art comes to terms with both the wounds of the world and the promise of resurrection and learns how to express and respond to both at once, we will be on the way to a fresh vision, a fresh mission."[37] Here, he specifically refers to "Christian" art, and even then he is quite unimpressed.[38] Wright continues, "art at its best draws attention not only to the way things are but also to the way things will be, when the earth is filled with the knowledge of God as the waters cover the sea," but he holds such a low view of popular culture that one will often find him using "popular imagination" in a negative sense, as if popular culture is excluded from theologizing or constructing a worldview.[39]

History teaches us, however, that popular culture can interpret belief in ways that can challenge church instruction. Interestingly, Wright's hermeneutic places a 'first step' value on the understanding of the cultural context, but then insists it always 'gets it wrong.' Wright seems to insist necessarily that the elimination of "misunderstandings" within the symbolical constructions of ancient culture is all the truth that can be gleaned from outside ancient Judaism, as if Judaism was working in some type of cultural vacuum.[40] Yet in other places where it suits his purpose, Wright argues that Christianity's collective memory must not steer it away from tradition, but "must be taken seriously in any eschatologically based and mission-shaped view of the church."[41] He adds, "of course beware of idolatry," which is, as Gordon Kaufman learned from his mentor Richard Niebuhr, "the fundamental theological task, as well as our most profound and difficult human task, [that] is to distinguish between God and the idols."[42]

Wright's observation of the many images of heaven is not ignored by heaven's proponents. Zaleski makes clear that the

---

35. Wright, *Surprised by Hope*, 6.
36. Ibid., 12.
37. Ibid., 224.
38. Ibid., 223–24.
39. Ibid., 224–25. Also, see Wright's, "Response to Markus Bockmuehl," 231.
40. Wright, *The Resurrection of the Son of God*, 84.
41. Wright, *Surprised by Hope*, 261.
42. Ibid. Also, see Kaufman, *The Theological Imagination*, 17.

proliferation and redundancy of images for postmortem existence is therefore the norm; the effort to cook them down to a single conception has never been shown to succeed. Indeed, if it were to succeed, it would render unintelligible many of the things people do for the dead. Again, this would mean the breaking of vital links between the society of the living and the dead-the outcome would be not clarity, but anomie and despair.[43]

In pinpointing a few of the concerns of Wright and others, Zaleski names the following "three knotty questions of Christian eschatology: anthropological dualism, the interim period between death and resurrection, and judgment of the dead."[44] In order to address the first contestation, where Wright finds Platonic dualism detestable, others have been honest enough to recognize a number of Christian responses are appropriate, especially surrounding issues of creation where Christians believe matter is not evil, but rather good and that creation is a gift, a "free act" of God, not an abortion or emanation.[45] Wright's strong push back against any type of dualism in order to secure a body-soul unity finds a slight, if not important disjunction. If the "real" person is experiencing "restful happiness," waiting for a re-embodiment, it is hard to get around at least some type of dualism.[46]

At the same time, to ignore the contribution of Platonic references is to ignore much of the history of Christian doctrine. For example, the continuity between the physical and spiritual is precisely the project Hans Boersma sets out to achieve in his work *Heavenly Participation*, where he argues that the *nouvelle theologie* saw the need to go back further than Thomism or the Neo-Thomist approach because "they recognized in the Platonist-Christian synthesis a sacramental ontology that they [such French thinkers as Henri de Lubac and Jean Danielou] believed had been lost through the modern separation between nature and the supernatural."[47] Boersma's work points to a growing emphasis on the need to "rediscover" or a "plea for a retrieval *(resourcement)* of a theology of heavenly participation."[48] If "the modern period has taught us to look to other sources as the main guides for establishing our life together," rather than theology, do the shapes of these sources or narratives help us in expressing God's presence with us or do

43. Zaleski, *The Life of the World to Come*, 66.
44. Ibid., 55.
45. Boersma, *Heavenly Participation*, 33–34.
46. Wright, *Surprised by Hope*, 171.
47. Boersma, *Heavenly Participation*, 15–16.
48. Ibid., 3.

they continue to encourage us towards the "dissident choice [which] has been to take temporal goods for ultimate ends?"[49] Boersma is honing in on a significant issue that carries implications for many categories within theology, not least anthropology. Zaleski also argues that "the body is also, in the Platonic tradition, the indispensable means by which we are to engage in our essential calling as seekers of truth and lovers of the good."[50]

Thirdly, Wright seems to be unintentionally aligning with culture's emphasis upon materialism. For example, he seems to overlook the way in which materialistic interpretations of the *eschaton* play well in accord with the culture's insistence upon materialistic understandings of the world. The very culture Wright is deeply suspicious of is at once the very culture conditioning notions of materialism based on "pervasive rational and technological qualities" that lead towards "reduced and truncated versions of the afterlife."[51] The type of suspicion Wright suggests can become a liability if we are unwilling to acknowledge, as Walter Brueggeman suggests, that every hermeneutical or listening posture, including our own, carries a "woundedness" that inevitably impedes certain communities from going "the way of our theological reading for reasons of lived reality."[52] Ironically, for different reasons, contemporary exegetes, as well as secular materialists, have determined "the drama of the future is decidedly this-worldly."[53] McDannell and Lang insightfully observe: "the denial of individual life after death agrees with the very substance of contemporary ideology which rejects the supernatural and insists that the true concern of humanity is life on earth."[54] It is important to emphasize at this point, in order not to be misunderstood, that I affirm the scriptures are true in their use of imagery, and that interpretations of what the future entails is firmly pointing to the totality of what God values in humanity, including the goodness of materiality in humanity and nature.

Further, Wright is concerned with much more than thinking correct thoughts about heaven. He is concerned with how people live now and the contribution that they will make towards restoring justice to God's good creation. He fears that escapism is too prevalent in contemporary eschatology, leaving the world in further shambles. In a recent *TIME* article, Jon Meacham features Wright in discussing the divergent interpretations of

49. Ibid., 19.
50. Zaleski, *The Life of the World to Come*, 55.
51. Lang, *Heaven: A History*, 351.
52. Brueggeman, "A First Retrospect on the Consultation," 344.
53. Lang, *Heaven: A History*, 352.
54. Ibid., 351.

heaven.[55] Meacham quotes Wright's dialogue with Stephen Hawking where Wright comments, "of course there are people who think 'heaven' as a kind of pie-in-the-sky dream of an afterlife to make the thought of dying less awful."[56] Wright continues, "no doubt that's a problem as old as the human race. But in the Bible, 'heaven' isn't the place where people go when they die. In the Bible heaven is God's space, while earth (or if you like, 'the cosmos' or 'creation') is our space."[57]

Interestingly, where Wright is concerned with the plight of humanity, some with similar concerns take an opposing approach. For example, Meacham quotes Cleophus LaRue of Princeton where he "points out the global South still believes in the miraculous. The poor cling to the hope of a future heaven to persevere through life's hardships."[58] Zaleski even goes further to observe that "the effort to starve out the will to imagine has not produced the humane fruits it was expected to bring. If anything, the contrary has been shown to be the case: totalistic efforts to create utopia on earth and to suppress pie-in-the sky thinking have ended by creating hell on earth."[59] Lewis also distrusted the "shyness" of mentioning heaven in a modern context:

> We are afraid of the jeer about "pie in the sky," and of being told that we are trying to "escape" from the duty of making a happy world here and now into the dreams of a happy world elsewhere. But either there is "pie in the sky" or there is not. If there is not, then Christianity is false, for this doctrine is woven into its whole fabric.[60]

---

55. Meacham, "Heaven Can't Wait," 36.
56. Ibid.
57. Ibid.
58. Ibid.
59. Zaleski, *The Life of the World to Come*, 48.
60. Lewis, *Problem of Pain*, 129–30. One may also consider some of Lewis' observations regarding hope: "Hope is one of the Theological virtues. This means that a continual looking forward to the eternal world is not (as some modern people think) a form of escapism or wishful thinking, but one of the things a Christian is meant to do. It does not mean that we are to leave the present world as it is. If you read the history you will find that the Christians who did most for the present world were just those who thought most of the next. The Apostles themselves, who set on foot the conversion of the Roman Empire, the great men who built up the Middle Ages, the English Evangelicals who abolished the Slave Trade, all left their mark on Earth, precisely because their minds were occupied with Heaven. It is since Christians have largely ceased to think of the other world that they have become so ineffective in this. Aim at Heaven and you will get earth 'thrown in': aim at earth and you will get neither." See Lewis, *Mere Christianity*, 119.

Lewis, in no less extreme fashion, picks up an argument that is playing out in contemporary theological discussion. Lisa Miller draws on the work of President Barack Obama's former pastor:

> Reverend Jeremiah Wright, complained about this in a 1990 sermon at his Chicago church. His "educated friends," he said, wished he wouldn't talk so much about heaven "because that's so primitive, you see." These friends, Wright said, believed heaven-talk detracts from the real message of the Gospels, which is justice. But heaven, [Jeremiah] Wright insisted, is at the center of Christian belief. "If I drop heaven, I'm going to lose the first verse in my Bible," Wright preached. "If I drop heaven, I'm going to lose two of my Ten Commandments. . . . If I drop heaven, I'm going to have to stop praying my favorite prayer, 'Our Father.' . . . If I drop heaven, I'm going to do away with the Second Coming; I'm going to have to get rid of Pentecost. I'm going to have to throw Revelation out of my Bible. . . . Don't make me drop heaven!"[61]

In his interview with Boersma, Matthew Miller asked how Boersma reconciles, "a reorientation of our vision towards heaven with the biblical notion that humanity was created for inhabiting the earth and that our final destination is a renewed earth?" Boersma's reply gave strong indication that replacing one doctrine for another was not the most promising way forward. Boersma is quoted as saying:

> I'm not suggesting that we *replace* an earth-focused spirituality with a heaven-focused spirituality. To be sure, according to Saint Paul, heaven is our home. But it is that because that's where our citizen-papers are housed, as it were. Heaven certainly ought to be our aim. But this is not a matter of *replacing* earth with heaven. If we did that, we'd still only have one side of the equation. What I am arguing for instead is a sacramental vision that genuinely values earthly, created realities, precisely by acknowledging that they are not ultimate. It is when we insist that earthly realities are ultimate that we lose their mysterious depth—precisely that which gives them their significance in the first place.[62]

N. T. Wright is consistent in stating his position that heaven and earth will come together at the resurrection, but as Boersma shares in the interview, "the problem with so much this-worldly talk about the hereafter is that it

---

61. Miller, *Heaven*, 211–12.
62. Miller, "Eerdmans 100 Interview Series: Hans Boersma," (2011).

unwittingly drags the separation between heaven and earth into the hereafter, while still focusing on the latter, even when it comes to the eschaton itself."[63]

Several strengths of Wright stand out. First, his concern to ensure truthful revelatory impact consistently shows up in his thoughtful work on the scriptures. Secondly, he is faithful in drawing careful attention to the need for a thought-out hermeneutical methodology, which prompts further work in constructive theology. Boersma also appreciates that Wright's "belief in the resurrection entails the transformation of earthly realities."[64] But, as is sometimes the case, our greatest strength, may limit us to move in ways that would be helpful to consider. As suggested earlier, what may be needed in contemporary theology is not a continuation of twentieth-century Protestant rehearsal of why God is inaccessible to the world, but a recognition that all theological constructs are interpretations of history and experience. Wright is creatively rejecting much of twentieth-century thought, but in the area of discussions concerning immediate survival in eschatology, he is still very much in line with those within that stream. Also, human experience is not just useful for context setting, but shaped the recipients of God's revelation where the human imagination is engaged in understanding this revelation. The trend within New Testament studies to pull interpretation of heaven in a different direction from the long tradition of two complementary aspects is one more example of the cultural situation. By apparently making heaven only relevant to an earth-bound material culture, this trend continues the process of a distrust of the immaterial God, and downplays interpretations from within culture which may actually have deep roots within the tradition that challenges these recent trends.

Wright serves as a good example of the current marginalization of the doctrine of heaven within New Testament studies. Before explicitly addressing the need for theology to engage contemporary popular culture and its capacity to retain insights from Christian traditions on the topic of heaven, I want to turn briefly to the trajectory of scholarship regarding heaven in Western culture, to include mention of a broader range of interdisciplinary pursuits among historians and philosophers. This will provide a wider context to our discussion.

---

63. Ibid.
64. Boersma, *Heavenly Participation*, 4.

WESTERN THOUGHT AND PERCEIVED INADEQUACIES IN THEOLOGIES OF HEAVEN

In 2001, McDannell and Lang published a second edition of their initial 1988 contribution to the history of attitudes towards heaven.[65] Prior to 2001, Jeffrey B. Russell also produced his 1996 work, *A History of Heaven*, in which he claims that "heaven, a concept that has shaped so much of Christian thought and so much of the Christian attitude toward life, has been strangely neglected by modern historians."[66] Russell makes reference to McDannell and Lang's work, along with Jean Delumeau's *Histoire du paradis*, but claims that McDannell and Lang's history provides "little grasp of the interiority of the subject," although he admits the sociological contribution.[67] Unfortunately, Russell neglects to adequately substantiate his criticism of McDannell and Lang's work, except for a quick comparison with Alan Bernstein's research on hell, where Russell merely mentions the reference.[68]

Although McDannell and Lang do not mention Russell's work in their second edition, they have added a preface, offering further reason for more research in heaven studies. The authors emphasize "a renewed curiosity about life after death," within Christianity and the larger culture.[69] The authors comment: "not to be outdone by popular culture, scholars have also constructed their own stories about heaven; their historical monographs have deepened our portrait of heaven but have not altered it."[70] The praise of historians is short lived as the majority of the preface is a critique, as much as an indictment against the lack of theological contribution to our thinking about heaven. What is perceived as an inadequate response by theologians in light of what many see in culture as a deeply embedded phenomenon leaves McDannell and Lang puzzled as to why theology has not given more consideration to heaven. One of the hinges of this indictment hangs on the

---

65. Lang, *Heaven: A History*.

66. Russell, *A History of Heaven*, xiv. More recently, Gary Smith has developed his history of heaven by highlighting American cultural shifts in attitudes "based in part on personal and social factors." Smith, *Heaven in the American Imagination*, 237. Importantly, Smith draws attention to a binary in McDannell and Lang's argument that overly polarizes theocentric and anthropocentric images of heaven (ibid., 230).

67. Ibid., xiv.

68. Ibid.

69. Ibid., xiii.

70. Lang, *Heaven: A History*, xiii.

"expectation that they [heaven proponents] will meet their loved ones after they die."[71] McDannell and Lang further their argument by adding:

> And yet professionals in the field—theologians and some clergy—are frequently critical of this anthropocentric heaven. While these may be amused at the speculations of Renaissance poets or Victorian novelists, they generally prefer a more abstract, theocentric heaven. Many seem perfectly happy to believe in a heaven that cannot be described. They deplore the silly movies and angel junk that people sell and buy. Even when we point out that many reputable Christian writers tell of husband meeting wife in heaven or friend meeting friend, they are not impressed. No, the professionals argue, the notion of "meeting again" is neither desirable nor theologically viable. It is merely naive. We, however, believe it is the theologians that are naive. It is the anthropocentric view of heaven that has been the most widely articulated perspective. The expectation of being reunited with family and friends in heaven is so prevalent throughout Christian history that it is not surprising that contemporaries see it as the "natural" notion of life everlasting. Although "meeting in heaven" varies considerably in detail and is shaped by cultural trends and individual tastes, the general contours are easily recognizable. That one meets family and friends after death requires, for most people, no explanation. What does need to be accounted for, what needs argument and explanation, is precisely the "professionals' heaven," the theocentric notion. It is the heaven of the eternal contemplation of God that requires more ink to be spilled, more biblical passages to be cited, and more elaborate descriptions to be drawn. The theocentric heaven has been difficult to sustain, in spite of the fact that Christianity originated as an ascetic community with a charismatic leadership and a mystical experience of the divine.[72]

The indictment against these theologians is supported by a positive example of Perpetua and Felicity in the account of their Martyrdom, as well as later readings of their account in Augustine's sermons.[73] McDannell and Lang observe: "*The Martyrdom of Perpetua and Felicity* was instrumental in disseminating the idea of heavenly reunion throughout the early Christian world and encouraged Christians to take seriously their dreams of other

---

71. Ibid.
72. Ibid., xiii–xiv.
73. Ibid., xiv–xv.

worlds."[74] These historians claim that modern theologians too often dwell on both sides of an unhealthy divide, "between the person as theologian and the person as lover," consequently, leaving their hearers with a vague and uncertain understanding of the afterlife.[75]

One of the variables at least, which is central to this project is that "reason is seldom combined with imagination," especially in contemporary theological constructions of heaven.[76] Kreeft, referencing Roth's *Story and Reality*, observes: "rational philosophers and theologians seem suspicious of the imagination, and poets and storytellers suspicious of reason—as if imagination would pollute the purity of reason or reason kill the liveliness of imagination."[77] Near the end of his own work, Kreeft asks a series of concrete questions. For example, "will my dead cat be alive in heaven?" or "will we have sex organs in heaven? If we will not, will we all be neutered?"[78] Kreeft argues that Thomas Aquinas (1225–74) would not have been afraid to take up a response, where "ninety-nine out of a hundred contemporary theologians would not touch such questions with a ten-foot pen."[79]

Far from being a negative that the history of theology has produced no unified version of heaven, one should be more concerned if one claimed to have the only version. Following Aquinas, Kreeft argues that "words about Heaven are like words about God, are neither univocal nor equivocal but analogical: partly the same and partly different. They are neither nonsense nor photographic reproductions, neither simple lies nor simple truths. They are symbols, metaphors, images of the real thing."[80]

Although Russell clearly advocates a historical approach as "the best approach" to heaven research, he also sees the danger and hesitates to narrow the subject by compartmentalizing the sources from which he draws, but rather he is adamant one needs to be "incorporating insights from all disciplines."[81] Russell admits being partial to "the history of concepts" approach out of an unwarranted caution against being limited by the confessionalism of theological approaches, but at the same time he admits:

74. Ibid., xv.

75. Ibid., xvi–xviii.

76. Kreeft, *Everything You Ever Wanted to Know about Heaven But Never Dreamed of Asking*, 254.

77. See Kreeft's use of Roth's, *Story and Reality* to describe the integral relationship between the imagination and reason, 254.

78. Ibid., 253.

79. Ibid.

80. Ibid., 257–58.

81. Russell, *A History of Heaven*, 16.

> The theological tradition is itself broader than abstract or academic theology, for it embraces not only formal theology but the life and thought of the entire community.
>
> Tradition is not repetition, but the transmission of a living reality, which must be renewed and rethought as the community develops.[82]

Russell wants to remain far away from what he names as "the dead heart of reductionism and the dead hand of deconstruction."[83] He published his second volume on heaven in 2006 with a reemphasis upon avoiding "closed dogmatisms on the one hand, and evaporative relativisms on the other" in an effort to address some of the opposing arguments and he skillfully "shows their limitations."[84] Once again, Russell opens a door for further work in heaven studies, "heaven has gradually been shut away in a closet by the dominant intellectual trends of the past few centuries."[85]

And yet, theology is in a good position to account for the imagery history has used to paint stories of heaven in the past, but also to account for the role of the imagination in this longer Christian tradition, as well as in contemporary culture. After all, the Christian tradition has always had a pulse for trying to get at the truth, as McDannell and Lang's illustration of Bonhoeffer and Rahner depicts, but the limitations often rear their head, not because the theologian does not have time for the question, but rather, because of the burden to lead the enquirer to truth is difficult if certainty is sought after without "fresh handlings of inherited traditions."[86] For example, Russell observes that, "Barth's understandable quandary was the difficulty of expressing 'heaven' in modern idiom—in any language."[87] McDannell and Lang, however, do not show much sympathy for these modern thinkers who were trying to communicate in a culture that did not always recognize as Dante did, that "language can leap."[88]

Among sociologists, Peter Berger and Anton Zijderveld have recently argued that "modernity relativizes" and as theologians have worked to talk about absolutes in relativized modern, now post-modern contexts, "the awareness of our eventual and inescapable death is probably the most

---

82. Ibid., 17
83. Ibid.
84. Ibid., 1–3.
85. Ibid.
86. Brown, *Tradition & Imagination*, 57. Also, see Lang, *Heaven: A History*, xvi–xvii.
87. Russell, *Paradise Mislaid*, 122.
88. Ibid., 155.

pressing absolute."[89] Even in light of this universal experience, in *The Theology of Death* Douglas Davies picks up on a similar concern where the church and society no longer hold consensus in knowing what to do with traditional religious beliefs, "and nowhere is it better manifest than over ideas of death, hell, and heaven."[90] Davies observes that, "many contemporary churches have members who both do and do not hold what might be conceived as traditional beliefs over heaven and hell."[91] At the same time, various beliefs surrounding the certainty of death and what comes next find limited convergence between what theologians learn from each other and what the church and wider public come to endorse.[92] According to Davies, "theologians and clergy seldom engage with the public at large," especially concerning questions of eschatology.[93]

Alister McGrath has found in this area an important and striking connection between theology and culture in that "the exploration of the idea of heaven in the field of Western literature was far more interesting than anything I found in works of systematic theology."[94] McGrath's history is admittedly more "thematic, rather than historical," allowing for freedom to move between literary sources without rigid strictures of chronology, while serving as an encouragement for further theological work in the field.[95] McGrath is very theological in his thematic approach, while at the same time paying close attention to one of his central claims; namely, "the Christian concept of heaven is iconic, rather than intellectual—something that makes its appeal to the imagination, rather than the intellect, which calls out to be visualized rather than merely understood."[96] Connecting the Greek Orthodox tradition of "public worship of the church [as it] represents a drawing close to the threshold of heaven itself" to the Isaiah 6:1–5 text, McGrath argues: "The central insight that many theologians gleaned from this passage is that human beings are simply not capable of beholding the worship of heaven itself; it must be accommodated to their capacity through being reflected in created things—such as the created order, the sacramental bread and wine, or the liturgy itself."[97]

89. Berger, *In Praise of Doubt*, 25.
90. Davies, *The Theology of Death*, 92.
91. Ibid., 81.
92. Ibid., 94.
93. Ibid.
94. McGrath, *A Brief History of Heaven*, x.
95. Ibid., ix.
96. Ibid., 166.
97. Ibid., 166–67.

Following McGrath's suggestion, I am arguing that based on a sacramental understanding of creation and in reaction to the marginalization of, as well as exegetical challenges to, heaven in some New Testament trends, theology must, while looking at scripture, also, look beyond scripture to engage cultural texts for its theological construction of heaven. The following section will first explore some definitions of popular culture before giving reasons for treating it as significant for the project of reimagining heaven.

DEFINITION AND SIGNIFICANCE OF POPULAR CULTURE

Scholars working at the intersection of popular culture and theology continue to refine definitions of "popular" within cultural studies, not least because of difficulties in identifying what is encompassed by the term. In his essay on the study of religion and popular culture, David Morgan expressed his distrust of the term by asking, what is there in contemporary life that is not popular?[98] By asking the question, Morgan is implying that the dilution of "distinctions between popular and high or "elite" culture has been effectively achieved and that Western culture markets, if not everything, nearly everything for mass consumption.[99] Similarly, Kelton Cobb argues that the technology of mass production has blurred the lines between "highbrow and lowbrow art."[100] Gordon Lynch is another advocate for tempering the "popular" category, his concern being that "using the term 'popular culture' can have the implicit effect of reinforcing the ideologically-loaded binary of high/low culture and of perpetuating a sense of marginalization for scholars working in the area of cultures of everyday life."[101] Lynch senses that "the barriers and unhelpful assumptions generated by this term often out-weigh its value now."[102] He adds, "the turn to culture in theology and religious studies means that studying cultures of everyday life is no longer a niche area, to be valued and protected under the term 'popular culture',

---

98. Morgan, "Studying Religion and Popular Culture," 21.

99. Taylor, *A Matrix of Meanings*, 17.

100. Cobb, *The Blackwell Guide to Theology and Popular Culture*, 48. William Dyrness has traced visual artistic developments in the West and senses that "this blurring of the lines" has as much to do with how artists understand their work as much as with their audiences that receive their work for interpretation. See Dyrness, *Visual Faith*, 103.

101. Lynch, "Some Concluding Reflections," 162.

102. Ibid.

but is becoming increasingly mainstream."[103] In other places, Lynch defines "popular culture, as the shared environment, practices, and resources of everyday life in a given society."[104]

Prior to Cobb's and Lynch's contributions in 2005, Craig Detweiler and Barry Taylor argued that "analysts of popular culture use broader definitions of the word 'culture' making fewer value, taste, or quality judgments. Movies, cartoons, comic books, T-shirts, ball gowns, symphonies, and rock bands *all* constitute 'culture.'"[105] These writers argue that "popular culture requires a mass audience created by urbanization and democratization along with technologies of mass distribution, in other words, mass media in all forms."[106]

In her essay on reasons for studying popular culture, Lynn Schofield Clark writes:

> Today, the study of popular culture brings together three different, yet related, concerns: culture, the popular, and mass culture. Culture is the term used to denote a particular way of life for a specific group of people during a certain period in history. It also references the artifacts, narratives, images, habits, and products that give style and substance to that particular way of life.[107]

Clark defines *mass culture* as "a term that highlights the profit motive that directs the production of certain products made available for commercial sale."[108] She follows by offering a simple, yet helpful definition of *popular culture*, which "usually refers to those commercially-produced items specifically associated with leisure, the mass media, and lifestyle choices that people consume. Items of popular culture can include products such as reading materials, music, visual images, photos, film, television, advertising, video games, celebrity culture, professional sports, talk radio, comics, ipods, and items on youtube."[109] An important expansion clause for popular culture, which Clark adds, includes, "what we might call 'high culture' things such as performance theater, art, musical arrangements and performances,

---

103. Ibid. Lynch does admit that those less familiar with the research or for the "important role in conferences, academic associations and courses in conveying that interest in a particular range of culture practices and resources" may also benefit from the term "popular".

104. Lynch, *Understanding Theology and Popular Culture*, 14.

105. Taylor, *A Matrix of Meanings*, 18.

106. Ibid.

107. Clark, "Why Study Popular Culture?" 8.

108. Ibid.

109. Ibid.

and museum installations designed for popular consumption. Popular culture also refers to a seemingly endless variety of goods, including modes of transportation, fashion, toys, sporting goods, and even food."[110] Essentially, in citing the work of Pierre Bourdieu, Clark concludes, "popular culture is anything that can be successfully packaged for consumers in response to their desire for a means to both identify with some people, ideas, or movements, and to distinguish themselves from others."[111]

Although, "popular culture" has no universally agreed definition, as Lynch has suggested, he is correct in further stating that "this is a reality no different to many other terms that we commonly use in theology or religious studies.[112] Concepts such as 'spirituality,' or indeed, 'religion' itself, do not have commonly agreed definitions."[113] I am in agreement with Lynch on this point, but I also want to add that the definitions offered in this brief survey do provide more coherence than disunity. Clark's comprehensive definition that includes all areas of lived experience will be endorsed throughout the current project.[114] The overarching inclusion of all aspects of culture fits within the overall framework of a kind of sacramental approach. As Smith affirms, "implicit in the materiality of Christian worship is this sense that God meets us in materiality, and that the natural world is always more than just nature—it is charged with the presence and glory of God."[115]

The scholar of popular culture is, therefore, "working not so much within a particular academic discipline, but within an academic 'inter-discipline'—force[d] to engage with theoretical and methodological resources from a range of relevant disciplines."[116] After briefly reviewing some of the current definitions of "popular" culture within the field, we return by a different route to the same conclusion reached in chapter one, namely that the appropriate stance towards the belief in heaven should be an interdisciplinary one. This leads to the unavoidable question "that any theological or religious study of popular culture must face": "So what?" What is gained by

110. Ibid.

111. Ibid., 9.

112. Lynch, *Understanding Theology and Popular Culture*, 3.

113. Ibid.

114. As Dyrness points out in a description of nineteenth-century Impressionist art movement, "people are always drawn by what is super in the natural. When one looks carefully at what is there, it is possible to know that 'the world is charged with the grandeur of God', even if, as is true of these artists, God does not figure in the equation." Dyrness, *Visual Faith*, 105.

115. Smith, *Desiring the Kingdom*, 143.

116. Lynch, "Introduction," 2. Also, see Lynch, *Understanding Theology and Popular Culture*, 41.

theology, a long-standing "scholarly discipline, practiced in university and ecclesiastical institutions" engaging a culture that is too often characterized as having "a penchant for delineating a manufactured, illusory, and escapist worldview"?[117] However, as Chris Deacy rightly argues, "this does not make the former superior to the latter," for "when it comes to questions of death and eschatology, theology does not exactly comprise a settled, consistent or coherent area of discourse."[118] Still, questions remain concerning what important reasons there may be why theology should engage popular culture in considering doctrinal constructions.

In the third chapter, I will move towards the sort of analysis I think will be most beneficial in theology's engagement with popular culture, but I am going to first delineate three important reasons why theologians should engage in mutual dialogue with popular culture.

Meaning-Making

Heaven's influence is clearly universal in scope. The critical juncture in our historical context calls for a serious reconsideration of how the images of heaven in culture are pointing beyond themselves to reveal the transcendence of the all loving God, our creator who has created us in his image (Gen 1:27). Our ability to make meaning is also a universal human endeavor. In order to answer the "so what" question, one should consider the vital role that the imagination plays in "world-constructing and maintaining behavior."[119] Dyrness drawing on the work of Mitchell Stephens', *The Rise of the Image and the Fall of the Word*, observes how resisting such a "visual turn" can generate a failure to recognize that many of the "tools to solve the cultural crisis" are within the grasp of a visual culture.[120] "Media are tools by which we can remake the world. Far from discouraging critical thought, therefore, images can be used in a positive way to break the hold of print and linear thinking. This is possible because interpreting images, Dyrness believes, requires more imagination, not less."[121] For instance, Dyrness observes how younger generations "see" much more in a film than older

---

117. Deacy, *Screening the Afterlife*, 29.

118. Ibid.

119. Morgan, "Studying Religion and Popular Culture," 27. Also, see Greg Garrett, *Entertaining Judgment*, 6. Meaning making is the "central premise of [his] book." Although less interested in constructive theology, Garrett offers a wealth of examples from popular culture to show how popular "imaginings are part of our process of creating meaning."

120. Dyrness, *Visual Faith*, 131.

121. Ibid., 131–32.

generations who have not been raised in a visual culture, but "the debate" concerns "what to make of it."[122]

The question still stands; how do people make sense of the world which they inhabit? As Clark suggests, "through its [culture] study, we may gain insight into how people construct and maintain the world in which they live, and how they are able to imagine a way in which to behave within that world."[123] Along these lines of trying to understand how images work on people and in society, I want to argue with Lynch that "popular culture as a medium for theological reflection can also provide an important means of exploring essential questions about our existence in ways that connect with the symbols, concepts, and concerns of contemporary culture."[124] Morgan elaborates:

> I find it important to trace the narrative life of an image from the mental schema, imagination, traditions, and commerce of making them to their purchase and display to the response they receive from one generation or context to the next. Meaning is restless, forever unfinished thing. In knowing what an image does at any moment, we have one meaning, but an even greater need to know what it might do in the next moment.[125]

The presence of Christianity in the West is undeniable in the sense that we have received doctrinal constructions which find wide expression and embeddedness in popular culture. Consequently, the study of these expressions allows for a much greater understanding of how images within the Christian tradition impact important shifts in culture. Clark expands the possibilities of what should be included in such a study:

> The study of popular culture enables the scholar to transcend popular culture and reflect upon wider issues of religion's role in society. Such studies offer insights into how various religions might be represented and understood, how various popular artifacts become adopted by religious subcultures as a means of establishing and reinforcing identity, how popular culture becomes a resource through which people can reflect and discuss with others their own views and practices, and how religious traditions might be meaningfully communicated to a future

---

122. Ibid., 129.
123. Clark, "Why Study Popular Culture?" 20.
124. Lynch, *Understanding Theology and Popular Culture*, 41.
125. Morgan, "Studying Religion and Popular Culture," 27.

generations through emotionally captivating stories, images, sounds, and rituals.[126]

Detweiler and Taylor argue in a similar vein, that "popular culture both reflects who we are as people and also helps shape us as people."[127] Further, they argue that "popular culture must be investigated theologically because it is already studied by the broader culture," not to mention that "popular culture serves as the lingua franca of the postmodern world, a point often missed by scholars."[128] Indeed, Mieke Bal argues that one cannot understand Western culture without acknowledgement that "Christianity is present" and is a part of the cultural imaginary, as well as other cultural structures that are creating ways for belief in a pluralistic environment.[129] Theology must not ignore the important role it contributes in society. It is within this world "that theological traditions and methods have a distinctive role to play in this process of evaluation."[130] Here, Lynch is referring to an essential theological task of "rigorous analysis of the truthfulness, meaningfulness, goodness, justice, and beauty of popular cultural texts and practices."[131]

Within this context of meaning making, transcendence is an essential element in a theological engagement with popular culture; especially for an earth-bound culture enveloped by a materialistic understanding of images that reduces meaning to reason and leaves imagination for children. Lynch comments on the observations of Pete Ward:

> For those theologically committed to particular notions of transcendence, such a culture turn need not involve reducing the transcendent to the cultural, but can instead be conceived of as the study of the ways in which the transcendent is mediated through culture. For both theology and the study of religion, the cultural turn has now broken beyond the confines of those interested in "popular culture".[132]

Transcendence is one reason that we will return to throughout this project, as Lynch proposes that the issue of transcendence is one of the

---

126. Ibid., 20.
127. Taylor, *A Matrix of Meanings*, 19.
128. Ibid., 20–21.
129. Ward, ed., *The Blackwell Companion to Postmodern Theology*, 5.
130. Lynch, *Understanding Theology and Popular Culture*, ix.
131. Ibid.
132. Lynch, "Some Concluding Reflections," 163.

primary reasons for theology to engage with popular culture.[133] "Religion provides a medium through which people are able to experience 'God.'"[134]

Taking account of developments in visual interpretation, as illustrated with great clarity by Dyrness in his work on visual art, provides some compelling features of the current culture that open further doors for theology to engage meaningfully. He offers what is a generous assessment of the current state, and I will mention the first two from his conclusions. First, an appeal to the "element of performance" in contemporary visual art, where "artists now want to say that meaning in art does not lie in the completed object—or better, it does not lie only in that one place."[135] Secondly, Dyrness raises the question of the "interactive character" of art.[136] He suggests that "artists are not just allowing but often insisting that their work be understood as embedded in some social or political reality."[137] In such contexts, Charles Taliaferro has reminded us, that "we do face a very difficult problem in deciphering those [authors'] intentions."[138] One of the narratives that run through the course of Dyrness' brief history of visual art is that of "meaning" and he does a good job of showing the historical connections to some of the contemporary approaches.[139] Part of the interactive variables within current visual culture finds "meaning, if it exists, [lying] in what the piece does rather than in what it represents."[140] Dyrness' second observation will be displayed in the following chapters, as we mine the strengths and weaknesses within the interpreted images of heaven, as well as asking how the metaphors work in order to represent an analogical way of considering heavenly possibilities.

Hermeneutics of Doctrine

Hermeneutics of doctrine, as a central consideration, should give ample ammunition for an engagement between theology and contemporary culture as it concerns heaven in the pursuit of a hermeneutic(s) that takes seriously how doctrine is received and preserved in culture, both in terms of belief and practice, as Thiselton and others have begun to work out, as well as the

133. Lynch, *Understanding Theology and Popular Culture*, 28.
134. Ibid.
135. Dyrness, *Visual Faith*, 123.
136. Ibid.
137. Ibid., 124.
138. Taliaferro, *Aesthetics*, 53.
139. Ibid., 126.
140. Ibid.

countless constructions that point to our need to constantly be at the theological task of interpretation.[141] As David Tracy argues: "to understand at all is to interpret. To act well is to interpret a situation demanding some action and to interpret a correct strategy for that action."[142] Rather than lamenting the need for continued interpretation or reducing the truth factor in areas of belief and practice, I want to argue that both theology and culture are at vital junctures. As Tracy reminds us: "at times, interpretations matter. On the whole, such are times of cultural crisis."[143] I find agreement with James K. A. Smith in his view that hermeneutics is not a matter of the fall of humanity, but rather, a part of our "situationality."[144] This point echoes some of what is drawn upon in my anthropology in chapter one, but it is appropriate here to emphasize Smith's perspective:

> Interpretation is not something that happens only when one reads a text; instead, interpretation occurs at every level of communication and is not limited to the textual or even the verbal (for even "body language" require interpretation). Interpretation "happens" at every level of relationship between situated beings. Every reading of the newspaper, every conversation at the dinner table, every rude gesture on the highway must be interpreted before it is understood. Every communication is filtered through a series of questionings, largely implicit, asked with the goal of understanding.[145]

Revelation

Finally, and, of course not exhaustively, I return to the opening section of chapter one where I sought to argue that God remains active in the world and the imagination plays a primary role in such an understanding of a theology of *revelation*. Within the development of the Christian tradition continues "the dynamic of an inherited past interacting with fresh stimuli for change from outside, from the wider surrounding culture" where "this new, imaginative narrative may provide a critique of key aspects of the historical narrative."[146] The church's understanding of what the Spirit is doing

---

141. Thiselton, *The Hermeneutics of Doctrine*. Note especially his early chapters pertaining to "Dispositional Accounts of Belief," 19ff.

142. Tracy, *Plurality and Ambiguity*, 9.

143. Ibid., 7.

144. Smith, *The Fall of Interpretation*, 161.

145. Ibid., 161–62.

146. Brown, *Tradition & Imagination*, 25.

in the world and how the church might best interpret the Spirit's activity, therefore, is clearly highly important. One of the primary reasons for theology to engage culture is to construct a hermeneutic of doctrine that takes into account the full range of God's creation and how analogical thinking as described in the work of Farrer, Brown and others shows a way forward in analyzing metaphors and images of heaven that have not stood still through time, but have shifted to bring further insight. Naturally, this leads to a further discussion concerning the best sort of analysis that might provide for such a theological approach to popular culture. This will be taken up in chapter three.

CONCLUSION

In this chapter, I have argued that one of the narratives coming from New Testament studies, as represented by Wright, disregards culture too quickly and does not take the long Christian tradition in general and, popular culture, more specifically, seriously enough in considering theological constructions of heaven. I have also traced some recent developments regarding the study of heaven more widely in Western thought among disciplines within the humanities that perceive inadequacies in the lack of theological reflection on heaven. Further, I have provided three areas that not only draw attention to the significance of popular culture for theology, but also help establish reasons why more work needs to be done at the interpretive level in order to consider the wide range of possibilities concerning heaven, along with the theological implications for Christian eschatology more generally. In chapter three, I will consider different approaches theologians have taken towards culture and ask the question: what sort of analysis is most beneficial?

3

What Sort of Analysis Is Most Beneficial?

After acknowledging and assessing some of the challenges to heaven raised by recent developments in New Testament studies, as well as from Western religious thought more broadly, I have also made a case concerning the significance of popular culture for theology. It is my contention that an imaginative hermeneutical approach, therefore, can offer significant contributions for further addressing some of the challenges, both in doctrine and culture regarding heaven. The next necessary component, then, of this book entails laying out a methodological approach that will guide the following chapters. I will begin by sorting through some of the most recent approaches that theologians have undertaken to understand the relationship with culture and, then, move towards what I consider the most effective way forward.

APPLICATIONIST

Theological engagements with popular culture in the latter half of the twentieth century, as well as the early part of the twenty-first century, typically pay tribute to Richard Niebuhr's work, *Christ and Culture*.[1] Niebuhr's five models describing Christianity's approach to culture allowed thinkers to evaluate and gauge the practices of particular groups under the types of, *Christ Against Culture, Christ of Culture, Christ Above Culture, Christ and*

---

1. H. Richard Niebuhr, *Christ and Culture*.

Culture in Paradox, and *Christ the Transformer of Culture*.[2] Lynch describes Niebuhr's approach as *"applicationist"* where "a basic assumption of this approach is that it is possible to identify core theological truths from a particular source (e.g., the Bible or church tradition) and then apply these critically to the beliefs and values of popular culture."[3] Although it is still important to acknowledge Niebuhr's contribution, Deacy has brought attention to where the five models cross over and intermingle. Some scholars have gone so far as to "claim that 'virtually every Christian and every Christian group expresses in one way or another all five of the motifs [in Niebuhr].'"[4] Graham Ward also draws attention to the limitations of Niebuhr's "binary problematic" seeing that "Christ is already a cultural event."[5] In other words, "we have no access to a Christ who has not already been enculturated."[6] In response, Ward proposes that instead of trying to provide "a typology of the various theological answers," one should "begin in a theological enquiry; begin that is, to think through the grammar of Christian believing on the basis that there can be no distillation of Christ from culture."[7] Ward goes on to argue:

> If all things exist in Christ, then the cultural is not something entirely separate from him; the cultural is that through which God's redemptive grace operates. Christ, we could say, is the origin and consummation of culture, in the same way as he is both the prototype and the fulfillment of all that is properly human.[8]

Deacy also recognizes limitations in Niebuhr's framework; "for there to be a proper dialogue, theology must expect to be challenged in the process, this is more likely to be achieved in models three to five than in the first approach, where theology resolutely refuses to engage with culture through fear of contamination."[9] Even Niebuhr's title draws the dichotomy that underscores the challenge for the Christian to think through what it means to be part of culture, not in some sense removed or outside of culture. As Garret Green observes: "for God has chosen to reveal himself in the world in a manner accessible only to imagination."[10] Therefore, culture must not be

2. Ibid.
3. Lynch, *Understanding Theology and Popular Culture*, 101.
4. Deacy, "Theology and Film," 65.
5. Ward, *Christ and Culture*, 21.
6. Ibid.
7. Ibid.
8. Ibid., 22.
9. Deacy, "Theology and Film," 67.
10. Green, *Theology, Hermeneutics, and Imagination*, 205–6.

bracketed out if we are to understand how Christ is in the midst of culture. As Dietrich Bonhoeffer loudly proclaimed, "God is beyond in the midst of our life. The church stands, not at the boundaries where human powers give out, but in the middle of the village."[11]

CORRELATIONAL

As mentioned earlier, Paul Tillich (1886–1965) is an example of someone favorable to the *correlational* model, which Lynch seeks to revise following the work of David Tracy and Don Browning.[12] Although Deacy criticizes Tillich for holding to a "highbrow" view of art, as well as Tillich's lack of mention of the "fledging medium" of film at the time of Tillich's writing, he does pay tribute to Tillich's "ultimate concern," which began to dissolve the religious/secular divide.[13] One should add that Tillich pointed to a theological aesthetics that left space for further possibilities. For instance, although Tillich laments Christianity's adoption of the symbol of immortality, which for him was a horrible "confusion of symbol and concept," his understanding of Paul's theology of the "spiritual body" allows us to talk about the "transformed total personality of man."[14] Tillich suggested that where "concepts cannot go beyond this," the "poetic and artistic imagination" can take us into further possibilities.[15] For Lynch, "Tillich clearly saw the role of the Church as that of maintaining a prophetic voice in the midst of wider society. But he also recognized that prophetic voices may come from that wider society which might challenge distorted beliefs and practices in the Church."[16] Where Tillich is limited is precisely where Deacy draws attention, in visual artistic expressions that have changed in the last decade, especially in the area of film, but this does not detract from Tillich's emphasis on the importance of the arts in theology.[17] For instance, it was Tillich who argued

---

11. Bethge, ed., *Dietrich Bonhoeffer*, 155.

12. Lynch, *Understanding Theology and Popular Culture*, 103.

13. Ibid., 72–74.

14. Tillich, *Systematic Theology*, 411–12.

15. Ibid., 412.

16. Lynch, *Understanding Theology and Popular Culture*, 103.

17. Jonathan Brant has in recent years revisited Tillich's theology of revelation through culture by observing how the reception of film works among a group of filmgoers in a Latin American context. See Brant, *Paul Tillich and the Possibility of Revelation through Film*.

for the "universe as God's sanctuary," where "essentially the religious and the secular are not separated realms. Rather they are within each other."[18]

REVISED CORRELATIONAL

A third approach is the *revised correlational* model proposed by Lynch.[19] By taking into account the descriptive, historical, and systematic aspects of doing theology, one is more able to find ways to avoid the "risks [of] becoming a form of abstract theological debate that does not lead into any tangible outcomes for the way in which people live their lives."[20] For Lynch, the revised correlational model takes "seriously the praxis models' concern for the effects of theological reflection."[21] One of the central characteristics of the revised correlational approach is that it "places a high value on taking time to understand both popular culture and religious tradition on their own terms."[22] Accordingly, Lynch constructs a definition of theology as being "normative, contextual, and dynamic" that asks and gives answers concerning the "meaning, values, and practice" and how these can be "related to our understanding of the absolute reference point of life."[23]

At the core of Lynch's project, as understood by Deacy, "theology and popular culture can both learn from and be challenged or changed by the other—they are not two discrete, monolithic or changeless entities."[24] Within his revised correlational method, Lynch puts forward a number of paths theologians are taking in an engagement with popular culture (noting that these paths are not exclusive, but interweave at points, as well).[25] For example, religion and media scholars often take their study "in relation to the environment, resources and practices of everyday life."[26] Thus, one can "study the ways in which popular culture may serve religious functions in contemporary society."[27] Further, at times, theologians will take "a missiological response to popular culture."[28]

18. Tillich, *Theology of Culture*, 41.
19. Ibid.
20. Ibid., 106.
21. Ibid.
22. Ibid., 108.
23. Ibid., 109.
24. Deacy, *Screening the Afterlife*, x.
25. Lynch, *Understanding Theology and Popular Culture*, 197. See endnote 2.
26. Ibid., 21.
27. Ibid.
28. Ibid.

Part I: Theologically Engaging Popular Culture

Of particular importance for my project, theologians may interpret popular cultural texts and practices as "a medium for theological reflection."[29] All these points can often cross over even within the same work. For instance, as this book is mainly concerned with images and questions concerning heaven and immediate post-mortem survival, so within Lynch's approach, he delineates between examining how culture uses scripture and how popular culture uses theological questions and concepts.[30] The two may overlap at times, but the starting point for this project is the exploration of theological questions raised by the doctrine of heaven.

Towards a further point of clarification, Lynch sets out areas of transcendence and hermeneutical questions within his second "correlational" approach, in understanding how religion functions.[31] For example, Lynch references Robert Johnston's work in film where Johnston wants to show how the theologian's too frequent obsession with finding meaning in a film can detract from the "possibility that the aesthetic experience of watching a film might serve as a means of encountering the divine."[32] In turn, Lynch argues that "in the same way that religious practices of prayer and worship can serve as media for religious experience, so arguably certain forms of popular culture can function as means of encountering transcendence."[33] Through discovering the work of Johann Gottfried von Herder (1744–1803), Cobb also observes the importance concerning transcendence as a search that has wide implications for people of many different persuasions:

> Through culture we seek to grasp, consolidate, and transmit a coherent order of values that we perceive to be transcendent and therefore worthy of pursuit. These values are discernible in the whole range of cultural artifacts, from poetry, music, and moral beliefs to economic practices, technology, and cooking utensils. The values that organize a culture are never static, but always struggling into new configurations.[34]

As Ward proposes, "there can only be culture where there is figuring. It is, then, because as human beings we are image makers that we fashion as expressions of ourselves the cultures we inhabit."[35] Theology must contribute to understanding how these new configurations of "popular culture such

29. Ibid.
30. Ibid., 39.
31. Ibid., 28.
32. Ibid., 32.
33. Ibid.
34. Cobb, *The Blackwell Guide to Theology and Popular Culture*, 44.
35. Ward, *Christ and Culture*, 22.

as television and film, as well as novels, comedy clubs, fashion magazines, and more, are locations in which these contradictions and negotiations are constantly played out through narrative and representation" to better understand religious experience and transcendence.[36]

SACRAMENTAL/INCARNATIONAL

Most recently, Clive Marsh and Vaughn Roberts have produced a significant contribution to the field of theology in and through popular culture as a part of the Engaging Culture series, a major project edited by Dyrness and Johnston. Marsh and Roberts are specifically interested in an engagement between theology and popular music, along with Marsh's many groundbreaking contributions in the area of theology and film. They are arguing that "popular music is a medium through which God can self-communicate to generate encounters with God that are genuine and wholly consistent with what happens in baptism and Holy Communion," in other words, a sacramental approach to culture.[37] They distinguish their contribution by drawing on the work of three key theologians, David Brown, Tom Beaudoin, and James K. A. Smith. Marsh and Roberts observe in Brown's work:

> One of the most expansive theological studies of the interaction between Christian tradition and human experience ever published. Across five lengthy volumes, and in particular in his trilogy—*God and Enchantment of Place: Reclaiming Human Experience* (2004), *God and Grace of Body: Sacrament in Ordinary* (2007), and *God and Mystery in Words: Experience through Metaphor and Drama* (2008)—Brown has sought to acknowledge and heed the implications of a "God active outside of the control of the Church."[38]

According to Marsh and Roberts, Brown and Beaudoin share a sacramental/incarnational approach to popular culture. Where Brown has theologically engaged a vast range of the arts, from classical art, to food, to gardening, to sport, to dancing, to popular music, Beaudoin's work has been most noticeable within theology and popular culture studies. Marsh and Roberts mention such works as Beaudoin's *Virtual Faith: The Irreverent Spiritual Quest of Generation X* (1998), *Consuming Faith: Integrating Who We Are with What We Buy* (2003), and *Witness to Dispossession: The Vocation of a*

---

36. Clark, "Why Study Popular Culture?" 9.
37. Marsh, *Personal Jesus*, 176.
38. Ibid., 32.

Postmodern Theologian (2008).[39] James K. A. Smith's work focuses less on how the "*cognitive* elements of human formation (ideas, beliefs)" shape our lives, and more on how "it is *desire* that drives us, and therefore our emotions, our guts, and our heart are what primarily steer us."[40] Although somewhat known for his popular works such as, *Who's Afraid of Postmodernism?: Taking Derrida, Lyotard, and Foucault to Church* (2006) and *Who's Afraid of Relativism?: Community, Contingency, and Creaturehood* (2014), Smith's contribution to the broader conversation between theology and culture can be found in his multi-volume Cultural Liturgies series, which focuses on the formation and education of human beings.[41]

Where Brown is an Anglican Priest, and Beaudoin, a Roman Catholic, Smith is more broadly a Reformed Evangelical. Marsh and Roberts observe the theological spectrum widening significantly in these three, even by the range of diverse traditions that they represent.[42] In Brown and Beaudoin, Marsh and Roberts observe an emphasis upon "God's commitment to human form [which] means that many channels of God's self-commitment through the human/material are feasible."[43] Their argument finds echoes in all three scholars, but especially in Brown: "articulation of a doctrine of incarnation falls short, then, when it does not have the whole humanity in view.[44] As referenced earlier, the theologian must "not be just at the edge of the church, but in the middle of popular culture," both asking and listening.[45] Further, "in Christian understanding, a sacramental theology provides a basis for any aspect of popular culture's becoming a channel of the self-revelation of God, or of the grace of God."[46] While much of the scholarship in theology and popular culture traced earlier has emphasized a correlational or revised correlational approach to culture with the desire to go beyond, by drawing attention to Brown, Beaudoin, and Smith, Marsh and Roberts are pointing to the necessity of the role of the imagination and embodiment in theological construction, which includes further nuances concerning revelation and tradition in developing new perspectives in theology. Still, more work needs to be done in the direction that Brown, Beaudoin, and Smith are pointing, along with Marsh and a host of others, in

39. Ibid., 34
40. Ibid., 35.
41. Ibid., 35–37.
42. Ibid., 37.
43. Ibid., 34.
44. Ibid., 169.
45. Ibid., 129.
46. Ibid., 37.

reflecting on theological constructions concerning specific doctrines. All of the necessary work preceding such an endeavor has paved the way to make these construction materials available. My project will follow in the stream of those placing their main focus on an imaginative approach.

IMAGINATIVE APPROACHES IN INTERCULTURAL THEOLOGY

I also want to draw attention to recent contributions in Christian theology that call for either an imaginative approach and/or are works by theologians doing theology with broad engagement in our pluralistic situation. Theological aesthetics is rightly becoming a significant area for constructive theology, as engagement between different cultures, religions, and philosophies are all interweaving in popular culture. Intercultural theologies tend to break out of the old debates between liberal and conservative stances in theology. They are not neatly characterized, nor should they be. Space will only allow for a sampling of the important theological work being done in intercultural engagement. For instance, rather than constructing a theology of religions, David Cheetham has attempted to resource the imagination by seeking ways in which different religions discover "new spaces for meeting."[47] For Cheetham, the imagination of the philosopher is key in a dialogical approach.[48] He is also alert to the possibilities resident within an aesthetic approach to theological inquiry. Cheetham observes: "it may be that reflecting on the 'aesthetics of encounter' between different religions and cultures is one constructive way ahead for the theology of religions which could create space that most people can inhabit wholeheartedly."[49] Cheetham is not alone in his imaginative endeavor, as William Dyrness and his team have conducted studies on visual arts and worship practices in Christian communities, and most recently within Buddhist and Muslim communities in Southern California.[50] A further example is Amos Yong in his work on the theology of religions, where he argues for what he describes as the "pneumatological imagination."[51] One final example I will offer is from the prolific systematic theologian Veli-Matti Kärkkäinen in his most recent constructive approach dealing with questions of Christology and reconciliation. In his usual multi-discipline, ecumenical, global approach,

47. Cheetham, *Ways of Meeting and the Theology of Religions*, 2.
48. Ibid., 19.
49. Ibid., 124.
50. Dyrness, *Senses of Devotion*.
51. Yong, *Discerning the Spirit(s)*, 225.

Kärkkäinen offers some prefatory remarks in support of wider engagement in theology: "it is about time for Christian theology to break out from its ghetto and engage insights and contributions from other faiths."[52] He is clear that a "naïve pluralism" is not as helpful, but also asserts, "that one remains faithful to one's own tradition does not of course mean an unwillingness to learn."[53] The goal of his five-volume series "is to provide a fresh and innovative vision of Christian doctrine and theology" and for Kärkkäinen, "doing theology in this way does not of course mean that Christian tradition is to be undervalued. That would be not only naïve but also counterproductive."[54] Rather, he is seeking after a "hospitable vision."[55] Kärkkäinen adds, "to do this task well, theology must engage in continuous ecumenical and interdisciplinary dialogue."[56] Kärkkäinen is after an approach "in the spirit of hospitality, [which] makes room for the other."[57] I too share Kärkkäinen's desire for an interdisciplinary approach of hospitality in theology. To add further incentive, likewise, George Newlands calls for an imaginative approach of hospitality. He offers some telling words of encouragement for a project in theology and popular culture:

> The relation between theology and culture will always exhibit a dialectical tension. Theology seeks to be self-critical, and not to confuse its critical engagement with culture with a triumphalist perspective which is often itself no more than the reflection of a particular cultural reading of Christian faith. It reflects on the scope and limitations of language and imagery of its tradition. It seeks to criticize culture in society which is inherently coercive, contrary to the central elements of the gospel, and which has sometimes been echoed and reinforced by theology itself. There is no escape from absorption in a particular culture for human language and human activity. The task is to try to remain as self-aware and as critically constructive as possible. This is most likely to happen through conversation and dialogue. This tradition cannot be faithful to its own best insights without radical renewal which involves critique of past tradition, openness to quite different and often conflicting traditions, an input from fresh sources.[58]

52. Kärkkäinen, *Christ and Reconciliation*, xii.
53. Ibid.
54. Ibid., xii, 20.
55. Ibid., 29.
56. Ibid., 12.
57. Ibid., xii.
58. Newlands, *The Transformative Imagination*, viii–ix.

Here, I want to highlight Newlands' emphasis on fresh sources for this, among other tasks, is what a constructive theology must attempt, especially an analysis and construction in theology and popular culture. Again, I underscore this sampling simply to lend support for a wider sphere of an imaginative approach to theology and popular culture, which leads to specific examples of focused work in the field of theology, aesthetics and culture.

STRENGTHS AND WEAKNESSES—FINDING A WAY FORWARD

In different ways, each approach has provided valuable and contextual insight for creating space to make these construction materials in popular culture available for theology. My project will follow in a modified stream of those placing their main focus on an imaginative, intercultural and sacramental approach.[59] This modification is in a sense a generous borrowing of sorts, but first, I want to observe some of the weaknesses in the applicationist, correlational, as well as revised correlational approaches.

Although providing multiple pictures for understanding certain perceived binary tensions between Christ and culture for discussion, I am unconvinced that furthering Niebuhr's project is a helpful way forward for constructive theology, for reasons mentioned under the applicationist approach (i.e., Christ as too detached from culture). On the other hand, although providing a wider understanding of revelation, Tillich's correlational strategy saw only the need for theology to correlate answers to modern culture's questions.[60] Revised correlational approaches made modifications "envisage[ing] a more complex conversation involving questions and answers from both culture and tradition."[61] From the revised correlational approach, Lynch has been especially helpful in analyzing ways in which popular art, religion, and religious experience all play important roles in our understanding the normativity of theology in popular culture.[62] Certainly in the field of eschatology, Deacy has begun to move beyond theoretical pro-

---

59. I have also not forgotten about important voices that have served to shape the field of theological aesthetics more broadly. For example, Hans Urs Von Balthasar, Richard Viladesau, Frank Burch Brown, among others. Recent works have also made significant contributions towards an imaginative approach such as, Trevor Hart's projected multi-volume work on the imagination and literary aspects. See Hart, *Between the Image and the Word*.

60. Lynch, *Understanding Theology and Popular Culture*, 103.

61. Ibid.

62. Ibid., 97.

posals into more constructive domains in recent years, which has opened up further possibilities for constructive theology and popular film. Also important to note is the similarity between revised correlational uses of the American pragmatist tradition as found in William James and C. S. Pierce and the imaginative—intercultural approach of Amos Yong, who makes extensive use of Pierce.[63] This similarity is important because pragmatists such as William James emphasized the role of personal religious experience over against collective forms of religion.[64] As Charles Taylor so adequately observes, "nothing prevents these two [personal and collective forms] from combining in one religious life."[65] Yet this emphasis is not something new in James, as Taylor makes clear, "when the psalmist, speaking for God, tells us to set aside our offerings of bulls and sheep and to offer instead a contrite heart (e.g., Psalm 51), we are already on the road to our contemporary notion of personal religion."[66] Although Taylor criticizes James for not being able or willing to "accommodate" what Taylor sees as "the phenomenon of collective religious life" it is this wider understanding of religious experience in James that theologians are beginning to interpret as critical, not for subverting the collective experience (i.e. tradition), but as renewing it from a wider understanding of culture.[67] The hermeneutic of imagery in popular culture that I will carry out draws broadly on the strengths of the revised correlational, sacramental, and intercultural strategies.

HERMENEUTICS OF IMAGERY IN POPULAR CULTURE

Having earlier set forth the objective to take up an imaginative approach to a theology of heaven, I now want to return to an earlier discussion in approaches to heaven that address the hermeneutical question concerning how to best understand and interpret doctrine. In doing so, I will also return to a focus on the Spirit's role in doctrinal development.

Doctrinal Relocation Theory

Conrad Ostwalt suggests that religious beliefs will continue to find a much more liberated existence in secular cultures. His theory of secularization

---

63. Yong, *Discerning the Spirit(s)*, esp. 111–15.
64. Taylor, *Varieties of Religion Today*, 4.
65. Ibid., 16.
66. Ibid., 11–12.
67. Ibid., 24.

does not include the disappearance of religious belief, but rather a relocation of belief from churches serving as the houses of doctrine to the free-range exploration of beliefs in a secular culture. Two ways of understanding this increasingly "perceived loss of authority or relevance by religious institutions" is to observe on the one hand, the over compensation of liberal theologians in the twentieth century to "stave off obsolescence" or on the other, how conservative religious institutions utilize secular forms for distributing doctrinal content.[68] In other words, by packaging theological content in changing forms developed within popular culture, there is the hope, and often assumption that theological content will be safeguarded and will be better received by believers and non-believers alike. Ostwalt rejects antagonistic models of secularization in favor of a relational understanding where tension remains since "one cannot exist without the other."[69] This "dance" metaphor between sacred and secular is effective in providing a relational image descriptive of the mutual conditioning between two spheres, but does not provide an interpretation for why, for example, post-apocalyptic images fail to offer the type of hope envisioned by this-worldly eschatologies (chapter seven will explore this weakness of post-apocalyptic images in greater detail).[70] According to Ostwalt, the hope in navigating the hermeneutical problem rests in bringing these differing worldviews into dialogue to create a space where, "we can avoid the pitfalls of uncritical approaches to watching films that are categorized as apocalyptic."[71] Although signs of a reception model are present in the dialogical approach, the significance of image failure is underdeveloped.

To some extent, Ostwalt is correct in drawing attention to the freedom which doctrinal beliefs experience when they are opened up outside of a bounded tradition. Since the imagination is free in popular culture, not controlled by any set of texts, some restrict or worse, refuse an imaginative approach any legitimacy. Yet, while the imagination is capable of all types of distortions under such conditions, the advantage is that sometimes the imagination succeeds in providing a truthful possibility for deeper consideration. As noted earlier, the Holy Spirit is without restraint and is active in the world beyond texts. While development of doctrine recognizes possibilities for error, it also understands responses to errors as significant turns in development that often serve to strengthen beliefs.

---

68. Ostwalt, *Secular Steeples*, 7. Ostwalt's popular examples include John A. T. Robinson, 34.
69. Ibid., 200–201.
70. Ibid.
71. Ostwalt, "Apocalyptic," 382.

Some exegetes in New Testament studies are too quick to assert that understanding culture has as its objective merely to get back to historical horizons in order to accomplish the real work of authorial intention. The goal is to master the material for the purpose of solidifying the correct interpretation in a particular horizon of scripture. In other words, popular art too often fails the public by reading the text incorrectly or by going too far away from the text. Of course, artists trying to construct an overly literalistic account or completely unattached versions can place obstacles for audiences in either direction.[72] The hermeneutic approach I am advocating, however, does not wish to discount the important elements gained from historical critical methods, nor condemn knowledge acquisition resulting from exegetical pursuits. On the contrary, I am proposing a constructive/contextual theology. Most often in modern thought, the hermeneutic problem shows itself in a variety of ways moving between two poles of emphasis. Anthony Thiselton describes the rough play between these two poles of understanding and explanation:

> While admittedly a rational dimension remains within the process of hermeneutical inquiry, the more creative dimension of hermeneutics depends more fundamentally on the receptivity of the hearer or reader to *listen with openness*. To appreciate and to appropriate what we seek to understand with sensitivity have priority over the traditional method of scrutinizing "objects" of perception, thought, and knowledge. This "listening" dimension is often described as part of the process of *"understanding"* in contrast to the more rational, cognitive, or critical dimension of *"explanation"*.[73]

For example, consider how the Apocalypse of John uses imagery and metaphor to describe the relational interaction between the visionary and the Son of Man (Rev 1:12–18); or a second example of the New Jerusalem coming out of the heavens (Rev 21:2). Are we to interpret all of these images literally or as pointing us beyond the image? I suggest the latter is a slower and more difficult process as the reception will vary from context to context, but this does not undermine the initial interaction in a negative sense. Understanding how the imagery has continued to be applied in various contexts takes us beyond, but does not cut us off from an explanation of the text.

---

72. A good example is found in Ostwalt's critique of the *Left Behind* films in ibid., 378.

73. Thiselton, *Hermeneutics*, 7–8.

The reception hermeneutic I am advocating, then, follows along similar lines to that of Ormond Rush: "According to a hermeneutics of reception, a text is dead until it is read."[74] Now, this language sounds more like a resurrection of a text, rather than Paul Ricoeur's retrieval of "symbols, metaphors, narratives and other texts through openness and listening."[75] Nevertheless, Rush's point is clear: "a reconstruction of the world behind the text and of 'authorial intention' is not by itself sufficient for a full interpretation."[76] It would seem that exegetes would appreciate the coming to the text afresh, but the unfinished interpretation of a text is unsettling for many an exegete searching for the *correct* interpretation. But I am not suggesting that the understanding and interpretation of a text are completely "arbitrary" and "free" from history.[77] In reference to Westphal's use of Gadamer, the example of the theater or concert hall illustrates the "assimilation of interpretation and performance."[78] Just as a performance is "bound" to the work in one sense, "performers who are historically contemporary give *different* interpretations of the *same* work, but also, performers tell us that no two performances of their own are the same."[79] Westphal asks the appropriate question: "doesn't hyberbole pass into arrogance whenever we present 'our' theology as the definitive interpretation of the Bible?"[80] One way to understand this performance analogy is to look more closely at the ways doctrine and cultures have developed through the centuries.

Hermeneutics and Development

What is meant by doctrinal development? Construction is development, but it does not follow that a construction is innovating a new doctrine.[81] Shifts and changes in emphasis can and do work to go beyond current constructions while, at the same time, development does include connotations of a receptive process within a tradition. Pelikan provides two examples

---

74. Rush, *Still Interpreting Vatican II*, 55.

75. Thiselton, *Hermeneutics*, 10.

76. Rush, *Still Interpreting Vatican II*, 33. Rush is referring to the documents and authors of Vatican two, but the same principle could be applied to any text, as he illustrates later.

77. Westphal, *Whose Community? Which Interpretation?* 104.

78. Ibid., 102.

79. Ibid., 103.

80. Ibid., 104.

81. See Cameron's introductory notes in Cameron, ed., *John Henry Newman's an Essay on the Development of Christian Doctrine*, 33–34.

portraying tradition more as a hindrance: Thomas Jefferson and Martin Luther.[82] Pelikan observes:

> Each in his own way, Jefferson and Luther were summoning their contemporaries to move beyond tradition or behind tradition to authenticity: Tradition was relative and had been conditioned by its history, Truth was absolute and had been preserved from historical corruption.[83]

Whereas the exegete is reaching behind the tradition for authenticity, the theologian of culture is interested in going beyond tradition, while remaining in creative conversation with the tradition. I have already addressed the epistemological question in chapter one, but Pelikan's conclusion on the matter is worth repeating here:

> The dichotomy between tradition and insight breaks down under the weight of history itself. A "leap of progress" is not a standing broad jump, which begins at the line of where we are now; it is a running broad jump through where we have been to where we go next. The growth of insight—in science, in the arts, in philosophy and theology—has not come through progressively sloughing off more and more of tradition, as though insight would be purest and deepest when it has finally freed itself of the dead past. It simply has not worked that way in the history of the tradition, and it does not work that way now. By including the dead in the circle of discourse, we enrich the quality of the conversation. Of course we do not listen only to the dead, nor are we a tape recording of the tradition. That really would be the dead faith of the living, not the living faith of the dead.[84]

Ostwalt's analysis of relocation concerning religious belief moving from institutionalized forms to wider cultural forms points to a growing awareness of a phenomenal shift in Western culture. On the other hand, one could argue that this relocation is part of the religious situation and has continually developed through the centuries, allowing for the type of creative interaction that Pelikan suggests. For example, Walter Hollenweger points out the adaptive relationship between beliefs and forms:

> Festivals (Christmas, Easter), and even the names of our days (Sunday, Monday, etc.), do not come from the New Testament, but from our Celtic and Germanic forefathers. So too with the

---

82. Pelikan, *The Vindication of Tradition*, 43–44.
83. Ibid.
84. Ibid., 81–82.

form of our sermons, and with our church buildings, which are often built on the foundation of pagan temples.[85]

Tom Beaudoin finds in these historical adaptations a type of "dispossession."[86] His example is the Roman temple, the Pantheon, which came to be "known as *Santa Maria ad Martyres*," but only "since its conversion to a church by Boniface IV in the early seventh century."[87] According to Beaudoin, "here in this place, is Christ positioned as much as positioner. Christ, as if by contamination of a pagan structure whose 'difference' from Christianity foregrounds its contructedness, himself becomes available to be seen as a built structure, a work of Pantheonic architecture."[88] Beaudoin adds, "how ought such a(n) (im)pediment of Christian theology be read?"[89] Hollenweger offers further examples including marriage and funeral ceremonies—"they too go back to pagan patterns. The New Testament Christians did not conduct funerals [at least not in the contemporary sense]. They did not dream of such things. 'Let the dead bury their dead,' they said. Christ disturbed every single funeral where he was present by raising the corpses."[90] Accordingly, "our Christian rites and festivals carry with them a great heritage from our pagan past."[91] Ostwalt's analysis concerning the relocation of religious belief from church to the wider culture does not necessarily suggest a new phenomenon, but does raise the question why these developments are integral for the church to go beyond the tradition; especially, since many times these "beyond" moments are viewed as attempts to cut from or to relativize tradition causing "threat to the authority of cherished beliefs."[92] Most would agree with Alister McGrath's assessment that:

> Beliefs are unquestionably conditioned by the social conditions of their formulations and the vested interests of those who formulated them; to suggest that they are necessarily determined by those conditions, however, is to move from the realm of the empirical to that of the purely speculative, verging on the dogmatic.[93]

---

85. Hollenweger, *Pentecostalism*, 134.
86. See Beaudoin, *Witness to Dispossession*.
87. Ibid., 147.
88. Ibid.
89. Ibid.
90. Hollenweger, *Pentecostalism*, 134.
91. Ibid.
92. Pelikan, *The Vindication of Tradition*, 47.
93. McGrath, *The Genesis of Doctrine*, 102.

The notion of a *possible* determinative conditioning too often stimulates a starkly defensive stance especially where theology is perceived and understood so as to ensure that interpretive pressure runs in one direction—from church to culture.

The hermeneutical question becomes, then, what happens when the culture no longer understands what the church is saying to itself about itself? Dietrich Bonhoeffer raised this question in the 1940s. He too recognized the need for the church to go beyond tradition in seeking new approaches. What he saw as an abridgement of the gospel in Bultmann and an overly positivistic theory of revelation in Barth became increasingly dissatisfying for him.[94] "How this religionless Christianity looks, what form it takes," consumed much of Bonhoeffer's later thought, but as Hans Schwarz observes, since Bonhoeffer's "theology was still very much in the making when he died—he has been claimed for various movements."[95] Nevertheless, significant for this study is the way in which Bonhoeffer understood theology in "the midst of life," rather than on the margins.[96] In this light, the culture is no longer at the center, but Christ is at the center of culture. Admittedly, the question remains, if the church is to find Christ at the center, rather than the margins—what does this mean for a theology of God's action from the center?

Understanding how this movement works has been the subject of David Brown's extensive work in doctrinal development, opening up significant opportunity for a reconsideration of this process. First, he addresses the question of God's action in both the past and present:

> Consistency with the historical narrative is important, but not, it seems to me, decisive. For if, as the Christian believes, Jesus is still alive, then the question has ceased to be merely what he did in the past, but how his presence and influence can be appropriated in the here and now. A better imaginative relation between believer and Lord, greater coherence to the story and so forth, all become relevant questions. The possibility is even there that, because later generations can open up new perspectives undreamed of in the first century, this new, imaginative

---

94. Bethge, ed., *Dietrich Bonhoeffer*, 156–57.

95. Ibid; 155. Also see, Schwarz, *Theology in a Global Context*, 318–19. For a brief history of the varied reception of Bonhoeffer among liberals, as well as conservatives within American Evangelicalism, see Larsen's recent essay, "The Evangelical Reception of Dietrich Bonhoeffer," 39–57. Also important is Lawrence's observation: "A key to understanding Bonhoeffer's thinking of religionless is to recognize that this is as much a hermeneutical question as anything." See Lawrence, *Bonhoeffer*, 106.

96. Bethge, ed., *Dietrich Bonhoeffer*, 155.

narrative may provide a critique of key aspects of the historical narrative.[97]

Secondly, my aim is to draw attention to the Spirit's work in culture, not just in scripture and tradition. This calls for a hermeneutically receptive disposition, imperative for thinking theologically, as was the aim of Bonhoeffer.[98] In fact, reception is an ecclesial attitude from the outset. We receive life, love, acceptance, forgiveness, the Holy Spirit, scriptures, gifts, the church, tradition, and so forth. At the same time reception is neither passive nor determinative. "In that sense, the receiver is a co-creator of the meaning of what is communicated."[99] Accordingly, Rush rightly observes: "the human receivers of revelation are to be portrayed as active participants in discerning the way forward, co-deciders with God's Spirit, assuring continuity through creative discontinuity."[100] Creative discontinuity is meant in the most positive sense here. Like Bonhoeffer, I find Barth's "like it or lump it" approach completely unsatisfactory.[101] In Bonhoeffer's terms, "there are degrees of knowledge and degrees of significance . . . ."[102] If Christ is at the center of culture, then movement can come from a number of directions. As Brown elaborates:

> If we accept that new insights can become available to later generations, then all this was to be expected, with the imagination not resting content with the same version of the narrative for all time, and that is exactly what we find both within Scripture and beyond. As for what stimulates such developments, sometimes the pressure will have come purely from within the tradition in a refocusing of the balance of how the existing narrative is read, but perhaps more commonly it will be a matter of the dynamic of an inherited past interacting with fresh stimuli for change from outside, from the wider surrounding culture.[103]

As stated earlier, my work seeks to understand the development taking shape through the reception of past with "fresh stimuli" in popular culture.[104] I will argue from the standpoint of Rush's "reception pneumatol-

---

97. Brown, *Tradition & Imagination*, 25.
98. Bethge, ed., *Dietrich Bonhoeffer*, 156.
99. Rush, *Still Interpreting Vatican II*, 55.
100. Ibid., 76.
101. Bethge, ed., *Dietrich Bonhoeffer*, 157.
102. Ibid.
103. Brown, *Tradition & Imagination*, 25.
104. Ibid.

ogy" in recognizing "the God-given responsibility of being active, creative, imaginative receivers of revelation—for God's sake."[105] In this way, I want to get beyond "reader-response criticism, reception aesthetics, and reception theory [that are merely] engaged in understanding the relations between readers/viewers and texts/films."[106] Of course, all of these relations are critical for understanding reception, yet at the same time, a reception pneumatology is interested in the relation between God and the world. Such a "model requires a reception pneumatology that not only gives adequate emphasis to *both* continuity and discontinuity in the history of the tradition, but conceives the Holy Spirit as *the very source of divine discontinuity,* for the sake of continuity with the great *traditio*. And the divine discontinuity may just be all around us."[107] Naturally, an analysis of images in popular culture will serve to illumine some of these areas of continuity, as well as discontinuity.

WHAT SORT OF CRITERIA MATTERS?

There is a key objection, however, to this approach: what are the criteria by which to base an evaluation of an approach that can seem to be both overly subjective at times and overly celebratory of areas that are relatively unexplored by theologians for various reasons? Lynch is right to point out "that aesthetic experiences are by their very nature subjective" and he draws attention to areas that should be avoided, along with a number of points concerning criteria for a well-balanced aesthetic judgment through engaging popular culture.[108] By no means do I intend to ignore the important work being done by those working on the reception of images through concentrating on commercial aspects of distribution. For example, this approach is characteristic of Morgan's writing, as well as the work of Clive Marsh in analyzing audience reception.[109] Reception studies in culture provide strong empirical reason for this type of work, which is absolutely critical. At the same time, the central concern with my current project is a hermeneutic of reception focusing on the way popular culture creates images of heaven and the interpretive possibilities for theological construction that may challenge assumptions and/or raise possibilities for a reassessment of the tradition,

---

105. Rush, *Still Interpreting Vatican II*, 79.

106. Staiger, *Interpreting Films*, 8.

107. Rush, *Still Interpreting Vatican II*, 79–80.

108. Lynch, *Understanding Theology and Popular Culture*, 189. Also see, Lynch, ed., *Between Sacred and Profane*. See Lynch's concluding essay, 157–63.

109. Ibid., 27–33. Also, see Marsh, "Audience Reception," 255–74.

"however valuable or true we may think our present assumptions to be."[110] I agree with Detweiler and Taylor, that "while theology must be faithful to tradition and rooted in Scripture, it also must speak to the times, not just vernacularly but in emphasis and focus."[111] Where both Word and Spirit are vital, "theology must move with the era and shift with the Spirit."[112]

The set of criteria outlined by Lynch towards a theological aesthetic is admittedly "merely provisional and open for further discussion."[113] Following the pragmatic approaches of John Dewey and others, Lynch desires to go beyond "esoteric or disinterested accounts of beauty," and, rather, to "ask whether a form of popular culture is catalytic in the sense of provoking constructive experiences, attitudes and practices that spill over into other parts of our lives or whether it simply promotes an enervating passivity in us."[114] He offers an extended set of questions in making aesthetic judgments and it is important for the current project to mention a few of these questions. Firstly, "does it [the cultural text] exemplify *originality, imagination, or creativity*? If it is a cultural text, does it go beyond or make imaginative use of standard conventions within its genre, or introduce us to something we have not previously seen, heard or thought about in the same way."[115] Secondly (where Lynch draws from the work of Simon Firth), "does it offer a satisfying *reflection of human experience*, and/or provide a means for empathizing with a range of different experiences?"[116] Thirdly, "does it offer a valuable *vision of the meaning of our lives*?"[117] Fourthly, "does it make possible a *sense of encounter with 'God,' the transcendent, or the numinous*?"[118]

Again, however, these evaluative tools only represent a host of further questions Lynch proposes and most cultural texts need to meet more than one to have some form of value.[119] I want to add two further points which are important for a theologically constructive project and certainly

110. Brown, *Tradition & Imagination*, 28.

111. Taylor, *A Matrix of Meanings*, 295.

112. Ibid.

113. Lynch, *Understanding Theology and Popular Culture*, 191. As mentioned, the list of criteria is not exhaustive, but always important to keep in mind is Westphal's observation: "it is nice to have a method or set of rules to function as the criterion for interpretation. But the question can always be asked: by what criteria are these criteria justified?" See Westphal, *Whose Community? Which Interpretation?* 34.

114. Ibid., 190.

115. Ibid., 191.

116. Ibid.

117. Ibid.

118. Ibid.

119. Ibid., 192.

fit nicely with Lynch's broad descriptive list. Firstly, how well does a text handle received traditions and/or doctrine? Here, I am not advocating a position that the history of interpretation of scripture, tradition, and culture are somehow uniform in method or outcome, but rather, that we are living with a multiplicity of interpretations and traditions. As David Jasper writes, "interpretation, therefore, is not a process along a linear trajectory from ignorance to understanding via the medium of the text."[120] Jasper draws from the work of Martin Heidegger where he describes a person entering into the hermeneutical circle and wants to argue that "what is important is not how we get *out*" and he goes on to add "(which, arguably, is impossible anyway), but how we initially get *in*. In other words, what idea do you start with—one based on faith or one based on suspicion, or, more likely, a mixture of the two?"[121] Jasper asks a critical question for the engagement between theology and popular culture, "which comes first—text or interpretation? The answer is neither and both."[122] Traditions continue to pass on interpretations often from a variety of texts, including the scriptures and it is not uncommon for those interpretations to have many different angles. Here, I agree with Merold Westphal and his use of Hans-Georg Gadamer in that, "the plurality of viewpoints is not a compromise of truth and objectivity."[123] Westphal argues that we should be weary of objectivism and psychologism, as well as understand that, "authorial intention is about the public, shareable meanings the author offers to us."[124] Of course, the public nature of art is one of the many reasons for not giving too much attention to the intentions of the artist.[125] Once again returning to the performance metaphor as, J. O. Young observes, "there is no guarantee that even a composer's own performance realized his intentions."[126] At the same time, one must not lose sight that "knowing something of the intentions and life of the artist can deepen one's experience of the work itself," not to mention the important work of understanding contextual issues.[127] Westphal wants to maintain, "here the multiplicity of interpretations stems not from the indeterminacy of the object but

---

120. Jasper, *A Short Introduction to Hermeneutics*, 21.
121. Ibid.
122. Ibid.
123. Westphal, *Whose Community? Which Interpretation?* 23.
124. Ibid., 48.
125. Taliaferro, *Aesthetics*, 51.
126. Quoted in Taliaferro, *Aesthetics*, 55.
127. Ibid., 54.

from the way it exceeds the ability of any limited perspective to grasp it in its totality."[128] He moves in a rather helpful direction in the following:

> We need not think that hermeneutical despair ("anything goes") and hermeneutical arrogance (we have "the" interpretation) are the only alternatives. We can acknowledge that we see and interpret "in a glass, darkly" or "in a mirror, dimly" and that we know "only in part" (1 Cor. 13.12), while ever seeking to understand and interpret better by combining the tools of scholarship with the virtues of humbly listening to the interpretations of others and above all to the Holy Spirit.[129]

Part of the challenge can be represented in Deacy's argument for a more syncretistic approach towards interpretations of film, for instance, simply because a number of traditions could be so-called competing within a single narrative.[130] He suggests by allowing the imagination to breathe properly, one will not be surprised to find a multi-sided conversation occurring, which only further points to the inter-conversation taking place in culture, especially concerning heaven, while simultaneously, the key for Deacy is to recognize that:

> Films—no matter how "secular", no matter how shallow or banal—function no less importantly when they enable us to ask whether the values that underpin our theological positions are really any more cogent, any more consistent, any more defensible just because they happen to be more established and have been around for longer than their cinematic counterparts. Can *All Dogs Go to Heaven* challenge Aquinas? Can *The Shawshank Redemption* enable us to revisit the way we categorise and understand "heaven"? Can *Working Girl* shed new light on the way we conceptualise the "New Jerusalem"? Surely they can, they must, and they already do.[131]

A second question to add to Lynch's list of criteria is, how does the interpretation of a text keep, as Brown suggests, "image, text and truth work[ing] together, not in opposition"?[132] A central component to the present book is the desire to keep the imagination and truth in an interconnected relationship in the interpretation of heaven. Lynch also provides

128. Westphal, *Whose Community? Which Interpretation?* 26.
129. Ibid., 15.
130. Deacy, *Screening the Afterlife*, 158.
131. Ibid., 164.
132. Brown, *Tradition and Imagination*, 376.

a helpful reminder from Johnston, that, "theologizing should follow, not precede, the aesthetic experience."[133] Lynch concludes by emphasizing "this ongoing need for the theological and cultural criticism of the everyday and for imaginative and constructive interventions in contemporary culture."[134]

As in any relationship, the ability to communicate and trust, as well as negotiate authentic challenges requires a watchful discernment within the engagement. Tom Beaudoin has argued that "both [Lynch and Cobb] seek to go beyond mere religious studies commentary, on the one hand, or a poorly theorized spiritual celebration or condemnation, on the other."[135] Lynch is certainly correct that studies in the area of popular culture and theology need to go beyond

> a thinly veiled attempt to indulge in an uncritical celebration and display of our curiosities and pleasures ("theologians talking about their record collections") then it can have a show and tell quality which may be entertaining, but ultimately unsatisfying in the broader academic terms. The study of religion, media and popular culture has much more to offer than this.[136]

In answering the challenge of dilettantism, Beaudoin has made the case, "dilettantes or not, theological or religious studies of culture are enactments of our relation to ourselves and others that re(in)habit the forms of experience that make us who we are."[137] Westphal argues that "we don't turn to the work of art (primarily) for pleasure we derive but to open ourselves to what it reveals to us about the real."[138] One should also consider the nature of "popular" and the process of interpreting a text on its own terms, as suggested earlier. For instance, Detweiler and Taylor note, "the popularity of a song, movie, or show corresponds with its ability to connect with viewers' core hopes, feelings, and desires, and it does not automatically dismiss those desires as base, sexual, or sinful."[139] Johnston's advice to theologize after experiencing a text does not release all directional pressure in favor of theology or popular culture. It merely takes human experience seriously in the interpretive process.[140]

---

133. Lynch, *Understanding Theology and Popular Culture*, 37.
134. Ibid., 193.
135. Beaudoin, "Popular Culture Scholarship as a Spiritual Exercise," 95.
136. Ibid., 157–58.
137. Ibid., 108–9.
138. Westphal, *Whose Community? Which Interpretation?* 92.
139. Taylor, *A Matrix of Meanings*, 296.
140. Lynch, *Understanding Theology and Popular Culture*, 37.

A further caution is offered by Cobb who has observed the danger which cultural critics find firmly planted before them in the temptation to follow such deconstructionists of the 1990s as Michel Foucault, who find the only worthy path to pursue in cultural analysis in uncovering "the political and economic power struggles that its production and consumption represents."[141] If one rests with Foucault's proposal, then, the normative theological factors are once again reduced to a political theology and power struggle, lacking transcendence.

Why Do Some Images Fail to Enliven the Imagination?

Keeping these critical components and preliminary cautions in mind, it is important to elaborate how questions of criteria and ways the imagination can be significant and/or insignificant for reflecting on heaven. In doing so, I want to address the ever pressing question facing imaginative approaches to theology: why are some images overlooked or discarded while certain other images are brought under brighter light for deeper consideration. Aside from the obvious qualification that one cannot begin to write every word that needs to be written in order to come a bit closer to understanding such an expansive terrain, my aim here is to offer a few comments that describe some flexible starting points (of course, not the only approach one might undertake) for developing criteria that address the failure of certain images to enliven the imagination. Such a framework will provide a generous, hospitable, yet discerning means of interpreting imagery in popular culture.

Now, failure in a strict sense entails a lack of energy to generate life, but in terms of the imagination, failure may produce new ways of seeing what it is that the image is pointing towards. In this sense, failure attracts different connotations that tend to be more positive, especially for theology. For example, theologians of culture such as Paul Tillich wanted to describe the "shaking" and "transformation" of "conditioned forms," in order to describe his key action metaphor for revelation, the moment of "breakthrough."[142] Austin Farrer was not as concerned as Tillich seemed to be in transcendence undoing the natural, so I find Farrer's approach more helpful where he emphasized the "breaking of descriptions," not for the sake of iconoclastic demolition, but rather, to modify metaphors leading one into a deeper understanding of doctrine.[143] More recently, David Brown has effectively

141. Cobb, *The Blackwell Guide to Theology and Popular Culture*, 70.
142. Tillich, *On the Boundary*, 28. Also, see Reimer, *Paul Tillich*, 182.
143. Farrer, *The Glass of Vision*, 68.

illustrated what he describes as the necessary collapse of images in order for one to move beyond tradition.[144]

In order to provide a more concrete description of image failure, I should also mention a more negative view towards reality. For example, Don Cupitt argues that any type of "metaphysical realism was permanently demolished by Kant," therefore, any notion of an image pointing to a deeper reality fails in this non-realistic approach.[145] This is not to ignore the contribution of non-realism in reminding us that "theology is mediated; and the transcendence of God (or the otherness of God) is maintained by this mediation."[146]

For Christian theology then, transcendent reality is not something that can be set aside by philosophers. Neither is this to ensure unconditioned interpretation, nor should it; but rather it acknowledges that God is making himself known to finite creatures. Any attempt to eliminate transcendence usually places a high value on the physical, but ironically de-emphasizes God's transcendent presence in human lives through the Spirit by placing too little emphasis on God's continued action in history, as well as everlasting participation and response in Christ's salvific work. Therefore, disregard for social aspects of heaven, such as reunion, memory, and fulfillment, including taking into account both continuity and discontinuity of an earthly existence will most likely fail to enliven the imagination. According to Fergus Kerr, "non-realism, in religion in particular, is of course at odds with ordinary people's beliefs . . . ."[147] This is one reason why near-death experiences, mystical experiences, and radical religious conversions are given much popular attention—they provide a framework for making meaning within a tradition that remains open to possibilities.

Those more positive features describing the modification of images, whether natural or unnatural, will be more prominent in later stages of my constructive theology, but at this point, I want to turn to some historical developments within imaginative approaches that provide a way of negotiating through the vast popular imagery of heaven and give some reasons for the *negative* ways in which images fail. Therefore, my aim in the following is twofold. First, I will add to the voices of caution by pointing out extreme positions (i.e. representationalism and constructivism), as well as extreme ahistorical attitudes that can serve as reasons why images fail to open up new ways for reflecting on heaven. These extremes just mentioned lack the

---

144. Brown, *Tradition & Imagination*, 51.
145. Cupitt, "Free Christianity," 15.
146. Ward, "Theological materialism," 146.
147. Kerr, "What's wrong with realism anyway?" 130.

ability to learn from the other, to perceive what Richard Kearney upholds: "the imagination both receives and recreates."[148] Although cautious not to steer too far from the receiving activity of the imagination, Smith comments, "I do think it is crucial that we be able to imagine the world otherwise than how we 'receive' it."[149] I am not interested in setting up binaries in order to categorize popular art, but rather, to show how *extreme* positions can limit interpretive possibilities. Where my examples have ranged over broad terrain throughout part one of this book, I will now begin to narrow my focus using specific examples regarding heaven and popular forms of art.

Secondly, I will conclude by offering three general criteria for navigating into a more theologically constructive disposition. Here, I will also offer some comments regarding the possibilities for theology to learn from popular forms of art, such as film.

Popular Art as Representationalism

In a 2012 interview, Kearney outlined some of the challenges that remain pervasive streams of thought within Western culture as pertaining to any link between the imagination and truth.[150] In response to the question, "why might the concept of imagination need to be seen in new ways?" Kearney replied by advocating an avoidance of "two traditional pitfalls," both of which hold significant implications concerning the question I am asking regarding the weakness of images to work in doctrinal articulations of heaven.[151] The first pitfall to avoid Kearney traces back to classical philosophy in Plato where the imagination is described as a "purely passive receptor."[152] Ideas are merely faded images of reality (Truth), therefore in Plato, once the poet delivers words to the parchment, the piece "is by nature at third remove from the throne of truth" and this, Plato adds, is true of all representational art.[153] This reductive view of the imagination immediately breeds suspicion of created pieces of art, especially of mass-produced popular forms, which can be critiqued for creating further faded copies of reality.[154] For some, the distance from reality to image can serve as a safety mechanism protecting conflation of the two, but this only seems problematic for communication

148. Kearney, "Imagination's Truth."
149. Smith, *Imagining the Kingdom*, 17n35.
150. Kearney, "Imagination's Truth."
151. Ibid.
152. Ibid.
153. Plato, *The Republic*, 425.
154. Kearney, "Imagination's Truth."

if a representation becomes the sole representation with no allowance for modification. I find it a helpful reminder that "whatever image it [the imagination] constructs, there is always some dimension of otherness which transcends it."[155] The question remains, how far can a representation move away from its origins and still remain an accurate representation of an object? To argue that the embodied form gives less of reality is problematic on many levels for Christianity, especially for key doctrines such as the incarnation of Christ.

As we have observed, an unfortunate shift has occurred in certain parts of contemporary theology, placing a wedge between aesthetics and theological conceptions of heaven. Heaven is often understood as a place for God, but no longer a place for humans. Earth is where humans live, die, and rise according to such theological accounts. Therefore, works of representation experience immediate detachment from reality. In such conceptual conditions, all representation becomes suspect and can produce severe conceptual strain for the doctrine. Intentionally or not, this plays a role in what Kearney observes as the postmodern tendency to distrust all representations, perhaps for more reasons than theological, but nonetheless, similar consequences unfold.[156]

On a more positive note, representations of heaven still continue to spark interest at the more popular level of culture, including the church, as a place for the resurrected Christ and those who participate in his resurrected life.[157] In this case, Plato's understanding of the world as a representation of reality or heaven has not been made completely obsolete and is still considered a valid model by some Christian philosophers.[158] In this sense, "the question of heaven, then, is a realistic question, not an escapist question."[159] The material emphasis, for example in some New Testament scholarship, which has little use for heaven except for providing a framework for the direction from which God is coming to earth, has not completely overshadowed the role that the spiritual plays in and through the physical; it does create, nonetheless, a type of tension where God only overlaps in particular historical moments, failing to acknowledge that it is through inspired works of the imagination, along with refinement through the intellect, that we better understand and know what is being disclosed throughout history.

---

155. Kearney, *The Wake of Imagination*, 396.
156. Ibid., 388–89.
157. Paul, *Heaven*, DVD (2005–6).
158. Kreeft, *Everything You Ever Wanted to Know about Heaven*, 258.
159. Ibid., 24.

At the same time, the wider current state of cultural affairs seems not overly worried about extreme forms of representationalism as Kearney observes:

> We seem to have entered an age where reality is inseparable from the image, where the original has been replaced by its imitation, where our understanding of the world is preconditioned by the electronically reproducible media of television, cinema, video and radio—media in which every "live" event or performance is capable of being mechanically recorded and retransmitted *ad infinitum*.[160]

Ironically, this is not only the case with the productive imagination, but representative art also faces a similar dilemma. Although creating space for the distinction between original and re-creation, representational art has to combat the urge towards shielding the light from seeing further possibilities. Decreasing the distance between reality and image does come with warning signals, which leads to a second extreme to avoid.

Popular Art as Constructivism

A second stream of thought eliminates the problem of representation by championing a position of non-reality.[161] More specifically, according to Kearney, an extreme case of constructivism is to adopt a stance where the individual creates all meaning.[162] In other words, there is no meaning outside of what human beings create and recreate; no higher reality. Constantly pushing the boundaries is not a guarantee for success, especially in film production, but one must at least be on the boundaries (to use Tillich's life metaphor) to see new horizons.[163] Ward suggests that "the theological difficulty of anti-realist 'theologies' is that theology requires some notion of realism."[164] Thus, "for theology to be *theology* its discourse must, in some sense, be saying something about God and God's relationship with the world which is true."[165] Kerr describes extreme forms of anti-realism as "picturing the world as a product—if the realist pictures it as preconceptualized reality (some kind of raw material that awaits our intervention), the non-realist

---

160. Kearney, *The Wake of Imagination*, 251–52.
161. Kearney, "Imagination's Truth."
162. Ibid.
163. Tillich, *On the Boundary*, 13.
164. Ward, "Theological Materialism," 146.
165. Ibid.

views it as a creation *ex nihilo* (all his [or her] own work)."[166] As mentioned earlier, my aim is not to continue a feud between realism and anti-realism, but to avoid extremes by bringing both closer together and extracting their strengths. As in the case of all fiction, for the story to function meaningfully, character development, music, narrative form, and visual affects all need to be interwoven contextually for effectiveness. According to Kearney, "we create out of what we have already discovered in reality," which leads to my third point concerning the ways images fail to engage reception history.[167]

Popular Art as Ahistorical

If it is true, which I take to be the case, that the imagination works within the space between both extremes of representationalism and constructivism, popular forms of art are created and recreated with materials that are received, but the form and content will and must shift if an image is to enliven the imagination within culture. As Brown observes, in order to accomplish this type of participation and response, images "must relate to the readers' [or viewers'] own life situations and dilemmas, not simply to the past."[168] In order for these images to adjust within different contexts, Brown identifies "the necessity for tradition to keep meanings alive not simply by preserving them but by allowing their constant adaptation . . . ," a feature which he rightly finds working throughout scripture and tradition.[169] Keeping extreme forms of representation and constructivism in mind, a third way in which popular images of heaven fail is thus by paying too little attention to the historical trajectory of the imagination. At the same time, even such failures may in some way contribute to the life of a doctrine by imaginatively engaging dormant or marginalized aspects of a doctrine. The specific case of the doctrine of heaven serves as a prime example since the imagination and the doctrine are too often characterized as detached from the historical drama. While certain depictions can exhibit escapist qualities, if one pays attention to the historical traditions, one will discover a range of doctrinal appropriations in popular culture that do not serve escapist caricatures. For example, afterlife films desiring to treat the theme of the nearness of the beyond or what could be termed, the nearness of heaven, such as *Charlie St. Cloud*, *Dragonfly*, or *Lovely Bones*, all direct attention to

---

166. Kerr, "What's Wrong with Realism Anyway?" 141.
167. Ibid.
168. Brown, *Tradition & Imagination*, 59.
169. Ibid., 72.

the earthly drama.¹⁷⁰ The narratives are at the same time other-worldly, yet remain engaged to the unfolding of history. Films run the risk of stripping out imaginative power if they either detach from traditions or do not work with stories that shape people's lives within the viewer context. One of the ways films can engage the historical tradition is by drawing on resources from different disciplines such as painting, music and literature. Films that too quickly resolve complexities limit interpretive possibilities and do not rightly attend to the "hermeneutic task."¹⁷¹

Another way popular art fails to engage history is through symbol deflation or disjunction. I am referring to the use of symbols or metaphors in contemporary art that fail to connect traditional symbolic reference to the stories of everyday lives. For example, the use of clouds in films to describe heavenly reality is a quite common image, but too often clouds end up as merely a part of the aesthetic ambiance, such as in *Bruce Almighty*, rather than charged with theological meaning and presence.¹⁷² Therefore, the image flattens out losing significance for a materialistic culture already aware of the material composition of a cloud. The cloud environment becomes more artificial and less charged with presence. In the Hebrew Scriptures and New Testament, "clouds represent the presence of God (Exod. 13:21; 19:9; 24:15–16; Matt. 17:5; Mark 9:7; Luke 9:34–35)."¹⁷³ Alva Steffler rightly mentions the importance clouds play in association with "Christ's ascension (Acts 1:9) and his Second Coming (1 Thess. 4:17; Rev. 1:7)."¹⁷⁴ Again it seems arguable that Terrence Malick was attempting to infuse such a meaning with camera flashes towards the clouds in the sky in his film, *The Tree of Life*.¹⁷⁵

The deflation of a symbol is not necessarily the problem, but where a leap in discontinuity is observed, the imagination wants to go further. For instance, many contemporary advocates of heaven might find great dissatisfaction if the defining image of heaven entailed a dwelling in white clouds with little or no other images making up the environment.¹⁷⁶ In the case of *Bruce Almighty*, subversion of the symbol may have been intended to make

170. *Charlie St. Cloud*, DVD (2010). *Dragonfly*, DVD (2002). *The Lovely Bones*, DVD (2009).

171. Kearney, *The Wake of Imagination*, 389–92.

172. *Bruce Almighty*, DVD (2003).

173. Steffler, *Symbols of the Christian Faith*, 5.

174. Ibid.

175. *The Tree of Life*, DVD (2011).

176. Meacham, "Heaven Can't Wait," 32–33. The article displays a number of images from paintings to films, to cartoon animations where clouds make up a significant role in differentiating heaven from earth.

room for a corporeal God (played by Morgan Freeman), but the dislocation of a symbol should open up space, not constrict.[177] Even where more natural elements such as clouds are portrayed, the artificiality of heaven as depicted in Western material culture leaves many with a vision that is comparable to an artificial flower shop, rather than the most beautiful Eden-like gardens. Flexibility of a symbol to continue operating can be an aesthetic challenge that certainly overlaps with religion. One critique common to film is the unwavering freedom to stretch a symbol beyond recognition, but Christian theology is not trying to become merely aesthetic, it seeks to grow in faith and understanding of a God that is beyond symbolic exhaustion.[178]

A fear remains in some contexts that "fantasy is [or will become] more real than reality," especially if the origin of an image is ignored or dies.[179] Kearney observes, "deprived of the concept of *origin*, the concept of imagination itself collapses."[180] He argues that to some degree the "imagination always presupposed the idea of origination: the derivation of our images from some original presence. And this position obtains regardless of whether the model of origination was situated *outside* of man (as in the biblical God of creation or the Platonic Ideas) or *inside* of man (as in the model of a productive consciousness promoted by modern idealism and existentialism)."[181] Kearney describes the postmodern situation as moving away from "the *mirror*" of pre-modernism "(which reflected the light of a transcendental origin beyond itself), and the modern by the metaphor of the *lamp* (which projected an original light from within itself)," to what he describes as "the *looking glass*—or the interplay between multiple looking glasses which reflect each other interminably."[182] Parodies of heaven such as *Heart and Souls*, *Chances Are*, and a more extreme image from the cartoon animation *South Park*, where "Kenny enters the gates of heaven to help God fight Satan with a video game," run the risk of either becoming too artificial for the imagination or so constructive that all historical continuity, narrative believability, and hermeneutical interest is lost.[183]

The complexity of selecting particular films over others, prioritizing certain texts or songs while leaving others aside, is never completely

---

177. *Bruce Almighty*, DVD.

178. Brown, *Religious Aesthetics*, 42.

179. Kearney, *The Wake of Imagination*, 252.

180. Ibid., 253.

181. Ibid.

182. Ibid.

183. *Heart and Souls*, DVD (1998). *Chances Are*, DVD (1989). See Meacham, "Heaven Can't Wait," 33.

resolved, but this does not alleviate the burden of trying to provide starting points. Brown, for instance, has provided nine such criteria where "more than one has been in use at any one time."[184] Among his criteria, he includes: the historical, empirical, conceptual, moral, criteria of continuity, Christological criteria, the degree of imaginative engagement, the effectiveness of analogical construct and finally, ecclesial criteria.[185] Gordon Lynch also has a list of nine, specifically targeting the area of popular culture and theological aesthetics.[186] His list includes: the level of technical skill, imaginative creativity, reflection of human experience, vision of meaning for our lives, genuinely pleasurable experiences, a sense of transcendence, and finally, the question of authenticity.[187] Conceding the provisional nature of such criteria, Lynch comments: "aesthetics of popular culture could be seen as hopelessly simplistic if it encourages the idea that there is a single, ideal form to which all popular culture should aspire. Such a notion is unrealistic, though."[188] Following Simon Firth, "different forms of popular music exist within an on-going field of tensions between 'authenticity and artifice, sentimentality and realism, the spiritual and the sensual, the serious and the fun.' [Lynch adds], there is no single correct way for popular music to resolve these different tensions."[189] Kearney observes, for those who have conceded no way to "determine a representational relationship between image and its original," degrees of "epistemological undecidability do not necessitate ethical undecidability" or what Kearney terms the "ethical-poetical imagination."[190] Kearney's decision to retain ethical dimensions of judgment is right in trying to combat the "sovereign subjectivity."[191] As mentioned earlier, Christian theology is not at a complete loss of a representational relationship to reality, especially in the resistance to moral relativism, except where new images are disallowed development or where the conceptual is cut out of the doctrine. My project insists that neither of these are sound options for the doctrine of heaven. Although more interested in the philosophical development of the imagination, Kearney offers three important factors that the theologian can strongly endorse and can be found working in the criteria of both Brown and Lynch for adjudicating between the changes, either for

---

184. Brown, *Discipleship & Imagination*, 389.
185. Ibid., 389–405.
186. Lynch, *Understanding Theology and Popular Culture*, 190–91.
187. Ibid.
188. Ibid.
189. Ibid.
190. Kearney, *The Wake of Imagination*, 388–89.
191. Ibid., 389.

failure or success of an image to work in doctrinal articulation. This interplay with philosophy also reminds the theologian not to "forget about other forms of aesthetics, whether philosophical or religious," even though the theologian is asking specific questions concerning revelation and doctrine within a religious tradition.[192]

Why Do Images Enliven the Imagination?

Kearney's broad categories for navigating the effectiveness of an image include three tasks, the *hermeneutic task*, the *historical task* and the *narrative task*.[193] All three fit well within a theologically constructive project. Kearney observes:

> The aim of such a hermeneutic is to discriminate between a liberating and incarcerating use of images, between those that dis-close and those that close off our relation to the other, those that democratize culture and those that mystify it, those that communicate and those that manipulate. This requires in turn that imagination undertakes a hermeneutic reading of its own genealogy: one which critically reassesses its own traditions, retells its own stories. Thus instead of conforming to the official censure of imagination in premodern thought, such a hermeneutic reading would brush this tradition against the grain, allowing repressed voices to speak out, neglected texts to get a hearing.[194]

Kearney offers St. Jerome, Origen, Gregory of Nyssa, and Maximus the Confessor as exemplary figures who endorsed the "creative play" of reading the scriptures and tradition.[195] "Rather than construing the premodern and modern interpretations of imagination as *either/or* alternatives, our postmodern hermeneutic would seek ways of integrating them—combining the ethical emphasis of the former with the poetical emphasis of the latter."[196] I am not quite sure why it is necessary to limit this emphasis to postmodernity, especially if we find examples in earlier periods (as mentioned above), and indeed even in the scriptures themselves. Nonetheless, Kearney provides an important emphasis. A constructive theology is also a hermeneutic of doc-

---

192. Brown, *Religious Aesthetics*, 194.
193. Kearney, *The Wake of Imagination*, 389–96.
194. Ibid., 390.
195. Ibid., 391.
196. Ibid., 392.

trine, full of descriptive possibilities. Since I am a student of theology looking to the arts, my concerns will naturally be slanted in a certain direction, just as in the case of the scientist, philosopher, or filmmaker. Frank Burch Brown has suggested that the theologian is at no less a disadvantage than any other professional in such aesthetic understanding.[197]

The second task of "history" will serve as an important criterion to include in adjudicating multiple interdisciplinary texts associated with heaven. Kearney writes: "any project for future alternatives to the paralysis of the present needs to remain mindful of the narratives of the past."[198] He later adds, "the concrete struggle to transfigure our one-dimensional society cannot dispense with the hermeneutic services of such an historically attuned imagination."[199] In the selection process of popular texts, a number of possibilities are open especially pertaining to questions of life, death, forgiveness, hope, fulfillment, joy, salvation, healing, just to name a few. Once heaven is allowed to be a place, associations of continuity and discontinuity with human existence become possible. As pointed out earlier, Brown has consistently communicated the importance of the historical tradition in doctrinal development. Following Ricoeur, Kearney offers "a reminder that the horizons of history are still open, that *other* modes of social and aesthetic [we might add, theological] experience are possible."[200]

Thirdly, Kearney advocates the narrative task. Certainly not unrelated to the hermeneutical and historical, especially in connection to this project on heaven, narrative dimensions of the individual are crucial to literary devices utilized in fiction media such as film. In this way, popular art serves as a way for the individual to interpret and reinterpret their life,

> By relating himself [or herself] in turn to the cathartic effects of those larger narratives, historical and fictional, transmitted by our cultural memory. The notion of personal identity is thus opened up by the narrative imagination to include that of a *communal* identity. The self and the collective mutually constitute each other's identity by receiving each other's stories into their respective histories.[201]

All three tasks help to answer the question of why images work to enliven the human imagination. Further, Quash develops a helpful description of the risk laden interplay between imagination and history, lending support

197. Brown, *Religious Aesthetics*, 191.
198. Kearney, *The Wake of Imagination*, 394.
199. Ibid.
200. Ibid.
201. Ibid., 395–96.

for a theologically imaginative approach that pays careful attention to hermeneutics, history, and narrative:

> There is a risk of overstating the primacy of the imaginative insight over historical evidence: the risk, perhaps, of using the claim that the worlds conjured by our imaginative powers are *truer* than the givenness of our day-to-day world to justify a certain naïve escapism from the intractabilitites of material and social life; or the forfeiting of an ability to judge between imagined possibilities, such that anything imagined is allowed to command uncritical credulity simply by virtue of being imagined. But caution in relation to these dangers ought not to disregard the theologically compelling fact—in a Christian perspective—that the imagined worlds of parables, apocalypses and prophetic speech are offered to be trusted. They are divinely licensed, and (like well-worn liturgies?) they can command assent because they seem to disclose the deep dynamics of reality somehow authentically, even if non-literally. In the case of parables of the Kingdom, they are revelation by the Son of what the Spirit is doing in service of eschatological consummation.[202]

Prior to these comments, Quash provides an excellent example of Jesus' approach with his disciples: "the fantastical actually affects and directs the historical (or 'realistic'). Jesus' disciples are transformed by his pictures and stories, as—in history—the members of his Church have repeatedly been transformed by them too."[203] I aim to show, through the images selected for interpretation, both strengths and weaknesses in the capacity to identify imaginative possibilities for a theology of heaven through engaging the tasks of hermeneutics, history, and narrative.

Even in light of these three categories, one could pose the question: what can the theologian learn from films or other popular forms of art about heaven? I have already addressed the question concerning the importance of the imagination in the Christian life, as well as the role culture can play in keeping dormant aspects of Christian doctrine alive. In addition, films for example, can provide imaginative narratives that deeply concern humanity. As having noted the importance of reading scriptures, history, and contemporary narratives in conversation, theology can learn how narratives go beyond scripture to offer plausible (of course in varying degrees) imaginative grasp of history that should not be left aside by theology. On a more functional level, films can help theology better understand the

---

202. Quash, *Found Theology*, 258.
203. Ibid., 257.

implications of theology for society. This does not mean that theologians will always agree on film selection, but this is true of any art form, including literary resources for theology.

Culture, Sub-culture, and Challenges of Film-Selection

Among questions of evaluation, the theologian of culture must still face important decisions regarding which examples provide support for establishing the argument. Since my overall contribution is in the area of theological studies, I will echo the words of Marsh: "readers expecting to find extensive film-critical analyses of the works considered will be disappointed."[204] Further, narrowing the selection to Western cinematic examples still leaves vast possibilities for materials available for inclusion. Marsh has been critical of the "pre-occupation" with certain films, which in turn have limited possibilities for less popular films to be brought into the conversation.[205] He mentions one film in particular that I have chosen to include: Vincent Ward's *What Dreams May Come*.[206] Although I concede Marsh's point and have even included examples with no eschatological focus to shine light on the subject, a number of reasons have provoked my inclusion of this text. Firstly, Ward's film raises hermeneutic possibilities for questions of appearance and human longing for reunion. These are well established questions within the long Christian tradition regarding heaven. Secondly, the film allows for an interdisciplinary engagement by raising questions concerning other forms of visual arts, as well as philosophical questions concerning appearance and the body. Thirdly, the film is still listed in popular media, as one of the top films on the afterlife.[207] Finally, but not exhaustively, the recent, tragic death of actor Robin Williams (who plays the main character in the film) has brought added attention to his work, in his role as an artist. All of this is to suggest that establishing selection criteria for films is likely to be accompanied by some criticism of choice. Nevertheless, Marsh rightly observes that more work needs to be done in Christian eschatology through engaging popular films.[208]

The vast amount of film material on afterlife themes remains problematic for reasons of cultural and sub-cultural adherence. Naturally,

---

204. Marsh, *Theology Goes to the Movies*, 3.

205. See Marsh's review in, Marsh, "Blick über den Tod hinaus/Seeing Beyond Death in Theology," 311.

206. *What Dreams May Come*, DVD (2003).

207. Greg Taylor, "Top Ten Movies On The Afterlife."

208. Marsh, "Blick über den Tod hinaus/Seeing Beyond Death," 311.

sub-cultures will gravitate towards certain types of films for greater preferred emphases, while others will make use of taste or value judgment to minimize the reception of certain popular films. For example, the 2014 release of *Heaven Is for Real* experienced a great attraction from within what is often known as the "Bible belt" of the United States, but also found acceptance within wider demographics, as well.[209] Cobb mentions several recent films also making their way onto popular lists regarding the afterlife, such as *Flatliners* (1990), *Ghost* (1990) and *The Sixth Sense* (1999).[210] Many films on the afterlife deal explicitly with the nearness of heaven or near-death experiences (NDE's). I have instead intentionally focused on issues of appearance, memory, and fulfillment as they relate to the Christian doctrine of heaven.

CONCLUSION

After providing a theological context and rationale for engaging popular culture and navigating some of the current challenges in contemporary theology towards the doctrine of heaven, I have set forth the argument that the human imagination is essential in the reception and hermeneutical process of developing a doctrine of heaven, and that by theologically reflecting on texts and practices in popular culture, the eschatological imagination can once again become enlivened for Christian theology.

Part 2 will feature a theologically imaginative approach to popular culture in relation to key areas of humanity's longing for reunion, memory, and bodily continuity, all of which have significant histories within philosophical and theological conversations in Western culture. By focusing on these three aspects of human identity, I am suggesting more than merely imagining disembodied experiences, such as remembering, "dream-like perceptions," as well as "joy, peace, and benevolence towards other beings."[211] Appearance in relation to reunion and reconciliation points further towards an embodied, social existence. In this way, Sherry suggests more fruits of the Spirit can be imagined to describe life in heaven as "gentle, patient and self-controlled, and as exercising love and kindness towards others."[212] Also, by focusing on these aspects of identity, one can imagine ways in which matters of "the body, the heart, and mind" are more closely related than is often the case.[213] As mentioned earlier, although many fruitful treatments

---

209. *Heaven Is for Real*, DVD (2014). Also, see McClintock, "Box Office" (2014).
210. Cobb, *The Blackwell Guide to Theology and Popular Culture*, 278.
211. Sherry, *Spirit, Saints, and Immortality*, 61.
212. Ibid., 61–62.
213. See Olthuis' essay, "Taking the Wager of/on Love," where he is quoting Luce

of the nearness of heaven have been considered as warrant for the doctrine, whether in discussions of near-death experiences or paranormal activity, within the limited space available, I have decided to focus on heaven and aspects of human identity.[214]

Although film is a primary media I am working within this project, I must also take theology and film's engagement with popular music and narrative aspects of literature seriously, thus showing the intertextual relationship between these disciplines.[215] Thus, while chapter four will focus on humanity's longing for reunion through a conversation between theology and film, chapter five will follow by looking at the question of memory through a conversation between theology, film, and popular music by highlighting music's role in film and theology. In chapter six, I will take up the question of bodily continuity concerning fulfillment and resurrection bodies by emphasizing theology and literature's intertextual relationship with film. In chapter seven, I will conclude by analyzing films that attempt to imagine a post-apocalyptic world, yet find it difficult in providing imaginative grasp for certain earth—bounded eschatologies. Film, music, and literature are key mediums through which culture has contributed significant images of heaven. Film often takes up literary theology, but when it does, the dynamics are a far more oral, visual, and musical way of story based theology.

With that in mind, I am aware that "theology *has* to work with some new materials, as well as old ones, in order to complete its task."[216]

Irigaray in *Gazing through a Prism Darkly*, 151.

214. Walls, *Heaven*. Especially take notice of Wall's chapter, "Heaven and Visions of Life After Life," 133–60. One of Walls' conversation partners has also written extensively in this area. See Zaleski, *The Life of the World to Come*.

215. Taylor also suggests further work needs to be done between theology and film by considering the roles of "story and sound" in his essay, "The Colors of Sound," in *Reframing Theology and Film*, 51–69.

216. Marsh and Ortiz, "Theology Beyond the Modern and Postmodern," 252.

PART II

IMAGINING IDENTITY IN A POST-MORTEM EXISTENCE

4

Humanity's Longing for Reunion

In chapter three, I argued that a more productive way forward in reflecting on heaven is through a hermeneutic of images that takes seriously art forms in popular culture, a culture in which heaven is still treated as a valid category for reconsidering post-mortem existence. This chapter develops the argument that popular films do not just make iconic stabs at expressing heaven, but can challenge conceptions that tend to make heaven less personal than earth. Theology, taking the lead from popular culture, can once again value and, indeed, privilege humanity's longing for reunion in heaven. By keeping the imagination as a partner, with faith and reason, in the knowing process, the critical reflection on films presents concrete questions concerning relationships and recognition in heaven.[1]

This chapter consists of four main sections. The first section introduces the specific relationship between film and the task of theological interpretation. In addition, by addressing recent criticism of the film and theology dialogue more generally, a more charitable analysis of different forms and genre of film can then be considered.

The second section addresses the question of why the relationship between friends and family should be any less, if not more important, in heavenly existence. I want to propose that some continuity, especially related with the exteriority of the human face, must remain between personal identity and recognition.[2] While keeping in mind the latter's importance for

---

1. Kreeft, *Everything You Ever Wanted to Know about Heaven*, 252–53.

2. The detailed account concerning the relationship between personal and/or social identity in psychology is far too storied to unfold in the current chapter, but it may suffice to add that the narrative hermeneutic of film under consideration and the belief in heaven expresses the need to consider ways in which a person continues to remain a

reuniting family and friends, the most interesting and vital component to the argument focuses on the transformation of relationships in a heavenly context. The ways in which different forms of film, such as non-realistic animation, both within comedic genres of animation (such as *Toy Story 3*), or dramatic fantasies (in the case of *What Dreams May Come*), will contribute to the argument by underscoring the importance of allowing some continuity of appearance recognition in connection to a person's identity, while at the same time moving beyond appearance towards a relational continuity between earthly and heavenly existence.

The third section offers further support for the previous analysis by taking into consideration the way particular metaphors work, using the narrative device of pretence as a way to exaggerate meaning for social identity towards a deeper imagining of relational dynamics in heaven. Parallel examples from OT narratives will also be analyzed, in order that a connection might be made between contemporary forms of art, such as film, and longer literary traditions where pretence can lead to disclosure.

Finally, the argument for heavenly recognition and relationship can lead to descriptive questions concerning space, where such reunions can occur. Therefore, in section four, I will argue that certain films can offer a way of analogically re-contextualising heavenly space by use of the creative imagination. For example, in the case of *What Dreams May Come*, the director Vincent Ward turns to the longer Western tradition and the history of interpretation to ask the common analogical question, what will heaven look like?

FILM AND THEOLOGICAL INTERPRETATION

In light of contemporary theology's interpretive release or dismissal of heaven to culture, popular art forms forge new and creative ways of thinking theologically about a heaven that is social, with communication and interpretation, as well as personal. At the same time, because of shifts in theology and culture (documented in part one of the book), heaven remains "open" as a doctrine, and is interpreted at many different levels and in different contexts.[3] Instead of removing the tension between faith and reason, alongside emotion and imagination, popular films integrate a combination

---

unique self in heaven and the process of social formations and relationships.

3. Thiselton, *New Horizons in Hermeneutics*, 477. Although Thiselton is addressing the literary arts, the discussion of open and closed texts is just as appropriate in the area of theology and the visual arts.

of hermeneutical/textual strands ("image, story, and sound"[4]), keeping the imagination as a vital component in the interpretive process of a doctrine, such as heaven.[5] Robert Johnston suggests, "film has become our Western culture's major storytelling and myth-producing medium. As such it has begun to invite the best (and worst!) of our theological reflection."[6] James K. A. Smith goes further to add, "film is the new *lingua franca* of not just American culture but, increasingly, global culture."[7] Christopher Deacy acknowledges the hesitancy among those who find little continuity between a theological discussion that is characterized historically by literary texts, and film, which necessitates more "visual sensitivity."[8] Without ignoring the difficulties involved, further methodological possibilities persist in the relationship between theology and film, especially regarding the theological potency to go beyond strictly correlational models of "looking for theological answers to cultural questions" to Gordon Lynch's revised correlational proposal in which understanding of the descriptive theology resident in a popular text is a first step in the dialectical direction where "theology can itself learn from (and be changed or challenged by) secular culture—even to the point that one may wish to reject aspects of one's theological tradition that are deemed to be deficient or harmful."[9] Popular films can provide a hermeneutic that uses a metaphor of heaven in a way such as to *defamiliarize* or *disrupt* "normal ways of seeing, perceiving, and understanding, to make room for new ways of apprehending and understanding the text."[10] Here, Thiselton draws on the work of Hans Robert Jauss and his "seven theses for a program of reception theory."[11] Thiselton particularly makes use of Jauss' understanding of "ongoing but also 'changing horizon[s] of experience'" where events and "inversion[s]" can lead one "from passive to active reception, from recognized aesthetic norms to a new production that surpasses them."[12]

David Jasper, who has offered criticism concerning a theology and film dialogue in the past, rightly concedes that "[Hollywood films] may, indeed,

---

4. Johnston, "Introduction: Reframing the Discussion," 19. Also, see Taylor's essay, "The Colors of Sound," in the same volume, 51.
5. Lewis, *Mere Christianity*, 124.
6. Johnston, "Introduction: Reframing the Discussion," 16.
7. Smith, *Who's Afraid of Postmodernism*, 24.
8. Deacy, "Theology and Film," 8–9.
9. Ibid., 68
10. Thiselton, *The Hermeneutics of Doctrine*, 99.
11. Ibid., 99.
12. Ibid.

contribute significantly to a proper revitalizing of the religious imagination in a time when the power of the word and the accessibility of theology are arguably less than in almost any other period."[13] His observation lies at the heart of popular culture's important contribution to a hermeneutic of images concerning heaven. Not without qualification, he is intent on drawing a distinction between paintings and plays "of the late Middle Ages in Europe" which possessed a particular "two-edged, ironic, difficult and ambiguous" quality making theological reflection more sustainable, while films remain trapped in the "commercial habit" of Hollywood.[14] Nevertheless, all cultural creations are at the mercy of the early recipients, where our classic remains their *kitsch* or vice versa. Therefore, one must be careful not to overlook the theological "disturbance" in films to stimulate fresh hearings of a doctrine for the imagination, even if it is not one's preferred mode.[15]

Films develop metaphors within these changing horizons, standing at times in stark contrast to McDannell and Lang's summary of Karl Rahner's take on heaven where "the mind [is] emptied of the 'trash' of its biography."[16] Films challenge such constructions by asking questions that allow for a continuation or further unfolding of a life story in post-mortem existence. The critique that film too commonly serves to "help us through the tedium of inactivity, and is supremely an art of illusion" falls short of considering the individual aspects of the religious experience of daily life, and not just its communal aspects.[17] It has not been uncommon for theology to receive similar criticism of being too escapist by emphasizing transcendent aspects of life, thus lacking historical grounding; whereas cultural historians are now asking why theology has ceased or at best postponed the pursuit to be "onto something transcendent, onto something mysterious,

---

13. Jasper, "On Systematizing the Unsystematic," 244. Marsh considers Jasper's critique as "one of the most widely quoted" passages from the *Explorations* volume. See Marsh's response to Jasper in Marsh, *Cinema & Sentiment*, 83.

14. Ibid.

15. Ibid.

16. Lang, *Heaven: A History*, 344.

17. Jasper, "On Systematizing the Unsystematic," 236. Marsh writes in response to Jasper: "The recognition of a necessary detachment from experience of immersion in an illusory world is, however, part of the experience of being religious and being a committed film-watcher. Christians know that bread and wine remain bread and wine, even whilst disagreeing amongst themselves about how to speak of the presence of Christ in relation to these elements of the Communion service. It is not delusory to view these symbols sacramentally: the interaction between them and those who consume them can do something to the people who partake. An experience of religious commitment of this type and an experience of film can sharpen perception." Marsh, *Cinema & Sentiment*, 85.

onto a reality that exists beyond life while having its presence already here in this life?"[18]

Still, some question how the medium of film can deliver such demanding, transcendent qualities. A literary example can be drawn from Walker Percy's character, Binx Bolling in *The Moviegoer*, as he is taken up in Ralph Wood's development on the topic of vocation: "The problem with the movies, according to Bolling, is that they create an artificial and distanced world that viewers enter at great cost."[19] The problem with Bolling's critique however, as presented by Wood, is that the same argument is often made concerning ecclesial settings that do not take seriously enough a hermeneutic of "doctrine that makes an impact on daily lives," where even participants struggle to understand how belief and practice come together.[20] Wood follows up Bolling's thought by commenting, "while the movies often manage to ask ultimate questions, they almost always fall short of ultimate answers" or, rather, in Bolling's terms, "the movies are onto the search, but they screw it up."[21] Plenty of theological critique lends itself in Bolling's direction of scepticism and disillusionment, but theology must move beyond such reductionism, and pursue a more nuanced understanding of the ways by which people understand and communicate what they believe.

For example, as "culture has made [its] turn toward the visual, and with the rise of new media, the visual image has come to occupy an unprecedented central place in our lives."[22] Dyrness aptly observes, "an American growing up today will watch at least seven thousand TV programs and a couple of thousand movies in his or her lifetime."[23] Dyrness contrasts his point by referencing that "a Puritan in early America listened to an average of five thousand sermons in his or her lifetime."[24] Heaven's non-sensory notoriety has not stopped creations from representing possibilities for ways of thinking theologically about spiritual space. As in the case of Ward's *What Dreams May Come*, films that display metaphors working in different directions within the same narrative show various possibilities where earlier thinkers held narrower views of concepts.[25] For example, McDannell and Lang place Schleiermacher in line with Kant's "suspicion of descriptions of

---

18. Wood, *Literature and Theology*, 16.
19. Ibid., 17.
20. Thiselton, *The Hermeneutics of Doctrine*, xvi.
21. Ibid.
22. Dyrness, *Visual Faith*, 156.
23. Ibid.
24. Ibid.
25. Ward, "What Dreams May Come."

heaven."[26] According to Schleiermacher: "we cannot really make a picture of it [post-mortem existence] either in the form of an infinitely progressive development or in that of an unchanging completeness; to such a task our sensuous imagination is unequal."[27] Contrary to Schleiermacher's suspicion, in a recent article, C. Stephen Evans defines a concept as "simply a possible way of being."[28] Film theory is thick with ontological speculation. In his essay, Smith comments, "I think the reason that most Christians are suspicious of movies is metaphysical, not ethical. At stake in film theory is an ontology (roughly, a philosophy of reality) which will determine how we understand the relationship between appearance and reality."[29] Critics claiming that art is too fixed and iconic to express transcendence will find difficult ground in film creation because films have the power to make paintings move, while the self faces and interprets the moving image. Smith suggests a more "incarnational ontology which maintains the distinction between appearance and reality while affirming continuity between them" with the end goal to move towards a more "revelatory film theory."[30] Smith is correct in drawing attention to the revelatory impact of art. For strict materialists, continuity is neither desirable, nor achievable, but film expresses human experience in such a way that social identity can be considered in spiritual contexts.

A key reason for selecting films such as *Toy Story 3* and *What Dreams May Come* as participating in the interpretive process of heaven is how, after thoughtful engagements, these films can challenge two questions that are common to humanity's longing for reunion: *1) How will people recognize the other in heaven?* and *2) What does heaven look like?* These two questions will serve to engage ways in which film practices a narrative hermeneutic that takes historical interpretations of heaven seriously, and offer some moments of surprise to provoke an unfamiliar reading of the belief in which a fresh consideration is possible. As Gooder reminds us, "a good theology of heaven is that it challenges us into the deepest act of poetic imagination."[31] How, then, might films that include comedic animation (in the case of *Toy Story 3*) and dramatic fantasy (in the case of *What Dreams May Come*) provoke fresh insight by applying a hermeneutic of popular imagery?

---

26. Lang, *Heaven*, 324.
27. Schleiermacher, *The Christian Faith*, 705.
28. Evans, "Wisdom as Conceptual Understanding," 372.
29. Smith "Faith in American Beauty," 181–83.
30. Ibid., 182.
31. Gooder, *Heaven*, 105.

RELATIONSHIP AND HEAVENLY RECOGNITION—HOW WILL PEOPLE RECOGNIZE THE OTHER?

Although not explicitly eschatological in nature, Pixar's *Toy Story 3* can serve as a good example of the way in which animation furnishes the imagination with other-worldly possibilities concerning questions of appearance and identity without undoing or creating an overly representational scenario that would reduce any variables of transcendence. In this sense, the non-realistic aspects of animation create a healthy tension between what is perceived as real relationship possibilities between the characters and, yet, point beyond the art form by opening up possible questions concerning the relationship between post-mortem bodies, face recognition, and reunion.[32] Kutter Callaway suggests that, "the sheer popularity of Pixar's films raises important questions about primary narratives within a culture with which children and adults can both engage."[33] *Toy Story 3* is not the only example of animation for theological consideration in this book, however. The film, *WALL-E* will be taken up for analysis in chapter seven and although Callaway is more interested in the music scores of the film, he is correct in making the following claim:

> *WALL-E* is more than a "children's" film. By inviting audiences of various ages to commit themselves emotionally to the plight of WALL-E and beloved EVE, it assumes the role of a shared narrative—a common story that is accessible across ages. On a concrete level, then, Pixar's films—especially their more recent films—are often meaningful in terms of the shared affective space they open up.[34]

The narrative of *Toy Story 3*, indeed, concerns a group of toys that are owned and played with by Andy, their human owner. Andy's imagination during play ignites all types of adventures for the toys and after Andy, or any human, sets them down and leaves the scene, each toy takes on a personality of their own, in which they become part of creating and acting out possibilities. In *Toy Story 3*, Andy is preparing to leave for college and has kept a small remnant (the main characters) all these years (some of which are documented in previous *Toy Stories 1* and *2*) in a toy chest. The toys are grieving not only because they fear that play time is over but, more importantly, because only two alternatives remain possible: first, they fear being

---

32. *Toy Story 3*, DVD (2010). The question of bodily continuity and discontinuity will be taken up in greater detail later in chapter six.

33. Callaway, *Scoring Transcendence*, 43.

34. Ibid., 46.

tossed out into the trash; secondly, the toys must consider an existence of being placed in a bag for life in the attic, devoid of their original purpose in being created. Other possibilities begin to open up, however, such as being sold in a yard sale (a theme explored at great lengths in *Toy Story 2*), as well as being donated to a children's day-care centre. Woody, a vintage cowboy character (voiced by Tom Hanks), argues that there must be another alternative: the toys must remain loyal to Andy, even if he banishes them to the attic. The majority of the toys, however, find the day-care world more appealing, seeing that they will be better fulfilling their purpose by having children play with them throughout the day. Woody tries to persuade them that Andy still loves them, in light of a fresh memory of an existence in the toy chest without the teenage Andy's presence. The film even opens up with the toys using a cell phone hidden in the toy chest to get Andy's attention and/or just to hear his voice. Andy's mom gives him directives to pack up all the toys and other items that he does not want to take with him to college. Later on, the mom takes the wrong bag to the trash corner and this possibility becomes actual, but Woody tries desperately to get the rest of the toys out of danger before the trash truck comes to take them away. The toys find a way to escape and make the trip back to the garage and end up climbing into the day-care box to be donated. Woody tries to offer a different interpretation of the account, claiming that the mom simply got it wrong and grabbed the wrong bag. The toys are neither convinced nor interested, until, after being donated, they find a dark world in an encounter with day-care culture. They find that the day-care world is run in a much different way than a home with an owner. The toys are treated poorly and eventually they make a plan to escape. Woody initiates the strategy and Mr. Potato Head finds himself locked up in a sand box.

    Something unique happens at this point in the narrative. Mr. Potato Head is a toy made up of a body and different parts that can interchange in different locations of his body. As part of the plan to spring Potato Head from lockup, a tortilla is slid under the day-care door. Mr. Potato Head's many body parts crawl away from the sandbox, leaving the potato body behind in order to take up the tortilla. All of the parts, such as the eyes, ears, arms, and legs poke holes in the tortilla allowing this now flat tortilla head to move around. But, this novel situation provokes the question: is this still Mr. Potato Head? Although the body is different, he can see, move, walk, smell, stand, and so on. A little time lapses until he gains the strength to overcome the new type of body, the "tortilla body." After he performs his part of the getaway plan, he meets up with the other toys. The film shows him walking up to the group of toys, but this time, his parts are embedded in a cucumber, "vegetable body." Along the journey, his tortilla body decayed, as he came under the pecking attack of a hungry pigeon, but still, crucially he remained himself. In other words, he did not have a crisis of identity, only an adjustment to a new body. He retained his same personality, memories, and purpose of mission, yet with a new body.

Mr. Potato Head (voiced by Don Rickles) comments on his new appearance, "I feel fresh, healthy. It's terrible." Mrs. Potato Head (voiced by Estelle Harris) flatteringly remarks, "You've lost weight and you are so tall." Interestingly, no one in the group of toys thinks he is someone different, even though he appears with a different body. He does not experience a loss of identity, even though his body is composed of a different material and in a different form. The continuity of appearance for Mr. Potato Head is found in his eyes, nose, ears, arms, and feet—all of the different parts that allow for the senses to operate properly with different bodies, not to mention the unique sense of humor that is embodied in the character's use of these parts. Perhaps, the eyes, which have played an important role in thinking about identity, hold a particular attribute for recognition; similarly, the many gestures of the mouth are especially characteristic of how a person is known.

Recognition is an important part of social identity in a theology of heaven and, yet, appearance recognition is pointing deeper towards the relational dynamics. For example, just because one has not seen the appearance of Jesus does not negate a loving relationship with him. As Oxford philosopher Henry H. Price (1899–1984) argued concerning not just different bodies in this life, but later:

> If a newly dead person is to be recognized by his friends who are in the Next World already, his post-mortem body must resemble his former physical body fairly closely, at least so far as its outward appearance goes. To speak extravagantly again, he must have more or less the same face as he had in his earthly life.[35]

Anthony Thiselton quotes from David Ford's work, *Self and Salvation*: "Each face is individual yet it is also a primary locus for relating to others and the world. The face as relating, welcoming, incorporating others is fundamental to social life."[36] Why should this concept of social identity be any less, if not more, important in heavenly existence? One would be remiss not to notice the representation in *Toy Story 3* of thinking about such possibilities, not only in the case of Mr. Potato Head, but even from the catch phrase of the popular, space astronaut, Buzz Lightyear (voiced by Tim Allen), "to infinity and beyond." Here again, one is more concerned with what Westphal

35. Price, *Essays in the Philosophy of Religion*, 111.
36. Thiselton, *The Hermeneutics of Doctrine*, 581.

would describe as "letting the believing soul speak to encounter possibilities rather than to establish certainties," where one is to open "oneself to the questions."[37]

Vincent Ward's film, *What Dreams May Come*, is based on the 1978 novel written by Richard Matheson. Ward's work provides a second example of work that attempts to navigate questions of personal identity in relation to appearance recognition and relational identification. Unlike *Toy Story 3*, Ward's film explicitly addresses questions of post-mortem existence. He combines genres of drama, fantasy, and romance. The narrative lays out a familial context in which Chris Nielsen (played by actor Robin Williams) is tragically killed in an auto accident where he had left his vehicle to help a person in need, only to be struck by another vehicle. Years earlier, Chris and his wife, Annie (played by actress Annabella Sciorra), had experienced the tragic death of their children. The story chronicles the difficulty for the Nielsens to make sense of and cope with their pain. The majority of the film focuses on Chris' journey through heaven to hell to find Annie, who had committed suicide a short while after she lost Chris in the accident.

Christopher Deacy makes an important and creative contribution to the discussion of Ward's film by establishing a connection based on what can be observed in Price's essay, *Two Conceptions of the Next World*, where Price explores the possibilities for post-mortem survival in a disembodied state or a "mind-dependent world."[38] Yet, even considering mind-dependent possibilities, Price stressed the importance of shared experience along these lines:

> For in the afterlife, if there is one, it is to be expected that only *like-minded* personalities will share a common world—personalities whose memories and desires are sufficiently similar to allow of continuous telepathic interaction. If so, each group of like-minded personalities would have a different next world, public to all the members of that particular group but private to the group as a whole.[39]

Deacy describes Ward's heaven as "simply a mental projection of whatever one imagines."[40] An important element implicit in Ward's depiction of the

---

37. Westphal, "Faith Seeking Understanding," 225.

38. Deacy, "Heaven, Hell, and the Sweet Hereafter," 190. Here, Deacy is engaging the work of John Hick and Paul Badham. Also, see Hick's work on H. H. Price's essay, "Survival and the Idea of 'Another World'" or what is termed, a "mind-dependent world" in Hick, *Death and Eternal Life*, 265–70.

39. Price, *Essays in the Philosophy of Religion*, 108.

40. Deacy, "Heaven, Hell, and the Sweet Hereafter," 190.

possibility of heaven is the relationship between earthly existence and the afterlife. Ward's metaphor illustrates the necessity to hold on to personal identity, meaning one must retain memory of time and space.[41] Price also concluded,

> Unless we "take our memories with us" when we leave the physical body, there can be no personal survival at all. For the same reason, we must "take" our characters with us too—the emotional and conative dispositions which we have acquired during our embodied life on earth. Otherwise we shall not continue to be the same persons after death as we were before. Let us suppose that in our disembodied state we also retain the power of imagination, even though we lose the capacity for having sense-experiences.[42]

Heaven, as a part of creation, is a doctrine which carries assumptions of memory. To use common metaphors such as reunion, reconciliation, and home in reference to place is to reveal something about relationships. Contrary to those who might have the conception that a pure soul, dream-like existence is not concerned with the here and now, Ward's depiction makes a strong case that reunion in the afterlife does have implications for relationships on earth. Several times throughout the film, memories serve to remind characters of conversations, along with relational struggles. Indeed, the role of memory serves as the catalyst for characters identifying the other even when appearance does not match the memory. "The material world in which we live now has what one might call 'unrestricted publicity,'" reminding humanity of the crucial dimensions the imagination and memory serve, especially for implications in a world where shared images are the only means for visualizing our longing for reunion.[43]

Although Ward lays stress on the mind-dependent image, "Price contended that we cannot rule out that a disembodied survivor could also engage in mental experiences."[44] Price suggests one dark conception in this direction: "conceivably a very dogmatic materialist might never succeed in realizing that he was dead and in the Other world."[45] Ward draws upon the similar notion that "hell is for those who do not know they're dead."[46] In

---

41. A more detailed account of social identity and memory will be given in the following chapter.
42. Price, *Essays in the Philosophy of Religion*, 104–5.
43. Ibid., 108.
44. Deacy, "Heaven, Hell, and the Sweet Hereafter," 193.
45. Price, *Essays in the Philosophy of Religion*, 107.
46. Ward, *What Dreams May Come*.

Part II: Imagining Identity in a Post-mortem Existence

other words, people who see no need to relate or be known by others, could possibly remain alone.

Although critics have found a conglomerate of comparative religious phenomena within the film, making the connection to Christian theology quite untenable at times, Ward stays quite closely aligned with many Christian conceptions of the afterlife by giving both heaven and hell space within the narrative.[47] Zaleski has been more pointed in her comments towards recent developments in publicly shared visions of the afterlife when as she writes:

> Most striking, of course, is the absence from most twentieth-century near-death accounts of postmortem punishment: no hell, no purgatory, no chastening torments or telltale agonies at the moment of death. The life review, when it occurs, is a reassuring experience, modeled on contemporary methods of education and psychotherapy.[48]

Although Deacy provides an excellent analysis in viewing Ward's film through Price's model, the conversation can be carried further in a slightly different direction along these visual lines. If humans retain memories of earthly life (which I will argue in chapter five), then, one should also take into consideration Price's comments concerning an embodied afterlife. All of the memories which Ward's characters retain involve sensory experiences from the viewer's visual perspective. Chris Nielsen's heavenly experience consists of ways he imagined the afterlife in his earthly existence, so his shared experience with others is very sense oriented. Price establishes the possibility of communicating in the afterlife in a telepathic type method, but he also goes further in illustrating how an embodied existence may be preferable in keeping our identity, even if this existence constitutes a "quasi-material" body.[49] Price deliberately approaches the subject of social identity in commenting:

---

47. See Deacy, *Screening the Afterlife*, 43. Here, Deacy is much more conscious of the negative critique concerning Ward's use of reincarnation as a theological conclusion to the narrative, as well as the reference of an absent God, "Somewhere . . . shouting down that He loves us," where he quotes Chris Nielson's spirit guide. Although admittedly, the conclusion is found wanting, Deacy's comment that, "there is nothing objective, or divine-oriented, about the [Nielson's] afterlife" does not necessarily take into account characteristics of God, such as invisibility, or the fact that the Psalmist also draws the image that God looked down from above to listen to the captives (Psalm 102:19–20). In many ways, not forming God into an image is staying true to the OT Decalogue.

48. Zaleski, *The Life of the World to Come*, 32.

49. Price, *Essays in the Philosophy of Religion*, 102.

It might be argued that no one can be a person unless he has social relations with other persons. According to Christian theism, the most important of all social relationships is the relation of loving, and no one can be a person unless he is at least capable of being related in this way to other persons.[50]

One of the central concerns of Ward's film, indeed, addresses the longing for reuniting the Nielsen family. Part of the challenge is not only to locate family members in the afterlife, but to allow them to recognize and communicate with each other. Ward carries the metaphor even further by making Chris Nielsen's son, Ian (played by Josh Paddock), appear in the afterlife as Chris' best friend and colleague in his earthly life (played by Cuba Gooding, Jr.), making it difficult for Chris to recognize his son in heaven. The unfamiliarity of such an image in relation to heaven reveals some of the hardened ground left uncultivated by contemporary theology. Could it be that Ward's stretch to code Ian's appearance serves a multifold purpose? First, Ian is the first human to encounter Chris in heaven. He later declares his intention that, by disguising himself, he imagined that Chris would be more willing to listen to him. Secondly, contemporary culture often assumes that appearance tells more of the story, but the lack of literalness in Ward's narrative flows out of a deeper concern for the characters to relate, pushing against materialistic reductionism. Thirdly, theological implications spring up in relation to issues of disclosure concerning personal presence.

What contemporary culture will not let theology forget, then, are the important elements of considering the role of the imagination in terms of continuity of these social components. When all possibilities of surviving identities are narrowed to a materialistic view of what it means to be human and recognizable, one has restricted the understanding of continuity to a limited sphere of knowledge, whereas the long Christian tradition, as a whole, has not. Wright is correct in arguing that "the new body will be incorruptible," but why must all further considerations of survival immediately after death be viewed as God "abandoning" creation?[51] Wright argues for a "transformed physicality" or what he calls "transphysicality"; and although he may consider such films as "mistaken for the real thing," such works of art continue to press the question of how one may survive and communicate in an afterlife, rather than postponing resurrection for thousands of years before "the real thing," as according to Wright's view.[52] Wright does not deny some type of immediate existence. In fact he writes, "I

50. Ibid., 110.
51. Wright, *Surprised by Hope*, 44.
52. Ibid., 44, 116.

therefore arrive at this view: that all the Christian departed are in substantially the same state, that of restful happiness. This is not the final destiny for which they are bound, namely the bodily resurrection; it is a temporary resting place."[53] He merely suggests that happiness and rest is not essentially the full person, but a happy existence. Here, Wright seems to be playing into what he most dislikes about versions of heaven that lend little weight to personhood and to our earth-bound condition, yet he still calls this a happy state, but shows slim room for the imagination to consider how one remains a social being after death.

Questions of human appearance or recognition by others in heavenly contexts are seldom addressed in contemporary theology. Perhaps speculative theology in this direction is too overwhelming for the imagination to consider. On the other hand, one does not have to go far into the church world to find those who gravitate to a more literal reading of heaven, imagining how the lame will walk again, the blind will see, and deaf will hear (Isaiah/Gospels), all conditions of sensory and bodily wholeness; not to mention a common-held practice for people to imagine themselves different in heaven than on earth, including appearance. Whatever insecurities people may wrestle with that can challenge value and/or perfection, it is not uncommon to imagine the opposite to be the case in heaven. At the same time, perceiving a post-mortem state where a consciousness can assume a different person's body, the challenge for recognition becomes that much more complex.

The ancient quest to answer the question, when does an individual change to a point that he or she is no longer him or herself? is also a topic that films explore and holds particular interest for those inquiries concerning immediate survival and philosophical thought in the area of metaphysical modality. In his work on the doctrine of heaven, Jerry Walls has observed that personal identity is "one of the most difficult of all philosophical questions."[54] The startling move by Ward to dress Ian in the body of Chris' friend in the hereafter, then, illustrates the profound problem with uniting a different body with a soul in the post-mortem.[55] Adler shows the unique character of this union by comparing angelic beings and humans, for this very reason, "theologians insist that angels and souls are radically different kinds of spiritual substances [because] an angel by its nature is

53. Wright, *For All the Saints*, 36–37.

54. Walls, *Heaven*, 93.

55. Deacy offers a prolonged discussion concerning reincarnation and other approaches raised by filmmakers in Deacy, *Screening the Afterlife*, 158–64. Also, see Freek Bakker's essay, "Reincarnation in Western Cinema" in *Blick über den Tod hinaus/Seeing Beyond Death*, 83–94.

not associated with a body that is its very own. Each soul is united with one body and only one, uniquely its own."[56]

The plurality of bodies is not necessarily a problem for Christian theology. Even for those who remain negative towards heaven, the resurrection displays a new body, yet at the same time a recognizable body.

The implicit question raised by Ward's film, therefore, is whether or not one's imagination can alter the way one is recognized, not necessarily known. Eventually Chris sees through the appearance to the presence of his son, as well as witnessing the transformation of Ian's appearance to a more recognizable state. The shared memories help share a public imagination for the two of them to recognize one another in spite of changes to the outside appearance. In some ways, the metaphor explores complex questions over social identity where the orientation of relationships takes on further nuances due to outward appearances, as mentioned earlier. Other films move appearance in the opposite direction, such as in Peter Jackson's film *Lovely Bones*, where the main character, Suzie Salmon (played by Saoirse Ronan), who is already in a post-mortem state, steps back into time and space, highjacking the body of Ruth Connor (played by Carolyn Dando), at least in appearance, in order for Suzie to experience a pre-death longing to kiss Ray Singh (played by Reece Richie).[57] If Smith is correct in his assessment of ontological importance for those viewing and experiencing film, the Christian tradition has long anticipated the decaying earthly body and the eternal new body with continuity. Even within Christianity's doctrine of God, plurality of language is central to core beliefs about the Divine. In fact, Walls even argues that "human beings can achieve fullness of being only by sharing in the life of the Trinity."[58] If Ward's metaphor for heaven loses some endorsement from the Christian doctrine of heaven, it is precisely at this recurring theme concerning personal identity and further bodies. At the same time, the way in which Ward delivers the metaphor with relational conflict between father and son being central to the social dynamic, the Christian theologian can certainly perceive how Ward arrives at this difficulty for Chris and his son to share a vision or a shared imagination in heaven. Where the metaphor breaks down a bit, the viewer is still called upon to wrestle with the necessity of imaginative work as social beings. Ward chooses to focus on Chris' son and the struggle to be accepted by his father. By imagining himself appearing as someone he believed his father respected and loved, Chris' son uses this appearance to guide his father into the new world. The relationship be-

56. Adler, *The Angels and Us*, 161.
57. *The Lovely Bones*, DVD (2009).
58. Ibid., 94.

tween Chris and his son plays a key role in lining up steps to eventually find the direction in which to venture for Chris to rescue his wife. While Chris' son battles his inadequacies in the afterlife with fractured imaginings, doubt remains for those (Annie for example) who appear to have body and soul matched quite nicely, but are found in hell, the place where one's imagination is not only unshared, but forgets how they look or worse, who they are.

One must not overlook the way in which the metaphor is working to show the problematic elements in one's earthly life by asking the question, how healthy are the family and friend relationships which one now enjoys? Recognition of appearance is a way of knowing, but it is only a partial way of knowing. Recent studies in sociology and identity have drawn some conclusions in the area of auto/biography, such as "a turn to intertextuality as significant: in producing a life story (one sort of text) we are always, implicitly or explicitly, referring to and drawing on other texts—other life stories, fictional and non-fictional, as well as a range of different kinds of texts."[59] Sharing a world with a personality that imagines looking like a different personality known from earthly experience is problematic for communication, but even more problematic is a heaven that does not take those relationships more seriously. In the complexity of trying to make the metaphor work, Ward depicts the possibility that the lives of others who have shaped our stories will have importance for the immediate afterlife. I am suggesting, then, that relational recognition may be a stronger indicator than appearance recognition but that, also, the face becomes gradually more significant in the relational dynamics.

PRETENCE, SECURITY, AND INTERPRETATION

In order to draw further attention to the significance of these relational dynamics in Ward's plot, other functions of thought such as Lewis' idea of pretence, comes into play. Ian is really Chris' son, but appearance and voice make him look and sound very different. The continuity that Ward uses to bridge the divide is a shared social imagination. The thoughts and conversations that plagued Ian and Chris' earthly life at home were vital in bringing recognition to their relationship in heaven, making heaven more like home. Lewis asks: "What is the good of pretending to be what you are not?"[60] In context, Lewis here is referring to "dressing up as Christ." He continues:

---

59. Lawler, *Identity*, 11.
60. Lewis, *Mere Christianity*, 163.

If you like, you are pretending. Because, of course, the moment you realise what the words mean, you realise that you are not a son of God. You are not being like the Son of God, whose will and interests are at one with those of the Father: you are a bundle of self-centered fears, hopes, greeds, jealousies, and self-conceit, all doomed to death. So that, in a way, this dressing up as Christ is a piece of outrageous cheek. But the odd thing is that He [God the Father] has ordered us to do it.[61]

Lewis is not referring to the type of pretence that is deceptive, but the kind of "pretence that leads up to the real thing."[62] Ward uses the metaphor of appearance or face to illustrate the complexity of seeing more than what is on the relational surface. Initially, Ian's face is a detraction from who he is, but Chris and Ian's shared life "leads up to the real thing."[63] Chris knows his son and his son is known and loved. He was Chris' son despite his appearance. Ward utilizes pretence to initiate relational tensions in the process of being reconciled. For knowledge to happen, one needs to know what is being inferred. Part of that knowledge is revealed in the unfolding of the narrative and the hard work of interpretation.

I have already mentioned the facial integrity of knowing the other, even if gradually, but here I am stressing the importance of the continuity of identity in relation to heavenly reunion. At certain junctures, the biblical narratives contain much more deceptive elements that "lead up to the real thing," either through repentance or shared experiences, such as in the case of Joseph, the government official in Genesis 41 compared to Joseph, the brother that is hesitant to reunite with relatives in Genesis 42.[64] Joseph's pretence can be partly explained by the time factor that shades memory of appearance. He is older and his exteriority has developed. Joseph uses pretence more deceptively to control the situation concerning recognizability. To reunite is to open the door of vulnerability that hiddenness secures and keeps intact. Joseph's pretence leads to the testing of his brothers' hearts, where Ian's pretence leads to Chris' respect and willingness to listen. Joseph's revealing eventually leads to reunion with his family, including his father, but only after his pretence impacts the whole family. Joseph's self-disclosure causes great distress for his brothers, as written, "could not answer him, so dismayed were they at his presence."[65]

61. Ibid.
62. Ibid.
63. Ibid.
64. Lewis, *Mere Christianity*, 163.
65. Gen 45:3b NRSV.

Tracing back the family line, two further examples of pretence are more seriously deviant, but eventually lead to reunion. First, Abraham pretending to be the brother of Sarai instead of her husband in Genesis 12. Out of fear of death, Abraham's pretence is more misleading so as to ensure safety for everyone, even at the cost of his wife, not to mention the illness brought upon Pharaoh's court. Secondly, Jacob covering himself in hair pretends to be his brother Esau in order to receive by deceiving (Gen 27). Jacob receives the blessing from his father, Isaac, and the narrative unfolds making reunion a more difficult prospect, but still leads up to further possibilities. Although Augustine's treatment of the account leaves one asking, "What kind of pretence by a man who tells no lies, unless we have here a hidden meaning conveying a profound truth?"[66] Augustine wants to read this story Christologically and move away from the deceptive imagery towards an unveiling, but either way, we are left with pretence leading to a further disclosure.[67] All three examples of biblical pretence come in the form of securing social identity either out of fear of being recognized or that the concealment of identity, if known, will unravel a string of implications for reunion.

On the contrary, Ian's motive from the narrative is to establish trust, although the hint of fear from past hurts may be pressing on the interpretation as well. Ian's pretence impacts his position from son to friend, as well as appearance and voice. Now, one may argue that in the case of Abraham, Jacob, and Joseph, we are dealing with earthly problematics. Should not all of these have resolutions in heaven? The answer is yes and no; observing the continuity of identity that later leads to reunion is an important piece of the puzzle. Ward's use of pretence in a heavenly context seems to be a better interpretation of heavenly reunions than some of the artificial visions that capture little essence of human relational complexities that use heaven as an eraser metaphor. In other words, heaven as a social context, working to bring reconciliation puts human fear, insecurity, and brokenness in a proper context that lead to healing and reconciliation.[68] By marginalizing heaven, relationships centered in love lose a piece of their eschatological imagination. If love is the key to understanding heaven, as I argue, along with Russell and Zaleski, then minimizing heaven is a start in an unloving

---

66. See the excerpt from Jasper, ed., "St. Augustine, *City of God*," in *The Bible and Literature*, 129–30.

67. Ibid.

68. Scriptural images such as "treasure" in Matthew 6:19–21 or of "inheritance" in 1 Peter 1:4 have too often been removed from their metaphorical connections to relationship in Christ in heaven, resulting in a misconstruction of heavenly materialism, not to mention the unfortunate connection to reunion with others.

direction.⁶⁹ At the same time, depicting heaven in familial terms, including reunion and reconciliation helps correct some of the more "love story" heavens where memory is erased or better overwhelmed by love and filled with an artificial type of love as depicted by Russell: "Suppose that when we go to heaven, we first encounter those whom we have loved. We enter with each of them into the totality of the love between us that we had wished for on earth but had never fulfilled."⁷⁰ But Russell then adds the further speculation, "now suppose that a third person, perhaps one we did not know on earth, observes the absorption of our love for A and A's corresponding love for us. Then that third person is drawn into the perfect love between us and A."⁷¹ The multiplication trail of absorbing and passing love, or rather, building loving relationships holds very little continuity with the cultural means of introductions and reunions. Perhaps Russell is more comfortable with the eraser type image to allow for such receptivity or, on the other hand, complete knowledge of the other where cultural constructions of introduction are no longer needed.

A final point concerning appearance recognition can be offered by considering Jesus' post-resurrection experiences. Being known and loved in heaven has in many ways been concerned with whom one knew and loved on earth, and, more precisely, in the salvific understanding of Jesus defeating death on the cross and through his resurrection; and the other professing faith in Jesus, known as the Christ. Recognition of Jesus as Lord is the entry point of following him to be where he is with the Father, which is in heaven (John 14:1–4). Where John Thiel wants to make the case for Jesus' continued reconciliation acts out of promise in his post-resurrection body, others have considered the all important aspect of recognizing and encountering Jesus' face.⁷²

Ford also offers some insightful comments in this direction by considering the face of the resurrected Jesus. He draws attention to "the obvious problem for a theology of the face of Jesus [being] its apparent vagueness. Nobody can see this face."⁷³ Ford goes on to press the question, "what sort of particularity and precision are required for theologically reliable reference

---

69. Russell, *A History of Heaven*, 189. Zaleski, *The Life of the World to Come*, 81–82.

70. Russell, *A History of Heaven*, 188.

71. Ibid.

72. Thiel, "For What May We Hope?" 537. Thiel writes in greater detail regarding the heavenly formation of our character in his recent work, *Icons of Hope*. Especially relevant is chapter five, "Forgiveness in the Communion of the Saints," 153–88.

73. Ford, *Self and Salvation*, 171.

to this face[?]."⁷⁴ Further, the Gospel narratives display "a strong sense of a disturbance of ordinary recognisability."⁷⁵ Ford continues:

> In Luke, "their eyes were kept from recognising him" (24.16) and "they were startled and thought they saw a spirit" (24.37). In Matthew, "when they saw him they worshipped him; but some doubted" (28.17). In John, Mary "did not know that it was Jesus" (20.4). In each there are verbal and physical signs of recognition but it is clear that, while the risen one is still Jesus, he is not simply the identical person. In Ricoeur's terms, he is "himself as another," and the other can be acknowledged as God: "Thomas answered him, 'My Lord and my God!'" (John 20.28); "And they came up and took hold of his feet and worshipped him" (Matt. 28.9). In Mark, the Gospel most reticent about the resurrection, the news that "you will see him" evokes a reaction in the women at the tomb which recalls awestruck worship: "for trembling and astonishment had come upon them; and they said nothing to anyone, for they were afraid" (16.8).⁷⁶

Ford's image of the resurrected Jesus follows in line with how others have tried to imagine other historical figures that leave no trace of photographic evidence. Even 1 Peter 1:8 elaborates on the idea that one can love (a form of knowing for 1 Peter) even though one has not seen (or has seen, but does not see in the present), which leads to joy. Ford comes at this from the following angle:

> This facing of Jesus as the facing of God is better seen as an intensification of facing rather than an indeterminate vagueness. The risen face of Jesus is a "revelation" not in the sense of making him plain in a straightforward manner. Rather, what is "unveiled" is a face that transcends simple recognisability, that eludes our categories and stretches our capacities in the way in which God does. It provokes fear, bewilderment, doubt, joy and amazement. It therefore is profoundly questioning and questionable. It generates a community whose life before this face is endlessly interrogative, and whose response to it leads into ever new complexities, ambiguities, joys and sufferings.⁷⁷

What initially appears to be a misstep in Ward's construction turns out to be a theologically creative move, not because Ian is a type of Christ but,

---

74. Ibid.
75. Ibid.
76. Ibid., 171–72.
77. Ibid., 172.

rather, his different appearance provides surprising and far-reaching implications for Chris and Annie. Ward's use of pretence is a form of protection to secure Ian's and Chris' interaction, which was uncharacteristic of their less communicative earthly life. Ward also faced the challenge early on in the film of creating frames of communication between Chris and Annie:

> Given it is a love story, the choice to make Annie a painter also meant there was more of a connection between the world of the dead and that of the living. It also provided a solution to the fact that Chris and Annie are not together for most of the film and allowed me to better visualize ways they could "speak" to each other between these worlds without using words.[78]

The lack of words is in large part because of the separation of the earthly life and afterlife, but, once characters are in the afterlife, all of the senses are awakened and people have bodies. One of the reasons why film is such an important conversation partner for theology, indeed, is because of the way in which it is able to talk about a concept and yet provide a visual metaphor at the same time. In other words, the film critic can observe how Ward depicts a mind-dependent world using anthropocentric, sensory-filled storylines. In many ways, this method echoes Price's attempt to show near the end of his chapter the convergence of both conceptions. Ward's film also illustrates a way of conceiving the convergence of the two conceptions, especially by making the plot about love crossing all boundaries, including heaven and hell to bring about healing and restoration of relationships. Price furthers his reflection in this direction:

> We now begin to suspect that this contrast is not quite so sharp as it seemed at first sight. For it turns out that in the disembodied conception of survival there is room for some sort of body after all. And a Next World composed of mental images, if it has at least some degree of publicity, is less dream-like and less subjective than it seemed at first. Indeed, I am inclined to think that these two theories of the Next World, which seem so very different, are complementary rather than opposed. They start as it were from opposite ends, but perhaps when both are worked out fully, they meet in the middle.[79]

Although Ward admittedly illustrates a subjective view of the afterlife, the use of film provides the visual for the critic to comprehend how body

---

78. Ward, "Concepts of An Afterlife."
79. Price, *Essays in the Philosophy of Religion*, 113.

and spirit can still somehow be related or how they "meet in the middle."[80] Film is a powerful means by its visual nature to convey a subjective, spiritual world by using a moving, physical metaphor, which tends to make the possibility of spirit-body continuity more real. As Peter Kreeft has observed,

> Pre-Cartesian cultures did not divide reality into the two mutually exclusive categories of purely immaterial spirit and purely nonspiritual matter. Rather, they saw all matter as in-formed, in-breathed by spirit, intelligibility manifesting intelligence, artistry manifesting an artist.[81]

According to Kreeft, "We [human beings] manifest the materiality of spirit as well as the spirituality of matter; in us, spirit is made incarnate."[82]

Although Ward's film presents the idea that "consciousness can be a world unto itself," the visual nature of film helps the metaphor work in a different direction, showing how quasi-material bodies can touch, and hug, as well as see and move in spacial dimensions.[83] Price argues that an "image body" for post-mortem survival is not out of the question, in contrast to the angelic beings (which are minds without bodies) in Mortimer Adler and Jean Danielou.[84] Price differentiates between the body as described by how the "artist conceives of it—the painter or the dramatist—and not the body as the anatomist or physiologist conceives it."[85] Price's emphasis is on the need to have a "face, but one need not have a skull, or cerebral cortex," in order to remain embodied.[86] As Tillich argued in a similar vein, "the individuality of a person is expressed in every cell of his body, especially in his face."[87] Paul's discussion in 1 Corinthians 13:12 where he uses a foggy mirror analogy to the completion of seeing "face to face" enforces his concept of being, not only recognized, but known. In Paul's analogy, he mentions the idea of not only "seeing face to face," but "knowing as being fully known." The importance of reunion and reconciliation between loved ones and friends can lead, then, to questions regarding the imagination and heavenly space where such reunions might occur.

---

80. Ibid.
81. Kreeft, *Everything You Ever Wanted to Know about Heaven*, 86.
82. Ibid., 86–87.
83. Ibid., 88.
84. Price, *Essays in the Philosophy of Religion*, 112. See, Adler, *The Angels and Us*, 183. Also in, Danielou, *The Angels and Their Mission*, 96.
85. Price, *Essays in the Philosophy of Religion*, 112.
86. Ibid.
87. Tillich, *Systematic Theology*, 413.

RE-CONTEXTUALIZING HEAVENLY SPACE—WHAT DOES HEAVEN LOOK LIKE?

Jeffrey Russell has been correct to persistently raise the question, "what is the most meaningful way of thinking of it [heaven]?" Film makers, such as Vincent Ward, have also wrestled with this same question.[88] In *What Dreams May Come*, Ward is open about these challenges in conceptualizing the afterlife:

> What struck me most about this project was the challenge of envisaging an afterlife so that it was not just cotton wool clouds or a white space filled with smoke. I also wanted it to be relevant and have a contemporary conceptual spin in an age where many people no longer believe in an afterlife.[89]

Although his last point is debateable, Ward's film explores a vast array of age-old topics from love, sadness, marriage, and children, to tragedy, death, suicide, heaven, hell, and redemption. Kelton Cobb describes Ward's depiction of "hell as a lake of fire with the damned swimming eternally in a smelly muck, while heaven is verdant meadowlands and lakes, monumental Arcadian cities, and reunions with loved ones."[90] Annie is an artist and Ward uses her paintings as a means to visualize the afterlife. In describing his attempt to describe the afterlife, Ward commented:

> To make it work [concepts of the afterlife] I needed to find a way to see it. The key here was choosing to make the afterlife a subjective world. Each paradise could be different so each paradise and hell could actually vary from person to person.[91]

The extent that Ward's characters experience the afterlife depends much upon how each character has imagined what survival will entail, but in order to tell the story, characters must share space. Ward's piece offers an interpretation that recontexualizes heaven as space where narrative still matters. Here, one is not forced to reckon with a heaven that is impersonal space, but one that challenges traditional assumptions that envision a heaven where "making a story out of life" is no longer an important part of being human.[92] Critical to Ward's plot is for the narrative to continue unfolding in

---

88. Russell, *Paradise Mislaid*, 160.

89. Vincent Ward Films, "What Dreams May Come: Concepts of an Afterlife," http://vincentwardfilms.com/concepts/wdmc/treatment/ (2009).

90. Cobb, *The Blackwell Guide to Theology and Popular Culture*, 277.

91. Ward, "Concepts of an Afterlife."

92. Lawler, *Identity*, 11.

post-mortem existence where the characters are still called upon to engage socially within their heavenly surroundings.

Still the challenge remains: how is one to envision a place where these social interactions become possibilities? Some disagree on which metaphors work better for the *polis*. For instance, Russell "concede[s] that the metaphors of the City of God and New Jerusalem, along with the essential idea of the communion of saints, are the main current of the Christian idea of heaven."[93] At the same time, he is not surprised that atheism thrives in places where "the greater part of humankind is wedged apart from God in noisy and light-polluted cities."[94] Where Russell finds the sea and the desert open spaces more accessible for discerning transcendence, Fiddes argues that, "the sea is a traditional Hebrew image (together with the wilderness) for the chaotic elements of the creation that seem to resist the divine purpose."[95] Ward's use of art pulls from the urban and rural to illustrate the vastness of heaven, exploring both contextual possibilities offering perhaps a more realistic environment.

Ward admits that, "by borrowing from painting in former periods I could invoke a time when people more commonly believed in such things, as well as make use of the visual language these artists employed."[96] Here, Ward is referring to the Hudson River School of the nineteenth century from which he borrows the paintings ascribed to Annie's work in the film. McDannell and Lang confirm the historical accuracy of Ward's move to glean his backdrops from this time period, arguing that the eighteenth and nineteenth centuries were marked by four characteristics concerning heaven: First, heaven was describable, with license to imagine concrete spacial contexts. Secondly, heaven was experiential where humans have new experiences. Thirdly, the person, in whatever form they persist, shall have a will that actively participates. Fourthly, humans will know God's presence in greater measures than in their earthly experiences.[97] The creativity of Ward to place these paintings in connection with the afterlife lend some deeper reflections.

---

93. Russell, *Paradise Mislaid*, 160.

94. Ibid. Gardiner also points to urban developments within early recorded visions of heaven where the authors of visions "were not sure about what went into making an ideal city, and perhaps their audiences were really more likely to associate a real city with hell" lending support in Russell's direction. Gardiner, ed., *Visions of Heaven and Hell before Dante*, xix.

95. Fiddes, *The Promised End*, 286.

96. Ward, "Concepts of An Afterlife."

97. Lang, *Heaven: A History*, 349.

Gene Veith has worked out an extended study to show, "as usually the case with Cole [Thomas], the human figures are small, swallowed up by the symbolic natural landscape."⁹⁸ According to Veith, those interpretations which tend to exaggerate "the human figure looking out over the land as signifying ownership, specifically the American domination of nature in the name of private property" miss the overarching aim of the Hudson River artists, which sought to "minimize the human to exalt the untamed land."⁹⁹ In the Hudson River School paintings, "human beings shrink almost to nothingness as they confront an objective order that they can neither control nor fully grasp."¹⁰⁰ Although the storyline is clearly centered on the anthropocentric aspects, Ward's film makes use of the Hudson River landscapes in order to open up eternal possibilities—for "in infinity any angle of hope ultimately opens up as widely as any other."¹⁰¹ Ward's work stays true to the transcendent emphasis in the landscapes by not trying to "analyze the Transcendent"; but rather, showing how one can discover how "the immanent is expressive of the Transcendent."¹⁰² Any success of the metaphor working in the film for the imagination to consider how one might envision the humanity and beauty of space coming together in heaven is much indebted to the use of the Hudson River landscapes. As Brown has observed, "by the way in which such artists present nature they can enable us to see the order, mystery, or transcendence that is not immediately perceptible to our own eyes."¹⁰³

Further, an important element regarding multi-layered or multi-integrated art forms concerns whether or not the multiplicity detracts from the singularity. For the purpose of constructing theology, multi-integrated art forms can lend more imaginative grasp to the communication of a doctrine such as heaven. Just as different forms and genre of popular film can offer unfamiliar degrees of fresh insight, certainly, the use of nineteenth-century paintings in film has not detracted from the value people place on these paintings.¹⁰⁴ Ward mentioned earlier the need to discover a historical con-

98. Veith, *Painters of Faith*, 51.
99. Ibid., 58–59.
100. Ibid., 59.
101. Russell, *A History of Heaven*, 189.
102. Schrader, *Transcendental Style in Film*, 8.
103. Brown, *God & Mystery in Words*, 63.
104. Kennedy, "National Academy Sells Two Hudson River School Paintings to Bolster Its Finances," (2008). The *New York Times* documented a sale of two Hudson River Paintings for more than $15 million. Within the same article, Kennedy mentioned the 2005 transaction by the New York Public Library, which sold one of Asher B. Durand's paintings for $35 million.

text in which to place the characters, so that the images of heaven would indeed be viable options for the imagination. A theme that will be explored throughout this project is the ability of popular art to recontexualize heaven by imagining social contexts that provide ways for the imagination to grasp heaven as a continuation of life, not as an impersonal post-mortem waiting room, as depicted in Tim Burton's *Beetlejuice*.[105] For such imaginative grasp to be achieved, one faces the formidable task of combating contemporary disbelief and nihilism.

As with the main concern for Dreyfus and Kelly's project, if one is to combat nihilism in contemporary culture, one must uncover the existential questions that human beings ask in every age.[106] Just as Ward relocates art into a new context that moves for reconsideration, Dreyfus and Kelly reinterpret classic works and ask, "how did we get from the fixed certainty of Dante's world to the existential uncertainty of our own?"[107] They proceed through the work to show where truth cracks the surface by interpreting historical texts and showing the applied possibilities.[108] Creatively, Ward is reinterpreting heaven by using historical pieces of art to live again in a new context, except this time, new characters fill in the narrative, making for a surprising turn of events that unfold through the narrative of the film. Christian theology, in its most effective moments, has affirmed that doctrine is living and speaks fresh in many different times and cultures.

One does not venture very far into the NT to find the example of the Apostle Peter altering interpretations due to his experience in Acts 10. Peter's vision ignites an altering of interpretations of eating practices and he comes into a new practice of narrative hermeneutics where the imagination sets the conditions for participation and obedience, and where Christian doctrine is now more revealing than the OT law. In other words, where the historical conditions for interpreting one's experience according to the OT laws and traditions no longer provide ways for interpreting the need for further relationships under divine guidance, Peter's dream provides the conditions for experiencing a new way of understanding. In the aftermath of his vision, he does not reconfigure his own story in Israel's narrative, but enters a new context with different characters, finding God's presence, not only in the past, but in the present, which helps him see Israel's history more clearly. In one sense, indeed, film is practicing a type of narrative hermeneutic

---

105. Tim Burton, "Beetlejuice," DVD (1988).
106. Dreyfus, *All Things Shining*, 20–21.
107. Ibid., 16–17.
108. Ibid., 21.

describing heaven as a place where one shares in a better interpretation of one's experiences and the memories of those experiences.[109]

As Marsh reminds us, "the history of Christian thought is a history of doctrinal change, as well as a history of continuity."[110] One of the challenges for Ward is to not lose the context of heaven in the narrative of the characters. Precisely, one of the many dissenting arguments about heaven focuses on the reader response interpretation of the individual's life. Each person interprets his or her story to give meaning to all of life's experiences. Ward explicitly displays a narrative where individual stories are interwoven and interpretation of those experiences does not end in heaven. Consequently, as Russell has argued following Derrida, "metaphors that die can come alive again when we enter into the worldview that produces them."[111] Ward sees within the worldview or horizon of the Hudson River School, particularly in the landscapes, a context where characters can recast a social context for thinking about heaven where characters do not get swallowed up into the divine. In so doing, Ward is able to offer a relational transcendence, which in turn allows the "language" of the artists to depict spiritual space or, better, a heaven where social relationships are reunited, restored, and can thrive.[112]

CONCLUSION

Where the long Christian tradition of being reunited with family members has fallen on some imaginative challenges for biblical scholarship, *Toy Story 3* along with *What Dreams May Come* offer two examples of imaginative contributions, ranging in form and genre, for our reflection on social recognition, but also concerning appearance and the challenges for thinking critically about reconciliation of troubled earthly relationships in heaven. Price's convergence of two concepts, starting with a disembodied post-mortem existence to the Christian preference for bodily post-mortem survival is helpful in interpreting Ward's imaginative contribution. Ward's work uses the narrative tool of pretence to illustrate the process of reunion, which leads to reconciliation of Chris and his son, Ian, in heaven. Here, Ward reconsiders how forgiveness, reconciliation, and reunion are possibilities in heaven. While this chapter focused on the issue of pretence, a further example of reunion, that would need to be developed further in a fuller treatment of the film, is the reconciliation of Chris and his wife (whose appearance was not

---

109. Issues of memory will be explored in greater depth in chapter five.
110. Marsh, *Theology Goes to the Movies*, 165.
111. Russell, *Paradise Mislaid*, 156.
112. Vincent Ward Films, "What Dreams May Come: Concepts of an Afterlife."

extremely altered), but who lost all memory of recognition in her despair and hellish experience. She did not recognize or know Chris until a re-filling of memory, rather than an emptying of memory occurred. Ward is able to create art that conceptualizes the possibility of heavenly space where social recognition is not only possible, but vital for reconciliation and reunion—a key metaphor for a theological construction of heaven. He does so by the use of the Hudson River School paintings and creating a film where the characters inhabit the moving space.

By reconsidering popular forms of art as important theological construction pieces, heaven can once again be a place that is understood by imagination seeking vision. Reconciliation is the heart of God and "God is love" (1 John 4:8). As Russell reminds us, "perhaps the most common modern concern about heaven is whether we associate there with those we love on earth."[113] Popular forms of art allow the imagination to once again grasp such possibilities.

---

113. Russell, *A History of Heaven*, 188.

5

Will We Remember?

In chapter four, I argued that the relationship between friends and family is just as, if not more, important in imagining heavenly existence than imagining a heavenly state where there is minimal continuity between heaven and the lives that contributed to the formation of a person's earthly existence. I suggested that some continuity, especially as related with the exteriority of the human face, must remain between personal identity and recognition. While keeping in mind the latter's importance for reuniting family and friends, the most interesting and vital component to the argument focused on the transformation of relationships in a heavenly context where the memory of the other proves vital for reunion. Secondly, I suggested that films can offer a way of analogically re-contextualizing heavenly space by the use of the creative imagination. For example, in the case of *What Dreams May Come*, director Vincent Ward turns to the Western historical traditions and the history of interpretation to ask the common analogical question, what does heaven look like?

In this chapter, I will carry out five main objectives. First, I will argue that specific narratives within contemporary theologies of memory in heaven have overly emphasized the annihilation of memories attached to sin and suffering. Although such purification models can be found within the Christian tradition, I will stay consistent with my argument in chapter four, where continuity between earthly and post-mortem existence is intricately intertwined with how our biographies are shaped by experiences within relationships. Secondly, to substantiate the validity of my claim, I will look at popular music as one way of contributing to the shaping of human experience, and a key factor in memory construction as a hermeneutic for interpreting life narratives, and how such interpretations can be applied to the wider phenomena of a hermeneutic of the doctrine of heaven. Thirdly, I will address the difficult interpretive factor of sentimentality, which can be associated with music, film, and other popular arts. I will take up the hermeneutic task of making a distinction between strong and weak sentimentality, rather than the narrow binary categories of true or false. Fourthly, by interpreting a piece of popular music as it is integrated in the narrative of a popular film, I will continue a theological construction towards an understanding of memory in heaven, which invites an interpretation paralleling the tradition found in Luke 23:43. By doing so, I hope not only to demonstrate the connection between music, film, and theology, but also, to focus on the critical aspect of memory in a theology of heaven and how music is often the memorial hermeneutic that enlivens one's imagination to think theologically about heaven. Finally, I will take the discussion of memory one step further by asking a series of questions concerning music and heaven.

My approach not only encourages creativity in the uncountable ways people practice remembering their dead loved ones, but also places weight on the importance of a reciprocal, relational remembrance. For some, perhaps, this will seem trivial as a rehearsal of the doctrine of grace, receiving favor where favor is undeserved which is of course common orthodox theologizing. Certainly, grace is prominent here, but the question of memory is usually surrounded by questions of forgetfulness as in the contrast between tragedy in earthly life, and blessing in eternal life or the doubt whether one can be truly happy in heaven without disintegrating all content connected to evil in earthly life.[1] As H. H. Price observed, even systems of reward and punishment make little sense if there are no memories left in immediate survival.[2]

FORGETTING AS "BLESSING" OR "CURSING"

Miroslav Volf has written a compelling account of his life experiences in an oppressive European context where he describes structures that were bent

---

1. Walls, "Heaven and Hell," 248–49. Jerry Walls' assessment of recent studies in philosophical theology summarizes one of the questions of whether or not a person can be fully satisfied in heaven if one is aware of the damned; which holds important implications for memory. As mentioned in the previous chapter, a further topic that needs exploration in Ward's film concerns how Chris' imagination will not be satisfied in a heaven where his wife is absent. This relational dynamic can bring further light to the question.

2. Price, *Essays In Philosophy of Religion*; 116.

on starving out human flourishing.³ In light of his experiences, Volf cannot fathom prospects of

> the *eternality of evil* in the midst of God's new world. If wrongs suffered are permanently inscribed in the minds and identities of the citizens of the world to come, would this not represent a peculiar triumph of evil rather than its complete defeat? Note the memory of evil is what many evildoers want; they do evil to be remembered.⁴

To defend his thesis, Volf utilizes three key figures, Søren Kierkegaard, Friedrich Nietzsche, and Sigmund Freud.⁵ Volf is after a view of new creation that allows all memories connected to evil to be eradicated or in his terms, "not-coming-to-mind."⁶ He finds that in Freud, "*nothing* in his account of psychoanalysis requires that *unrepressed* memories of wrongs suffered be kept alive instead of being allowed to sink into oblivion."⁷ For clarity, Volf is not concerned with immediate survival, as much as with a postponed, earthbound, new creation. He wants to alleviate any notion of escapism, asking:

> Is the non-remembrance of wrongs suffered that I propose a flight from the unbearable memory into the felicity of oblivion? No flight is involved. According to my conception, each wrong suffered will be exposed in its full horror, its perpetrators condemned and the repentant transformed, and its victims honored and healed.⁸

He recognizes in Nietzsche that forgetting includes different types, yet Volf separates himself from Nietzsche's flights by advocating a forgetfulness that is a "divine gift of a new world."⁹ It is not as if Volf's approach lacks faith; on the contrary, Volf's vision entails a new self, a new creation that carries no emotional baggage. He is content to resolve, however, that our experiences on earth are of little value after crossing the "finish line." The selective eternal memory is a gift and acts as a divine memory. Interestingly, Volf concludes his vision in a comparison with music. He humbly acknowledges

---

3. Volf, *The End of Memory*.
4. Ibid., 213.
5. Ibid., 152.
6. Ibid., 158.
7. Ibid., 153.
8. Ibid., 214.
9. Ibid., 58.

that his vision is not the only vision and he may be surprised on "that day," but he comments:

> I think of that life as like being absorbed in a piece of arrestingly beautiful music—music that captivates my entire being and takes me on an unpredictable journey. That's what that world of love will do for its inhabitants. It will bar the pathways through which the wounded past, a past marred by wrongdoing and suffering, enters the present, and it will set them free to explore the truth, the goodness, and the beauty of that world—each on their own and all together.[10]

I suggest the way Volf imagines "arrestingly beautiful music" for shaping a narrative as a more constructive starting point for theology than trying to quantify and qualify forgetfulness. Volf's thought experiment comes to an end with his own admonition to "rein in the imagination" and to allow for the element of surprise.[11]

Although the increased awareness of evil in the world makes Volf's approach tempting, his line of thought is not without limitations. In fact, Jane McArthur has written an entire dissertation in respectful refutation of Volf's thesis.[12] McArthur's protest takes shape around a key idea that "in all of our lives certain key events are so formative that to forget them would surely make us different people than we are."[13] Along with Volf, McArthur is after a postponed new creation, rather than an immediate survival in a new world, but regarding the role of memory in the new creation, she is arguing that theologians need to give more attention to those "memories from personal experience which are constitutive of personal identity."[14] Although memories of knowledge and of skills acquired play a role in shaping our identities, she does not rule out the prospects of reconciliation that are central to our identity constructions.[15] McArthur argues that "Peter would not have been the same person after his denial and re-installment."[16] Surely,

---

10. Ibid., 230. I must concede that Christianity does have traditions found for example in Tundale's vision of the afterlife where the voices and music are so beautiful that Tundale "forgets" "his own sinful past," yet the aftermath shows a transformed Tundale that not only can recall his experience, but recognizes the transformative changes by comparison. Russell, *A History of Heaven*, 108. For a much fuller account of Tundale's vision, see Gardiner, *Visions of Heaven & Hell Before Dante*, 149–95.

11. Ibid.

12. McArthur, "Memory in the New Creation."

13. Ibid., 123.

14. Ibid., 95.

15. Ibid.

16. Ibid., 123.

forgiveness and forgetfulness are not co-equals. As creatures whose biographies are shaped by many different variables, including sin, will we be forgotten by the other or will we be remembered in a way that is undeserving? These considerations raise the question, in turn, of God's memory. According to Lawrence Hoffman, "unlike human beings, God is never racked with bad memories; and that in the end, divine memory is covenantal memory, whereby God attends to pointers that bring down grace upon Israel."[17] Hoffman observes in the worship regulations of the *Seder Rav Amram* that "God is implored to do the remembering, even though it is God also who is the object of the memory."[18] Although God may not be "racked" by bad memories, to use Hoffman's term, it would be quite astonishing to think that God does not have memories that break his heart. As St. Ephrem musically responds, "blessed is He who through His Cross has flung open paradise," which simultaneously carries the horrific memory that the "blessed" "was pierced and so removed the sword from the entry to Paradise."[19]

Contrary to Volf's approach, lack of memory seems not to be a gift, as much as a human ailment. For example, the great sin according to Islam is of humanity's forgetfulness of God. "Muslims speak of '*gaflah*' (forgetfulness)."[20] According to Kreeft, "it's their version of original sin: an innate, universal human tendency to forget God."[21] Fiddes argues that "forgiveness is a voyage of memory, a calling to mind. As a path of discovery, forgiveness is not forgetting. Memory is subversive, calling the present situation into question."[22] Suffering seems to be the hermeneutic driving Volf's theology, even if it means that all experiences somehow tainted by evil are completely annihilated. Harvey Cox makes an important contribution to the issue of suffering and meaning-making:

> There is one thing the critics of experience-based theologies overlook when they claim that culture and language always precede and shape experience. They overlook pain. They forget that some human experiences are so intense that they defy words and compel us to create new worlds, sometimes whole new worlds. Of these world-creating experiences, perhaps the principal ones are spiritual and physical suffering.[23]

17. Hoffman, "Does God Remember?" 42.
18. Ibid., 44.
19. St. Ephrem The Syrian, *Hymns on Paradise*, 85, 109.
20. Kreeft, *Before I Go*, 235.
21. Ibid.
22. Fiddes, *Participating in God*, 201.
23. Cox, *Fire from Heaven*, 316.

Cox observes that "suffering is sometimes expressed in available cultural motifs, but sometimes it also forces us to reconstruct our worlds. Pain changes us. It compels us to break out of our normal modes of thinking and to see life in a different way."[24] Perhaps the query for Volf, then, is to imagine why God would not want to reconstruct our constitutions to be people prior to those experiences of evil. The teacher in Ecclesiastes 4 advocates a similar stance in that those who are never born are better off not existing to see the suffering under the sun, but this is a very negative way to remember. Where McArthur wants to argue for a better hermeneutic in remembering suffering in the new creation, Volf imagines this type of existence as old, oppressed creation. If pain functions as the realistic regulator to avoid an overly sentimental understanding of heaven, theodicy becomes the driving force of one's doctrine. He is not necessarily alone; DeCou argues that "the creative genius of the artist always arises out of suffering, without which it would not be true art."[25] Yet, hope resulting from the negation of suffering is limiting, if it does not give proper attention to the joy of memory. Therefore, a theology overemphasizing ethics and the alienation of humanity from God reduces possibilities for an aesthetic engagement treating the joy of memory.

Hans Urs von Balthasar partly credits Søren Kierkegaard's followers for allowing a residual breach not only between aesthetics and ethics, but even wider on the Kierkegaardian hierarchy, "a meeting between aesthetics and religion."[26] In his classic analysis of aesthetics and ethics in *Fear and Trembling*, Kierkegaard places concealment under aesthetics and disclosure under ethics, where he contends: "aesthetics called for concealment and rewarded it. Ethics called for disclosure and punished concealment."[27] In the context of Abraham's crisis, navigating a command of God to sacrifice Isaac, Abraham did not have the luxury of resting on the borderline, which in Kierkegaard's terms is the *"interesting"* or rather, "a category of crisis."[28] For Kierkegaard, this category "marks the boundary between the aesthetic and the ethical."[29] According to Balthasar, this breach between the aesthetic and ethical is unfortunate as "the word 'aesthetic' automatically flows from the pens of both Protestant and Catholic writers when they want

---

24. Ibid.

25. DeCou, *Playful, Glad, and Free*, 103. DeCou is referencing Barth here, but also within the context where she uses Barth to show how the theological task is a joyful task.

26. Balthasar, *The Glory of the Lord*, 50.

27. Kierkegaard, *Fear and Trembling*, 101, 104.

28. Ibid., 99.

29. Ibid., 100.

to describe an attitude which, in the last analysis, they find to be frivolous, merely curious and self-indulgent."[30] Kierkegaard suggests that the aesthetic too easily "contradicts itself as soon as it is applied to reality. Ethics therefore demands disclosure."[31] Here, I am in agreement where Balthasar finds such an attitude "unacceptable."[32] At the same time, as I have shown earlier in the discussion of Kearney's work, one is not necessarily forced into choosing between polarizations. Kearney is an example of one who has attempted to hold together the aesthetic and ethical.[33]

Kierkegaard was right to a narrow extent for wanting to stress Abraham's ethical dilemma. Jürgen Moltmann too concedes that "the life of Jesus in the gospels stands under the signs of manger and cross, homelessness and murder. In the face of such suffering, aesthetic categories fail rather abruptly."[34] However, even in the early 1970s Moltmann saw the necessary interpenetration of ethics and aesthetics. He observed: "Only those who are capable of joy can feel pain at their own and other people's suffering. A man who can laugh can also weep."[35] Theodicy, although containing varied categories pertaining to evil, places a large degree of attention on ethics. In an earlier chapter, I referenced McEwan's research that found to a considerable degree an overemphasis upon the alienation of humanity from God, leaving the twentieth century with limited theological resources emphasizing the transcendentals of beauty, goodness, and truth. Writing in the early 1970s on the relationship between theology and joy, Moltmann is helpful in this regard, since within his theological framework he leaves room to address the need for theological aesthetics. Moltmann writes of his context:

> Theology does not have much use for aesthetic categories. Faith has lost its joy, since it has felt constrained to exorcize the law of the old world, with a law of the new. Where everything must be useful and used, faith tends to regard its own freedom as good for nothing. It tries to make itself useful and in so doing often gambles away its freedom. Ethics is supposed to be everything. Yet the theological tradition is permeated with aesthetic images and categories.[36]

30. Balthasar, *The Glory of the Lord*, 51.
31. Kierkegaard, *Fear and Trembling*, 105.
32. Balthasar, *The Glory of the Lord*, 50.
33. Kearney, *The Wake of Imagination*, 388–89.
34. Moltmann, *Theology & Joy*, 49–50.
35. Ibid., 52.
36. Moltmann, *Theology & Joy*. Balthasar spends time in his introduction tracing the developments of this lacking aesthetic element of theological inquiry since the Reformation period in, *The Glory of the Lord*, 45–78.

David Jenkins offers these prefatory remarks to Moltmann's work on joy in his extended introduction: "Now, to suppose ethics to be everything is to make a fundamental and dangerous mistake about both God and man. Man is trapped in 'usefulness' and God becomes either an oppressor or an irrelevance."[37]

A further implication can result in theodicy becoming the sole interpretative factor for a theology of heaven. Christian traditions that are more testimonial driven for purposes of evangelism, or witness to God's saving and transformative work in a believer's life, often encourage believers to retell their personal story, which can and usually does consist of remembering a pre-conversion life. It would seem strange to reflect on a heaven that does not in some way continue the journey where memory plays such a significant factor in remembering not only who we are, but the God who has brought deliverance. If the current discussion in contemporary theology focuses on the relationship between forgetfulness and forgiveness in the individual, what are the further alternatives?

SOUNDS OF MEMORY

Volf's emphasis on the descriptive image of music invites a more general discussion of the role of music in theological construction. I find his analogy interesting in the sense that studies have shown music to be among the final remnants of memory.[38] Marsh and Roberts argue that "music not only manifests memory as a process of the mind; it can also bring back embodied memory—memories that are linked to physical and social encounters from the past."[39] Drawing on the work of Jeremy Begbie, Saliers suggests, "considered rightly, music can also offer insights on how theologians may re-think questions of time, temporality, and the experience of grace," all of which play into our understanding of memory.[40] Music theorists, such as Bob Snyder observe:

> That long-term memories could be permanent may seem to be inconsistent with the idea of forgetting. It is believed, however, that what is lost in forgetting is not the memories themselves but the *associative connections* between them (Fuster, 1995: 11). These connections are what create the recall "paths" to a particular memory. For example, a performer who forgets a

---

37. Moltmann, *Theology & Joy*, 10–11.
38. Marsh, *Personal Jesus*, 63.
39. Ibid.
40. Saliers, *Music and Theology*, 66.

particular phrase in a piece of music may be unable to go on because the performer has lost the cue for the memory of the music that follows.[41]

John Locke (1632–1704) maintained that even if we lose a large portion of our memories on earth, two ways of perceiving are not equal, but what is the link between actual sensation and memory?[42] What if the associative cues are recontexualized, so that the memories are not gone, just as the Christ-event is still *memoria passionis* for Christians at the table, while simultaneously praying and hoping that Christ remembers us in heaven?[43] I suggest that music can serve as a connecting link between what Locke described as the actual sensation and the perception from memory.[44] Saliers asserts, "paying attention to what music elicits and evokes also opens up two interrelated powers: music without words as having theological import, and the fusion of words and music forms to carry us beyond what the words alone signify. Both of these 'powers' of music are related human experiences of time and space."[45] Locke wanted to be sure to clear up any misunderstandings between the pain or pleasure felt in any type of actual present existence and pain or pleasure that we have experienced in the past. He sought to ensure that continuity of consciousness remained, even in light of the decaying body.[46] Rather than focus on the forgetfulness as stemming from age development or impairment, of course not minimizing these life-changing aspects of being human, I want to begin by focusing on that part of the self as constructed in culture, specifically the role of popular music.

41. Snyder, "Music and Memory."

42. Locke, *An Essay Concerning Human Understanding*, 407.

43. Christians practice *"memoria passionis"* a term John Caputo borrows from Johannes Baptist Metz who describes situations in which the church recalls, "dangerous memories of the sufferings of Jesus." Dangerous "to a world that wants to close over and close off and repress those memories of past injustice." Caputo, *What Would Jesus Deconstruct*, 61. Prior to Caputo, Paul Ricoeur made use of Metz' idea in his essay, "Toward a Narrative Theology," in Wallace, ed., *Figuring the Sacred*, 238. Also see, Kellaher and Francis, *The Secret Cemetery*. Western culture is well versed in remembering the other at death and aftermath, as well illustrated in ethnographies of memorial practices in *The Secret Cemetery*, but the Christian tradition has also carried a view somewhat forgotten these days that the blessed dead are remembering the living. In their well-documented study of burial and memorial practices in the UK, Kellaher and Francis open up significant reasons why people visit cemeteries. Of course, the variety of ways and motives people bring to remember their loved ones is extremely broad, but for some, talking with their dead loved one is part of "keeping the dead parent 'alive,'" 157. A popular belief persists that the dead are "listening," 157.

44. Locke, *An Essay in Human Understanding*, 407.

45. Saliers, *Music and Theology*, 66.

46. Locke, *An Essay in Human Understanding*, 214–15.

Before launching into my examples, a critical aspect to consider is how biographies are generally constructed. Drawing on the work of Stanley and Morgan (1993), Steph Lawler observes:

> They [Stanley and Morgan] see a turn to intertexuality as significant: in producing a life story (one sort of text) we are always, implicitly or explicitly, referring to and drawing on other texts—other life stories, fictional and non-fictional, as well as a range of different kinds of texts. This should not be taken to suggest that the resulting narrative is "false", but simply that, in telling a life, people are simultaneously interpreting that life. Narrative analysis is embedded within a hermeneutic tradition of inquiry in that it is concerned with understanding: how people understand and make sense of their lives, and how analysts can understand that understanding.[47]

Lawler is interested in how "identities can be understood as being made through narratives."[48] She is suggesting that "identities can be seen as being creatively produced through various raw materials available—notably, memories, understandings, experiences, and interpretations."[49] The implications of Lawler's proposal for theology are critical if one takes meaning making seriously. James McClendon was correct in redirecting the question concerning "experience" of God away from the "compressed, the non-durational, the abstracted products of actual or durational experience."[50] He argued that the question should be "whether the ongoing story of [human] lives makes more sense when the involvement of God in that story is recognized or when it is bracketed."[51] I would add that theology must emphasize that humanity does not know what it is like to live in a world where God is absent. God is present and active, so we must pay attention to everyday elements that shape our stories.[52]

Tom Beaudoin claims in the preface to Marsh and Robert's work that within the conversation between popular music and theology too much focus has been directed towards the lyrical content, rather than on how music works on people.[53] I think to some extent Beaudoin raises an important matter, so I have chosen two examples of what Marsh and Roberts describe

---

47. Lawler, *Identity*, 14.
48. Ibid., 11.
49. Ibid.
50. McClendon, *Biography as Theology*, 190.
51. Ibid.
52. Brown, *Tradition & Imagination*, 1–2.
53. Beaudoin, "Foreword," in *Personal Jesus*, x.

as the seventh function of popular music, "to shape lives" and "the practice of use" in popular music.[54]

An initial example can be witnessed throughout Cornel West's memoir, where he references popular music as the interpretive framework to describe how God was shaping his life.[55] According to West, "the knowledge and insights could be found in textbooks, but they were also just as powerfully present in music. The music contained the paradoxes, expressed the paradoxes, and exploded the paradoxes with such a sense of heightened joy and rhythmic wonder that all we could do was dance the night away."[56] As Judith Casselberry reminds us: "musical freedom is spiritual freedom, which connotes an intimate embodied relationship with the Divine."[57] West elaborates in detail:

> It was 1971, working and studying and dealing with an America in the throes of massive confusion, that I heard Marvin Gaye's *What's Going On*. It was everything I wanted, everything I needed. It was the ideological/theological feast of funk that got me—and countless others, black and white, yellow and brown—through these years of uncertainty and fear. Marvin worked with uncertainty and fear. They were his emotional clay. He molded them into things of lyrical beauty. His answer to the profound question "What's going on?" was in the imagery of his songs. Police brutality. Ghettos ravaged by drugs. Boys going off to die in an unconscionable war. A planet ravaged by greed and waste. A political landscape of hopelessness. Yet hope comes. Hope emerges from his gut-bucket black Christian faith, a faith powerful enough to transcend the sins of his own Christian father and have Marvin believe—to the very end of his life—in the transformational miracle of love seen from the cross.[58]

West recalls a time when he was preparing to go out to an Al Green show when his interest was suddenly redirected by opening "*Wittgenstein's Vienna* by Allan Janik and Stephen Toulmin, a depiction of the cultural world of Ludwig Wittgenstein that included classical composers Johannes Brahms and Gustav Mahler, and the historical sociologist Max Weber."[59] His description of this evening is musical: "It wasn't that I forgot about Brother

54. Marsh, *Personal Jesus*, 132.
55. West with Ritz, *Brother West*.
56. Ibid., 76.
57. Casselberry, "Were We Ever Secular?" 175.
58. Ibid.
59. Ibid., 78.

Al—no one could ever forget Brother Al—but this dang book was absolutely riveting. I tried to stop reading, but couldn't. Wittgenstein's courage and genius go to the core of who I was and wanted to be. I never did get to Al Green's show, but Wittgenstein's performance in the text was astounding."[60]

From Stevie Wonder, to the Spinners, to Barry White, West's narrative is defined by the popular music which filled his soul:

> The Maestro, Barry White whose soaring orchestral flights of fancy were anchored by deep bottom grooves that had us half-crazy. "Never, Never Gonna Give Ya Up," the Maestro declared. "Can't Get Enough of Your Love, Babe," he swore. "Let the Music Play." As the music played, as I dance my existential blues away, as I lost thoughts of entangled philosophical systems, I found myself at one with pure motion. Barry elevated the funk—gave sheen to the funk—without abandoning the funk. That was his artistic mission. He understood on the deepest level that the funk can be a springboard for beauty. Funk faces brutal reality and reflects its raw consequences. But in doing so, funk is transformation, even redemptive. Funk is liberating.[61]

Even in tracing his intellectual development at Princeton University, West describes Gadamer as "like a master jazz musician, he spun the words out of his spirit. He improvised magnificently. He was the Count Basie of philosophy."[62] West's story is shaped by popular music, and critical for my argument is the fact that one is given a glimpse of a critical thinker who understands the way popular music created meaning for his life.

Turning to a second example of the way in which popular music shapes lives, Rodney Clapp's interpretation of the story of America through the songs and specific themes of Johnny Cash serves as a musical biography of a nation.[63] According to Clapp,

> Like America in general and the South in particular, he [Cash] was God-haunted. He didn't always live up to his convictions but, even at his drug-addled and beastly worst, he never relinquished them. Christian convictions and practices profoundly mark his work, which still rings out across the country and the world—in radio, films, and television commercials.[64]

60. Ibid.
61. Ibid., 85.
62. Ibid., 91.
63. Clapp, *Johnny Cash and the Great American Contradiction*.
64. Ibid., xvi.

In choosing a country artist, Clapp is arguing for a popular poetry that extends to a wide demographic:

> Country music centers on its lyrics. Jazz and classical music are fundamentally instrumental, and in all events draw fewer listeners than country. Rock music's recorded or live sound mixes frequently subordinate vocals to electric guitars and percussion. For country music, the vocalist's words and intonations are paramount. Even rap, which certainly puts a premium on lyrical invention, is mixed so that bass lines and percussion often overshadow and obscure the rapper's words. (And rap appeals to a tighter age demographic than country.)[65]

One theme that stands out in Clapp's interpretation of Johnny Cash's music is derived from Cash's 1994 rendition of Tom Waits "Down There by the Train," which "taps into the longstanding country and gospel traditions of the train song."[66] Clapp's interpretation of the many contradictions that America tries to hold together is summarized in the following:

> Interestingly, this train doesn't stop at the station, but only "goes slow." Perhaps it is an ongoing, unending boxcarred parade, always available for boarding by anyone who makes it to the station. After all, you can hear this engine's whistle from "the halls of heaven to the gates of hell." For eternity's railroad schedule, arriving any time is "on time." Perhaps this train's promise is exactly its ability to move, to transport riders to another, better place, on a ride that can never begin too soon and so can never end or fully stop at any earthly destination. In all events, the train is open to every comer, and the lyrics emphasize that those who board must ride not by merit but by need—the passengers are "whores" and other shameful, forsaken souls. No one can buy a ticket to board this railroad. You must not be too proud to bum a ride, to slip onto the moving train like a penniless hobo. Passengers ride by grace, not by anything they have earned.[67]

Clapp illustrates the parallels between the popular music of Johnny Cash in the song's use of Judas Iscariot and John Wilkes Booth, as they both murdered "great men."[68] Clapp writes, "both are actors living out desperate 'roles'—Booth quite obviously, as a thespian assassinating Abraham Lincoln in a theatre; Judas meeting Jesus' strange expectation that he would assume

---

65. Ibid., xiii–xiv.
66. Ibid., 17.
67. Ibid.
68. Ibid., 18.

the role of the Messiah's betrayer (John 13.21–30). Both are dividers."⁶⁹ Clapp masterfully unpacks the richness resident in the song and squeezes every bit of interpretive impact out of these lyrics. A standout image arises in Judas carrying a limping Booth to the train. A dramatic image indeed to note, "this train runs on rails not made by mortals, crossing all national borders. It is best recognized by those who see shared humanity most acutely in our mutual need, who look at the other not as a scapegoat or a demonic 'other,' but as a fellow sinner and potential copassenger."⁷⁰ Clapp's interpretation and application to the contradictions he sees in American life, exemplified in Johnny Cash, through the artist's music serves as a corporate construction of memory pointing to further possibilities. Even where country music relies on lyrics, the images of Booth and Judas making their way to the train move us beyond words.

Music does not necessarily serve to rewrite the memory, then, but to take the memory or biography of a life further than the words or symbols achieve, especially into new contexts for interpretation. In theologizing about heaven, one can observe this function of popular music as a common hermeneutic framework in ceremonies such as funerals and memorial services, where making associations with music can be the interpretive vehicle. Jeff Keuss points out James Loder's observation that a moment of hearing singers such as "Marvin Gaye or Johnny Cash singing for the first time" can serve as a "life-defining event" in which "acts of faith" function in that space where "both the secular and sacred come together."⁷¹ Secular and sacred also come together in the human experience of death, as an "ontological essential," in Julian Hartt's terms.⁷² Music as a memorial hermeneutic allows participants at funerals to observe "art [as] a kind of action—it does something."⁷³ McClendon argued that "the theologian of culture must understand exactly what is being enacted in a given art-form and bring that action under gospel light for better understanding."⁷⁴ For example, as Keuss was preparing to officiate a memorial service in his church for a young woman, he was looking over the song selection for the service and found music by Sarah McLachlan, as well as Metallica, among others.⁷⁵ He recalls

69. Ibid.
70. Ibid.
71. Keuss, *Your Neighbor's Hymnal*, 19.
72. See McClendon's summary of Hartt's approach to culture in McClendon, *Systematic Theology*, vol. 3, 41.
73. Ibid., 178.
74. Ibid.
75. Ibid., 28.

James Hatfield's (lead singer for Metallica) "Nothing Else Matters" fitting perfectly in the service as "the song is about longing for something more."[76] Keuss remembers:

> As the song ran its course, arms covered with more ink than a stack of comic books were rubbing their eyes and waiting for something beyond James Hetfield's simple tune as we looked toward the cross that hung over that casket. "Nothing else matters" opened the way, for "something else" must matter amidst all this sorrow. When people ask me what pop music has to do with theology, it is moments like these I wish I could bottle up and hand to cynics.[77]

I recall a similar experience, where a young lady came to my church office needing help with a memorial for her father who died in a horrible accident. She wanted her father's memorial in the church and I was glad to serve her in this way. Leaving his daughter and two young boys with the preparations, I recall a song selection which included Lynyrd Skynyrd's "Sweet Home Alabama," Puff Daddy's "Missin' You," Eric Clapton's "Tears in Heaven," Randy Travis' "Forever Amen," Usher and Alicia Keys' "My Boo," and Amanda Perez's "I Pray." Not many attended the service, but one thing was certain, these were songs that shaped their Dad's life and how they remembered him. The music provided the memorial hermeneutic, but the question can easily be asked, from what direction is interpretational pressure being applied and is this not just another example of exaggerated sentimentalism?

SYMBOLS AND SENTIMENTALITY

Sentimentality has always been a risky, even unsteady hermeneutic variable, but as I will argue, sentimentality should not be cast aside for fear of reckless observance, just as memory should not be cast out of heaven in fear that paradise will somehow be vaguely satisfactory if one were to retain memories of an earthly life associated with pain.

Interestingly, both the memorials discussed above occurred in churches, where issues of content and form (especially where music is concerned) have long histories and present expressions of contention. A possible dulling of the edges between these dividing markers may be found in moments of key memory associated with death that moves one beyond taste to a place

76. Ibid.
77. Ibid., 29.

of possible true or strong sentiment attached to relationship. Trust within such relationships establishes an epistemological field for cultivation. When trusted forms of mediation are seen as being displaced or relegated to unfamiliar space, the fear is often that perception will become vaguer or veiled. I would not be painting a full enough portrait if I failed to acknowledge the awareness of false sentimentality exposing a possible weakness in symbols that show too much vulnerability towards fabrication.[78] In his article, *Beauty, Sentimentality and the Arts*, Begbie seeks to emancipate beauty from the tethered grip of sentimentality.[79] He argues:

> Sentimentality is neither a superficial nor an inconsequential matter but a deep, pernicious strand in contemporary culture and in the church, and that the arts have often played a leading part in encouraging it.[80]

To Begbie's credit, he does not ignore the fact that "almost any piece of art" (not just popular forms of art) has the potential to be used for manipulative purposes.[81] In his efforts to distance sentimentality from the arts, Begbie concentrates on "three traits" of sentimentalism to show the demise of sentiment, as well as offering a "countersentimentality" through the lens of Christ's death, burial, and resurrection.[82] For Begbie, "beauty can only be purged of sentimentality by appropriate attention to these three days, read as an integrated yet differentiated narrative."[83] At the same time, Begbie's proposal cannot and should not summarize all sentimentality into what he describes as a "kind of art that—as the saying goes—seems to 'wallow' in some negative emotional field and perhaps encourages us to do the same."[84] For example, a brief analysis of Begbie's three traits using the memorial examples above will dispel some of the supposed tension between popular music and sentimentality. First, an "evasion or trivialization of evil" is far from the pastoral response given in Keuss' case, as well as of the sentiment

---

78. Cobb summarizes Tillich's criterion for how symbols should be identified and understanding their function. See Cobb, *Theology and Popular Culture*, 114–19. For Tillich, *symbols cannot be artificially produced*. Only time, openness, and willingness prepare the ground for a symbol to take on sacred authority becoming reliable for a culture or sub-culture (114). Cobb uses Clifford Geertz' idea that "meanings are 'stored' in symbols" (116).

79. Begbie, "Beauty, Sentimentality and the Arts," 45.

80. Ibid.

81. Ibid., 49.

82. Ibid., 45–46.

83. Ibid., 61.

84. Ibid., 52.

of loved ones present at the memorial.[85] Yes, of course, people can make a life (or death for that matter) seem more ideal than the case may stand. In a memorial context, rather than an evasion, the probability seems to land more clearly on the side of what Begbie is in support of, that is, experiencing "another's pain as pain," but in further adding the Christian dimension of a hope that transcends even the present pain—the hope of heaven.[86] To consider this act evasion or simply escapism would be to miss a prominent role Begbie gives to "countering" sentimentality by paying attention to the "three days of Easter."[87] Secondly, I would not characterize memorial services as "emotionally self-indulgent."[88] If one were to apply his observation of a sentimentalist, as one who "appears to be moved by something or someone beyond themselves but is to a large extent, perhaps primarily, concerned with the satisfaction gained in exercising their emotion" to someone remembering a loved one in a memorial context, insensitivity would seem more dangerous than sentimentality.[89] Thirdly, sentiment as "avoidance for appropriate costly action" may or may not pertain to a memorial context.[90] We are not determined to "restrict ourselves to the pleasing or undisturbing aspects of a situation, and disregard the rest."[91] To the contrary, memorial situations can stimulate reevaluations of what is true, beautiful, and good. Begbie uses the cross and resurrection as his main thrust, as does Keuss who, in my example, also points to the cross. Remembering those who die or those who mourn is not avoiding costly action, it is, rather, entering into the type of situation that Begbie is calling for. In my mind, rather than 'true' sentiment remaining the voice of an "exaggeration of what is good or pleasing . . . ," it seems to me a better way forward is to explore how the arts encourage sentiment that is meaningful, beautiful, true, and indeed, good. A more meaningful distinction may be to think in terms of true or strong sentiment differentiated from false or weak sentiment.

One of the reasons in support of music as a means to shape key memories in a person's narrative, as well as the potential for offering a hermeneutic of memory, is music's tendency to stimulate the emotions, even to the point where words seem to be insufficient. Don Saliers observes:

---

85. Ibid., 47.
86. Begbie, "Beauty, Sentimentality and the Arts," 51.
87. Ibid., 61.
88. Ibid., 50
89. Ibid., 51.
90. Ibid., 52.
91. Ibid., 48.

Theology respects the going beyond words because the object of theology is not captured in the web of language. It is no accident that when poets or great theologians wish to speak of the deepest realities, they move toward poetry and music—heightened speech—as an attempt to "sound" spiritual matters.[92]

The connection between the spiritual and musical is historically embedded, then, in a theology of heaven. Music and heaven share a narrative—a story that is tightly interwoven into the narrative of Western culture, but this shared story is not without contestation. Historical observance provides an analysis for the changing forms that are trusted by some and are signals of apostasy for others. From Ulrich Zwingli's extreme iconoclasm during the Reformation period of moving from musical instruments to voices alone, to contemporary contexts where the inspiration of electric guitar riffs and drum solos in some contexts are understood to be more conducive for spiritual experience, at times even set up against more traditional hymns accompanied with flutes and cellos.[93] Intentionally driven by taste or trusted inherited traditions, people often interpret the spirituality of a subculture by the different variables related to music.

In an effort to make a case for imagining an "ecumenical taste" in music, Frank Burch Brown suggests by "keeping in mind the distinctions between perceiving, enjoying, and judging—we can say that the goal of ecumenical musical taste is not necessarily to enjoy, personally, the arts and worship styles favored by various other people and groups."[94] He later adds:

> The greater and more useful goal is to try to perceive for oneself what others are perceiving in forms of art and worship that one finds alien; to go on to enjoy their enjoyment (without necessarily liking what they enjoy); and eventually to appraise provisionally those more "alien" tastes in relation to the arts and worship styles one finds more congenial. That approach, when applied to liturgy, can make it possible for people with different tastes to worship more fully together, setting aside the music (for instance) that is most questionable on all sides, and discerning together what is more promising.[95]

---

92. Saliers, *Music and Theology*, 72.

93. Brown, *Religious Aesthetics*, 2. Although as Brown observes, Zwingli's contention was necessarily against "traits" in music as much as the case that "music was absent from the primitive church and was not positively commanded by God." 2.

94. Brown, *Good Taste, Bad Taste, & Christian Taste*, 192–93.

95. Ibid., 193.

The fixed certainties for spiritual mediation in one generation become uncertain and disruptive in a new generation. Not only are people "bringing to the music and the images an inappropriate set of aesthetic expectations, such listeners often bring prejudices related to class and age."[96] In 1981, Hans Küng posed the question, "should not art of the future again become *open to religion?*"[97] Popular art forms in 2018 have affirmatively answered this question in the positive, but what are the implications for a culture that ceases to "make use of the traditional symbols of transcendence?"[98] At once, a culture is conditioned with an "anticipation of meaning," yet yearns to describe the "unconditioned."[99] How is a culture to express "a new firmly established basic trust?"[100]

David Martin points to the complexity of such an array of cultural attitudes towards music in the church. He observes:

> For some churchmen [and women] in some periods, the seductions of music have led Christians away from the uncreated light; for others music may be a suitable handmaid to religion, provided she is kept in her place and behaves herself seemly; for others music is a direct mediate of divinity and the closest a person may come to the joys of heaven.[101]

Most pertinent in this context of popular music for theological construction is what Martin designates as the "demotic" tradition.[102] In the demotic tradition:

> The notion of musical worthiness is pushed to the background. It is not so much a question of "right" qualities in the music itself, though one may note a religious potential in this or that piece *en passant*, as its helpfulness in gaining and maintaining assent or conversion. Almost anything will do whatever its origin or style, provided it gets the message across. Clearly this approach is close to the view of language as the means whereby a message or a core of raw meaning is conveyed, the verbal mode itself being quite extraneous.[103]

---

96. Ibid., 16.
97. Selection from Küng's "Art and the Question of Meaning," 256.
98. Ibid.
99. Ibid., 258. Here, Küng references Tillich's notion of the "unconditioned."
100. Ibid., 256.
101. See Martin's essay, "Music and Religion," 47.
102. Ibid., 49.
103. Ibid.

A general critique sometimes leveled against traditions emphasizing spiritual experience is the lack of attention to shared tradition, as well as an over-emphasis upon emotional criteria. I am arguing that changing musical styles is one of the great strengths of a tradition: to change in order to develop further.

It may be helpful, at this point, to develop Martin's insight concerning the category of "sincerity" in order to understand the demotic tradition more fully.[104] While Martin is concerned that a sort of "amateurism" or "lack of technical prowess," can lead to lack of "play" (which for Martin only comes through "superabundant energy of a mind and a heart which has so mastered both technique and self-indulgence that it becomes free and untrammeled, almost godlike"). He is right to suppose that "sincerity is concerned with matters of the heart, which accounts more for the salvific sign of happiness."[105] Martin observes: "the demotic approach identifies happiness not so much with blessedness or with rapt attention as with outgoing jollity, preferably en masse. Once the criteria of being heartfelt, hearty and jolly are emphasized, a great deal of the art music of Christianity and, indeed, liturgical action as such, comes to seem sad or over controlled."[106]

One broad example showing signs of demotic tendencies is found in the range of music styles within contemporary Pentecostal churches. These traditions can emphasize emotional criteria, such as the "warming" of a heart, or the "tears" of joy, or the "peace" of mind, or the "laughter" of thankfulness. These are all signals of divine encounter and most often experienced through music and can be recontexualized in any setting even beyond ecclesiastical structures because the Spirit transcends boundaries. This in no way implies the only criteria Pentecostals use to describe religious experience. One of the great strengths that I find in Pentecostal/Charismatic contexts is the willingness to adapt cultural changes to forms within the church. Old stories are told alongside and integrated with new stories (oral theology), in song styles that emerge directly from the wider culture. Of course, these shifts in attitude are not without tension. No cultural change is free from this type of stress.

Music can highlight the sentimental value that people place in particular bands, genres, styles, along with further variables that are descriptive of a subculture, such as fashion, language, ethics, not to mention the theological divergent conceptions of what "moves" people to experience the divine through the medium of music. Central to my concern is the important role

---

104. Ibid., 49.
105. Ibid., 49–50.
106. Ibid., 49.

of the imagination in thinking about heaven. *Moments of key memory associated with a loved one's death can move one beyond taste to a place of possible true sentiment.* Robert Solomon observed that sentimentality came under great suspicion during the nineteenth century. He argues, "it is charged that sentimentality is distorting, self-indulgent, self-deceptive. I [Solomon] argue that all of these charges are misplaced or themselves distorted and betray a suspicion of emotions and the tender sentiments that is unwarranted."[107] Solomon elaborates his case for true sentimentality:

> I take sentimentality to be nothing more nor less than the "appeal to tender feelings," and though one can manipulate and abuse such feelings (including one's own), and though they can on occasion be misdirected or excessive, there is nothing wrong with them as such and nothing (in that respect) wrong with literature [or music in this case] that provokes us, that moves us to abstract affection or weeping. Sentimentality implies no deficiency in one's rational faculties and does not imply any inappropriateness, unwillingness, or lack of readiness to act. Sentimentality does not involve any distortion of the world, and it does not impede, but rather prepares and motivates, our reacting in "the real world." It is not an escape from reality or responsibility but, quite to the contrary, provides the precondition for ethical engagement rather than being an obstacle to it.[108]

Following his summary concerning Kant's dislike and further attack on sentimentality, Solomon describes the argument indicting "sentimentality [as] kitsch."[109] For some moral philosophers, this type of kitsch "substitutes cheap manipulation of feeling for careful calculation of form or judicious development of character."[110] Rightly, Solomon argues, "sentimentality as kitsch and sentimentality as an ethical defect are two very different charges, and part of the problem in the general condemnation of sentimentality is that it too readily identifies the two and treats them together."[111] Solomon makes this distinction:

---

107. Solomon, *In Defense of Sentimentality*, 1. Begbie finds Solomon's "minimal construal of sentimentality" as the "'tender' emotions" unconvincing and "strange." Begbie, "Beauty, Sentimentality and the Arts," 46. As already noted, Begbie is among those wishing for a severe break between art and sentiment.

108. Ibid., 4.

109. Ibid.

110. Ibid.

111. Ibid.

Part II: Imagining Identity in a Post-mortem Existence

> Bad art is one thing and sentimentality is another, and while bad literature [or other art forms] in particular may try to prove its redeeming value by evoking tender feelings, its sentimentality is neither the cause of its badness nor a species of immorality. Sentimentality in certain circumstances can be in bad taste, of course, but sentimentality as such is not always (or even usually) in bad taste and bad taste does not always (or even usually) reflect bad character.[112]

In light of Solomon's comments, how can pieces of popular music allow for strong sentimentality in remembering the blessed dead, yet still set up impediments for the imagination to theologize about heaven?

The impediments are heavy with cultural meaning. For example, introducing Metallica into a culture that is very unfamiliar with thrash metal may not always make the same associative cues that someone with familiarity may indeed grasp more fully. In Keuss' example, the description of "ink covering arms" may indicate that a portion of the subculture were present and were not only able to make the connection with where the song was pointing, but also to interpret this young woman's life, as Keuss expounds, as one remembered for "her laughter, her love of the sunshine, her passion for music, and what it means to live out this love with others and in the presence of God who lives with us now."[113] This example also illustrates the important work of pastors/theologians, such as Keuss, in helping people make these important connections. People who knew the girl may have anticipated a thoughtful memorial to incorporate the music that shaped her life.

As noted earlier in Frank Brown's work, expectations and anticipations of experience with the divine make a significant impact on one's perception, simply because trust and confidence play a role in our receptivity.[114] Yet, in spite of the charges against the frivolity or triviality of popular music as a resource for theology, Gavin Hopps' observation is correct: "it seems hard to find any absolute and secure criteria according to which pop music as a genre may be deemed *intrinsically* trivial."[115]

For this reason, I advocate a hermeneutical approach to theology, rather than more rationalistic models that treat a text as an "object of knowledge" or something to be mastered.[116] Although the rational is

---

112. Ibid., 8.
113. Keuss, *Your Neighbor's Hymnal*, 30.
114. Brown, *Good Taste, Bad Taste, & Christian Taste*, 16.
115. Hopps, "Infinite Hospitality and the Redemption of Kitsch," 158.
116. Thiselton, *Hermeneutics*, 8.

never untethered, "the more creative dimension of hermeneutics depends more fundamentally on the receptivity of the hearer or reader to *listen with openness.*"[117] C. S. Lewis' famous reference to the act of surrender steers in the direction concerning how a work of art acts on us:

> We sit down before the picture in order to have something done to us, not that we may do things with it. The first demand any work of any art makes upon us is surrender. Look. Listen. Receive. Get yourself out of the way. (There is no good asking first whether the work before you deserves such a surrender, for until you have surrendered you cannot possibly find out.)[118]

Advocating a surrender to art, not only foreign to a subculture, but suspect concerning factors of creative motivation, as well as religious devotion, whether or not the creator intended particular inferences, still plays a considerable role concerning the value of certain pieces of art, more specifically music.

Conrad Ostwalt asks, "what can we make of this contemporary sacralization of secular music?"[119] He maintains that secularization is a two directional process, but this does not happen without sacralization because he does not argue that religion is fading, but rather religion is showing up in different spaces, texts and images. Therefore, he answers the question by arguing that "it [sacralization] witnesses the extent to which our society has become religion-saturated throughout its popular culture in and through venues that are distinct from religious institutions and official religious bodies."[120] Later he asserts:

> The possibility exists that religion dissipated throughout the culture, arising authentically in the hands and creations of representatives who are removed from the restrictions of orthodoxy, can become a religion that empowers and functions to grant meaning to a more diverse population than can official religious bodies alone.[121]

Ostwalt concludes his observation of the phenomenon with a question, "if this in fact is happening, is there something about music that inspires a more powerful religious response than other cultural forms?" Ostwalt takes his lead from the work of Jon Michael Spencer in that "secular music contains

---

117. Ibid; 7.
118. Lewis, *An Experiment in Criticism*, 19.
119. Ostwalt, *Secular Steeples*, 195.
120. Ibid.
121. Ibid., 195–96.

layers of theological meaning."[122] Not unlike other arguments in disciplines such as history, as witnessed earlier in the work of Jeffrey Russell on heaven, Spencer advocates secular forms with religious content over against sacred music because for him, "sacred music is defined by, bounded by, and limited by doctrine and dogma," whereas "secular music has no such limitations."[123] Therefore, for Spencer:

> It is in secular music that we learn what we really believe, and it is through our response to secular music that we can fashion an ethic that is meaningful and relevant. Secular music, therefore, provides a more reliable measure of authentic belief, relevant ethics, and real commitment than sacred music, which can be defined by standards of belief that are no longer owned by those in the tradition.[124]

The freedom of expression that is often championed in secular spheres also runs the risk of not paying close enough attention to the process of cultural conditioning. If freedom refers to allowing room for forms and content that allow for true development and understanding, then Spencer's argument is unwarranted simply because all spheres are places of the Holy Spirit's involvement. At the same time, if freedom from confessionalism is understood as being without presupposition, once again, Spencer's argument as understood by Ostwalt is not paying close enough attention to consumer consumption, ideologies, and nihilism that characterizes a pseudo unrestricted honesty.

A better way, perhaps, to understand this type of authenticity is to pay attention to how popular music elicits "religious experiences that crosscut region, nationality, ethnicity, gender, and spiritual belief."[125] Symbols die in culture just as quickly as in subcultures, such as the Christian church. Following Tillich, Cobb observes, "history is strewn with dead symbols, and those which die usually do so at the hands of the religions that gave birth to them in the first place."[126] Cobb also observes: "a symbol can go into hibernation, ready to be awakened when the conditions are right," although he doubts Tillich "anticipated" such an awakening. As Brown has shown in multiple volumes, the text has been moving, rather than remaining static.[127] Therefore, one should not be surprised to find theological layers both

---

122. Ibid., 197.
123. Ibid.
124. Ibid., 197.
125. Casselberry, "Were We Ever Secular?" 180.
126. Cobb, *Theology and Popular Culture*, 117.
127. Brown, *Tradition and Imagination*, 169.

outside and inside of the church. Too often theology uses words such as "application" to refer to a type of repetition that merely invokes a durational construct that is itself unaware of change in the way people understand the world. This is by no means an ahistorical approach; rather, I am advocating a contextual theology that takes into account historical development.

Ostwalt contends that "religion in America became popularized in order to compete in the free market" and suggests that the U.S. exhibits a "popular culture that is more infused with religious images."[128] He also insists that "secularization equals secularizing the sacred as well as sacralizing the secular."[129] Regardless of spherical origin or direction of change, this two-way movement "between religion and culture [is what] steers our search for meaning" and to the extent one witnesses this phenomenon, the "blurring of boundaries has taken place."[130] Ostwalt claims "that the Christian tradition has been secularizing since its beginning," by providing numerous characters and movements initiating such innovation.[131]

Ostwalt's observations are helpful to an extent, but he does not answer any questions pertaining to whether or not the "powerful force" of secularization will prove as a "strengthening force that will allow Christianity to grow and thrive or perhaps a weakening force that will destroy Christianity as a distinctive voice in the cultural landscape."[132] My suspicion rests in Ostwalt's lack of engagement with thinkers such as Tillich who saw the "boundaries" as meaningful not merely for designating spheres, but showing where certain emphases arise. For example, Tillich's use of the "intentionality" of religion "toward substance," as well as culture's intentionality "toward form," but Tillich goes further to show the interconnectedness by arguing that "the substance, representing unconditioned meaning, can be glimpsed only indirectly through the medium of the autonomous form granted by culture."[133] Ostwalt's insistence that the secular is becoming more sacred in that it contains honest religious content in ever changing forms is an insight to consider.

Even more helpful, in my opinion, is Brown's work on tradition and change because he is attuned to the changes in tradition from different directions, while recognizing what he refers to as "triggers," whether from

---

128. Ostwalt, *Secular Steeples*, 6.
129. Ibid., 34.
130. Ibid., 34 and 95.
131. Ibid., 46.
132. Ibid., 72.
133. Tillich, *On the Boundary*, 70.

inside or outside tradition.[134] Where Ostwalt pulls up short, offering no judgment, and Tillich's view of transcendence gets covered up by immanence, Brown is aware that different spheres operate with different "canons," and he is willing to analyze "triggers" from all directions to better understand God's activity.[135]

I have been suggesting that music is a vehicle for shaping lives and a memorial hermeneutic for understanding lives, as well as providing room for a holistic understanding of the human person, including emotions, which allows for the possibility of true sentiment. I now want to tie together my initial point about memory in heaven to show the importance of popular art in imaginatively considering memory in a heavenly context. To illustrate my argument, I will provide two final examples exhibiting the interwovenness of popular music and visual art. Firstly, a popular song takes on new life in a new context as it gets embedded in a remembrance video becoming associated with those who have died. Secondly, I will analyze a popular song about heaven and the way in which film adopts the song to use during a specific scene dealing with the issue of identity, more specifically memory.

HEAVEN AS A PLACE OF REMEMBRANCE

As I have shown, in one sense, music is often the hermeneutical vehicle that is used to interpret cultural movements and particular historical periods in the life of a nation. In a similar way, music is closely connected to the memory of deceased love ones, therefore providing a way in which to interpret a life. For example, popular music artist, Sarah McLachlan's song, "I Will Remember You" found life and reception in connection with the visual arts on the soundtrack for the 1995 film, *The Brothers McMullen*. Later in 1999, the song exploded with popularity with the release of her live album, *Mirrorball*, which has since been re-released.[136] The phenomenon of text development and revival was on display at the 2009 Sixty-First Primetime Emmy Awards where McLachlan performed live, "I Will Remember You" during the "In Memoriam."[137] The unpredictable element of textual reception elicited a innovative hearing, as the older song was brought into new

---

134. Brown, *Tradition & Imagination*, 32.
135. Ibid., 31–32.
136. McLachlan, "I Will Remember You."
137. "In Memoriam" refers to the portion of the award program where the Academy of Television Arts and Sciences honor and remember their peers that died during that year. As is a common option in many funeral homes in contemporary Western culture, services are offered to family and friends to submit pictures, film clips, and music to be mixed into a presentation as a part of the memorial ceremony.

associations with memory, imagination, and the hereafter. Popular artists and fans alike, celebrated the diversity of beloved and now, missed voices, including pop music artist Michael Jackson, actor Patrick Swayze, and actor Paul Newman, amongst a wide cast of artists. McLachlan's song and performance served as a memorial hermeneutic that gave meaning to the question, what does memory sound like? Those present will now have associative cues to think about those now in post-mortem existence. In this context, memory is now associated with belief about what comes after death and for many that place is heaven.

Remembering as Love for the Other

A further step is to unpack a popular song that is already working with these ideas. Some may argue, that the interpretive criteria for such a move is too slim to substantiate theological warrant, but as Christian Scharen argues in his *Broken Hallelujahs*, theology at its best, "aims to reorient Christian imagination."[138]

My song selection comes from The Fire Theft, an Indie/Rock band from Seattle, Washington that has attracted many within Emo culture. They released their song, "Heaven" in 2003.[139] What begins as a ballad rises into a passionate cry for heaven, where Jeremy Enigk (lead singer and guitarist) takes listeners on an unpredictable journey. Not only do the lyrics point to unpredictability, but the music bursts with emotion at points, especially in the middle phrases where Enigk releases gut-wrenching expression.[140]

The characteristic octave changes and emotion driving the narrative resonates in a popular culture that is often described as being left alone. From educational reforms to political initiatives, people are crying out for a remembrance that is intent on considering the other in decision making positions, not to mention the interesting trust that humans place in areas of authority. The thief on the cross can't navigate the abyss before him, but he asks for remembrance in a paradise that is waiting at the door from the one hanging on a cross next to him. The metaphor of love in the song is most appropriate for thinking theologically about heaven. As Russell observes: "every human from the beginning has one fundamental question that underlies his or her whole nature. The question is: Do you love me?"[141] Memory in heaven is not simply a forgetfulness of all that has gone on before, but more

---

138. Scharen, *Broken Hallelujahs*, 99.
139. The Fire Theft, "Heaven."
140. Theft, "Heaven."
141. Russell, *A History of Heaven*, 186.

importantly, memory is a blurring of the boundaries between secular and sacred, summarized in the relation to the thief on the cross in Luke 23:43, and being remembered by Jesus who is near, who is listening, and who is reconciling.

A similar search for the way forward is found in John 14:1–4, where one discovers Jesus preparing a place for the disciples—a place where they will be welcomed—where they will be remembered. The ambiguity sensed by the disciples is answered with Jesus' assurance that because they know him, they know the way. The disciples do not want to be left alone. Jesus proceeds to draw their attention to the sending and the activity of the Spirit, in order that knowledge of "the way, the truth, and the life" will not be silenced and that trust in him is possible. The journey forward is still full of ambiguity for the disciples, but as Caputo reminds us:

> Real journeys are full of unexpected turns and twists, requiring a faith that can move mountains and a hope against hope, where one does not see what one was trying to do until the journey is completed, which postmodernists call the "absolute future." Deconstruction, like the Christianity of Kierkegaard's Johannes Climacus, is not a Platonic "recollection," a getting back to where you already were or a recovering of a possession that you did not realize you possessed all along. It is not a matter of becoming who you already are but of becoming something new, a *metanoia*, a new creation, which eye has not seen nor ear heard nor heart imagined, an openness to the coming of the other, which we don't already possess.[142]

Knowing the way to this place is a journey of faith as the biblical narrative unfolds, but Jesus ensures the disciples that because they know him, they know the way. Later, Jesus refers to the Spirit's activity in all creation, so that knowledge of "the way, the truth, and the life" will be remembered.

I have raised the question: what if memory in heaven follows from what we don't deserve, rather than on reward and punishment? Such a view would allow for us to understand memory, not merely in terms of past events or sufferings, but intentionality to remember the other (the example of Jesus remembering the thief on the cross). "I can feel it when it shines"—is the writer describing "heaven," "love," the "simple things," or possibly all of the above. Russell may very well be describing heaven when he writes, "heaven is acceptance of love, which burns through and shines through the pain, transforming it. Love would rather go through hell than to go to heaven

---

142. Caputo, *What Would Jesus Deconstruct*, 52–53.

without us."[143] It is very hard to imagine that the thief on the cross would forget his longing for Jesus to remember him and the context in which he finds himself. Even in the midst of his pain—deliverance was near. Memory in heaven is not a failure to recall, as a blessing or gift (e.g., Volf's account), but a remembrance of healing that does not involve the same pain recall (Rev 21:4). John's Apocalypse paints a picture of tears being wiped away because death is defeated and there is no more pain. Yes, the old is gone, but the narrative is being fulfilled, not erased. Memory is dynamic in that the true sense of forgiveness is interpreted and understood more clearly. Popular music can contribute to the process of understanding one's journey as it crosses boundaries to once again inspire the imagination to think about what it is like to remember and be remembered in heaven.

Film, Music, and Heaven

The Fire Theft's song took on new dimensions when it was integrated into the 2011 film *Beastly*, directed by Daniel Barnz.[144] The film is based on Alex Flinn's novel *Beastly*, a retelling of the older narrative, *Beauty and the Beast*. Barnz's work displays many of the marks of the earlier tales in that the story centers on true love. Kyle Kingson (actor Alex Pettyfer) plays a seventeen-year-old high-school student that is "beastly" in his relations to others. His actions epitomize self-centeredness, lacking any remembrance or consideration of others living up to what is revealing of his ugly heart. Kyle's popularity stems from his outward good looks, charm, and power to control his circumstances. He meets his match once he encounters Kendra (actress Mary-Kate Olsen) who is not an ordinary teenager. Kendra is a witch and she infects Kyle with a spell, which creates a hideous appearance on Kyle that illustrates his complicated inner struggles to be loved. The stipulation for healing Kyle's condition involves someone loving him for who he is on the inside, which would entail looking beyond the unattractiveness of his appearance. Kendra's spell forces Kyle to transform and disclose this transformation to someone in such a way that love will go beyond his "beastly" appearance—something must transcend his outer repellence.

At first Kyle is completely overwhelmed by his new situation, but, through a number of circumstances, Kyle builds a friendship with a girl he knew in high school; but he goes by a different name, Hunter. Throughout the film Lindy (actress Vanessa Hudgens) and "Hunter" grow closer in their relationship. If someone does not love Kyle within a certain duration, he

143. Russell, *A History of Heaven*, 187.
144. *Beastly*, DVD (2011).

152   Part II: Imagining Identity in a Post-mortem Existence

will remain permanently in his situation, as "beastly." After spending an enchanting afternoon together, there is a romantic scene where Hunter (Kyle) catches Lindy in his arms and is about to kiss her when her phone rings. Upsetting the moment, she answers the phone and devastatingly learns that her father has overdosed on drugs. They rush her to the train station and Hunter leaves her with a handwritten letter describing his feelings for her.

As the train departs, Lindy opens the letter and The Fire Theft's "Heaven" begins to play. More than accompanying the narrative, the song is shaping the narrative identity of Hunter. Lindy is reading the disclosure of Hunter's inner beauty, but the music takes us beyond the message to a place calling out for *heaven*. The descriptive potency of integrating artistic forms creates the remembrance of both characters for each other and take on new meaning for their situations. Saliers observes, "music in its deeper range cannot be confined to background sound, try as we might to keep it that way—a kind of constant accompaniment to our hours, or as accepted entertainment."[145] The music tells us more about the message contained in the letter and about Hunter (Kyle) than we would have otherwise known. Should "Heaven" be understood as merely love searching for a connection? One could suspect a reductionist approach from popular culture, but such a critique would miss the way the song has been attached to pictures through the art of film, illuminating a new audience with images that connect the concept of heaven as transcending our abilities to remember the other who is broken and ugly, according to some standards. The thief surely did not recognize in Jesus a beautiful face, but one in a position to point the way beyond his death. Lindy does eventually declare her love for Kyle, discovering a miraculous transformation into the young man that held the appearance of a selfish, non-considerate student. By looking into his face, she sees in his eyes the Hunter she had grown to love. His inner self had experienced a transformation and his once good-looking appearance, along with selfish attitude was no longer an impediment. Lindy remembers Hunter (Kyle) as the one she loves.

LISTENING IN ON HEAVEN

The examples I have offered throughout this chapter certainly overlap with the imagination in relation to heaven, especially those examples drawn from funerals and memorials, which can elicit strong imaginative responses. Yet, at the same time, it could be argued that these examples are still this-worldly

145. Saliers, *Music and Theology*, 67.

oriented. In what follows, I will ask a series of questions that will take this discussion to a further imaginative depth regarding music and heaven.

Firstly, it is not uncommon for one to posit a heaven where everyone sings the same songs together at the same time. This may very well be one of the reasons for contemporary disbelief in heaven, not just a reason for a lack of attendance at church worship services. As we have observed the ways music shape human lives, one can develop an understanding of the internal criteria that different types of music retain for listeners. In this way, heaven is not limited to one song, in one style.

It is also not difficult to imagine heaven with the best music, so this in turn raises a second question concerning the development of heavenly taste. One of the more famous examples utilized by theologians of culture is Karl Barth's heavenly taste for Wolfgang Amadeus Mozart. Barth asked the question:

> Why is it for the receptive, he [Mozart] has produced in almost every bar he conceived and composed a type of music for which "beautiful" is not a fitting epithet: music which for the true Christian is not mere entertainment, enjoyment, or edification but food and drink; music full of comfort and counsel for his needs; music which is never a slave to its technique nor sentimental but always "moving," free and liberating because wise, strong and sovereign?[146]

Vildesau begins his major work on theological aesthetics with this quotation from Barth.[147] Patrick Sherry also begins his theological aesthetics with Barth's preference for Mozart.[148] But most pertinent to my inquiry is Frank Burch Brown's observation:

> When this modern Protestant theologian thought of heaven, he immediately thought of music. Barth speculated that, in heaven, when the angels go about their task of praising God, they may play only Bach; but—Barth was quick to say—when playing for their own enjoyment, they surely play Mozart. On those occasions, too, according to Barth, God listens in with special pleasure.[149]

Although Barth's use of "the receptive" is strikingly limited as observed in the earlier quotation from his *Dogmatics*, one can certainly understand his

---

146. Barth, *Church Dogmatics*, vol. III.3, 297–98.
147. Viladesau, *Theological Aesthetics*, 3.
148. Sherry, *Spirit and Beauty*, 1–2.
149. Brown, *Good Taste, Bad Taste, & Christian Taste*, 160.

desire for allowing room for Mozart, alongside of Bach. His point raises the question whether or not one can imagine having a depth for likes and dislikes in heaven. Certainly, those Barth secondarily wished to meet up with in heaven, such as Augustine, St. Thomas, Luther, Calvin, and Schleiermacher would vary on likes and dislikes.[150] One wonders whether or not the sensibilities of an Ambrose, Augustine, or Barth shaped uniquely by the sounds of their times could tolerate listening to a Metallica or The Fire Theft (which break most, if not all classical rules), rather than their favorite chants, Bach and Mozart. Yet, one can certainly imagine a unity without violently imposing one taste, for one place (just as different forms of popular music become integrated with the shaping of a person's identity).

Some may suppose, however, that a type of transformation, violently imposed or not, must take place for unity to abound. Certainly, heaven is the most ecumenically, unified space we can imagine, but we need not fall into a sort of shallow view of unity that misses the important analogical ways one can conceive of unity in diversity of musical taste. A significance of understanding the neighbor is profoundly challenged by the question of musical taste, but unity of understanding the body does not then entail making every member of the body the same (1 Cor 12). The implication for the ways in which music shapes our lives has a great impact on how we imagine music shaping us in heaven. Perhaps each person's sound-track will vary. It is not a far stretch to suggest that even as our likes and dislikes develop in this world, we can conceive of our tastes developing in the next world in the most glorious ways, including carrying aspects of memory.

CONCLUSION

In this chapter, I argued that specific narratives in contemporary theologies of memory in heaven have overly emphasized the annihilation of memories attached to sin and suffering. Conceding that pain should be addressed in a theology of heaven, it must further stand that suffering should not be the driving force behind how memory functions. Suffering is one interpretive framework, but other narratives are possibly more useful in understanding how memory is important for relationships, such as more positive narratives of goodness and presence of life. Through examples of music as the hermeneutic vehicle for memory in understanding life experiences, I have made connections between memory and popular music for understanding one's own life story and even a nation's story. I have also taken into account the difficulty where differing musical horizons meet in specific contexts

150. Ibid., 161.

such as memorial and funeral services. I suggest that although sentimentality can be weak, it can also be strong and theologically meaningful, as well as useful in keeping memory alive.

Through an interpretive analysis of The Fire Theft's "Heaven," as it is integrated with the popular film *Beastly*, I have argued that such musical and lyrical content can help establish ways of imagining remembrance in heaven where one is not forgotten. To think that heaven is a place where there is no more adventure, no more experience could easily slip into a notion of non-memory.[151] Rather than being remembered for what we deserve, we are remembered by Christ who loves us. In continuing my argument from an earlier chapter, Luke's account in 23:43, as well as the discourse in John 14, describes a journey of forgiveness and memory that is reconciled, not divorced from the person. As McArthur argues in her thesis, "Christ kept his scars, so will we."[152] As much as pain unleashes the desire to forget memories of suffering that shape us, one must not forget transcendence. After showing the many ways that transcendence is related to Christian doctrine, Marsh and Roberts argue:

> Within whatever framework of meaning a music listener may then locate an experience of transcendence, theological and religious frameworks are close at hand. To speak of an experience of transcendence as revelatory, then, can legitimately be interpreted as an experience of God (a deity/divine reality) in whatever form "God" is understood.[153]

Jerry Walls reminds us: "We will remember the story of our sin, our failed relationships, our forgiveness, and our transformation by grace. We will know how we have responded to God's grace and all the ways we were changed by that response. Thereby all of us will know who we are."[154] Theology, music and film encourage us to imagine heaven as a place where we are known, where we are remembered and, as I will argue in the next chapter where we are fulfilled.

---

151. Thiselton, *The Hermeneutics of Doctrine*, 577.
152. McArthur, "Memory in the New Creation," i.
153. Marsh, *Personal Jesus*, 147.
154. Walls, *Heaven*, 112.

6

Fulfillment and Bodily Continuity/Discontinuity

In chapter five, I argued that memories associated with earthly existence are not necessarily obliterated in heaven. I am not suggesting that one's recall of bad memories becomes a necessary evil, where we repeatedly experience pain of memory as the price for being elevated to a heightened, heavenly state. Neither are we gifted with some supernatural suppression enabling us to conceal those memories. Such concealment would foster a condition of entrapment, rather than love, freedom, and joy. But, rather than reducing the joy of heaven, central to my thesis is a heaven entailing memory that is intrinsic to a reunion and reconciliation characterized by exceeding love and joy. Reunion presupposes memory of human relationships that are constructed by our life-choices and the choices of others that impact us. As Brown insightfully observes:

> What matters is not our actual calendar past, but our willingness to reorder that past into a narrative in conformity with the story of Jesus. This will mean demoting events which we now regard as landmarks in our lives, and exalting others which are apparently insignificant. Nor is it a process which will likely to cease with death.[1]

My treatment of heaven is thus firmly addressing human experience, or what Lang broadly terms as the "human side of heaven."[2] Part of my concern is that theology must learn to articulate pastoral questions and reflections

---

1. Brown, *Continental Philosophy and Modern Theology*, 209.
2. Lang, *Meeting in Heaven*, 33.

that arise in culture. This is not, then, an example of theological infiltration by popular culture to promote a heaven full of human pleasure devoid of God. Rather, along with those whom Lang refers to as "prudent authors," I seek to highlight those aspects of human life that are meaningful in relation to the triune God in a heavenly environment. In fact, by approaching doctrine as a response to experience of God, I am seeking precisely to focus on the relational aspects of God and humanity where one is in a better position to account for the pervasive overlap and continuity between earthly and heavenly existence. Even though we cannot know what heaven is like with any certainty, it is important to underline the perspective of how God's presence might "interpenetrate *our* living space, bringing a constant challenge into what otherwise would be a self-enclosed existence."[3] Heavenly life is not necessarily stagnant, nor repetitive, nor a "case of losing oneself in mystic meditation and adoration."[4] Rather, our imagination of heaven should include its characteristic portrayal in popular art as "reunion—emotionally charged reunion."[5]

Chapter five explored the interrelation of music and film envisioning heaven; the first section of this chapter considers the interrelation of film and literature in providing imaginative narratives for the afterlife. Rather than trying to show the continuity of cinematic interpretations with literary works and their contributions to theology (e.g., as in Peter Jackson's recent interpretations of J. R. R. Tolkien's *Hobbit*), this chapter explores the narrative dynamics concerning human endings. As Melanie Wright observes: "religion is (amongst other things) a narrative-producing mechanism, and in this respect can be likened to both literature and the cinema."[6] It is important to acknowledge and explore (especially in recent years), indeed, the vital role of film as "Western culture's major storytelling and myth-producing medium."[7] The second, and principal, section of this chapter analyzes selected popular films working with afterlife themes, I will show where certain films challenge, as well as fall short of particular views of bodily continuity/discontinuity in theological discourse. I seek to enliven the contemporary imagination in regards to constructing a theology of heaven that is based on how Tugwell described a "two-stage rather than a three-stage eschatology. There is this life and the hereafter, not this life, the hereafter and then,

---

3. Fiddes, *The Promised End*, 262.
4. Lang, *Meeting in Heaven*, 33.
5. Ibid.
6. Wright, *Religion and Film*, 4.
7. Johnston, "Reframing the Discussion," 16.

as it were, the thereafter."[8] Such a challenge raises further significant questions, which include, but are not limited to attitudes towards *1) Death and judgment, 2) Resurrection bodies, 3) The value of heavenly perfection,* and *4) Heaven as home.* I will give each point separate space for consideration.

For reasons explored in earlier chapters, contemporary theologians have been overly cautious of talking about heaven as fulfillment and, consequently, add multiple stages to their eschatologies for reasons that range from or combine perceived needs of a unified, resurrected person (unity of body and soul), a faithfulness to the biblical witnesses, as well as ensuring a multiple stage judgment. Tugwell observed: "fairness to the whole tradition is certainly not any better served by simply reversing the bias and stressing the public eschatology at the expense of private eschatology, highlighting the drama of the universal judgment by playing down the decisiveness of the death of individuals."[9] With so many in our global situation being displaced due to natural disasters, war, economic crisis, and persecution, there is arguably an urgent need to re-imagine a home that is neither broken nor spoiled (1 Pet 1:3–9). Peter Kreeft observes that an important reason for the decline of belief in heaven is that "our pictures of heaven simply do not move us; they are not moving pictures. It is this aesthetic failure rather than intellectual or moral failures in our pictures of heaven and of God that threatens faith most potently today."[10]

Undoubtedly, issues surrounding appearance recognition and bodily fulfillment share significant overlap as does my argument that memory in the hereafter is essential for personal identity. Rather than restate my position concerning bodily appearance and humanity's longing for reunion, this chapter seeks to explore further questions of fulfillment or human happiness. T. R. Wright's observation serves our central purpose: "one way of defining the area of overlap between theology and literature [and I would add film] more precisely is to focus on the role of the imagination in both."[11] In this way, I am considering a model of interpretation that is a "reading [or viewing] in progress, not for final interpretation."[12]

---

8. Tugwell, *Human Immortality and the Redemption of Death*, 149. Tom Wright is adamantly against what he calls a "one-stage post-mortem journey" because, for Wright, heaven is just another dimension of our present life," so he adds a further stage by subscribing to "life after, life after death." See Wright, *Surprised by Hope*, 19,148.

9. Ibid., 137.

10. Kreeft, *Everything You Ever Wanted to Know about Heaven*, 19.

11. Wright, *Theology and Literature*, 7.

12. Bennett, *Afterlife and Narrative in Contemporary Fiction*, 39.

THE INTERTEXTUAL/NARRATIVE RELATIONSHIP BETWEEN THEOLOGY, LITERATURE, AND FILM

If music and heaven share a narrative, literature and heaven form an even closer bond in the history of Western thought and culture.[13] Although biblical and theological literacy is according to Jasper, "arguably less than in almost any other period," in other places he offers a more telling report:

> That the study of literature and theology has begun importantly to suggest that our own time is experiencing not so much a dilution of belief as a shift away from traditional theological and ecclesial forms of belief and that literature is (and perhaps always has been) a major expression of religious beliefs and experience that have often been suppressed by the very guardians of theology.[14]

From the Bible throughout the long Western tradition, literature and religion provide integrated accounts of belief and practice. For example, poetry has been a central means of "build[ing] our knowledge of the unknown by comparison with the known."[15] Both Jasper and Detweiler support their claim with the example of Pico della Mirandola who "believ[ed] that the artist as poet is the best theologian and that aesthetics and religion are properly inseparable."[16] At the same time, it is arguably difficult to show how theology and literature, or any of the disciplines placed in relation to theological construction, are indelibly linked. If the overlap can be drawn from understanding the central role of the imagination, which I am convinced is a primary case, then theology must work to understand, "the interplay of all cultural forces," especially in our contemporary context where "it [reli-

---

13. In their introduction, Jasper and Prickett point to William Tyndale's contribution in translation of the Bible, which in turn "gave to English literature a treasury of phrases and language which ensured that it found a central place within the wider canon of poetry and prose. Even as the Bible was set apart as the sacred text, so it became embedded in the broad culture of 'secular' literature." See Prickett, ed., *The Bible and Literature*, 2.

14. See Jasper's article, "The Study of Literature and Theology," 29.

15. Wright, *Theology and Literature*, 11.

16. Detweiler and Jasper, eds., *Religion and Literature*, xiv. Worthy of mention, especially for narrative approaches to theology, such as being undertaken in the current project is Detweiler and Jasper's description: "our approach to literature and religion here might best be described as a hermeneutic or interpretation, which takes up both the forms of aesthetics and the content of knowledge, and holds them in tension, not discarding either too quickly. To know, to see, and to feel the beauty of divinity are to be taken together and can never, finally, be separated. In this tension is played out the telling of the story—that is, *narrative* lies at the center of our task," xiv.

gion] is back not as the totalizing foundation and confirmation of all reality. It is back as warring and wounded sovereignties without sure domains to rule. Literature [visual and aural arts, as well], can and must, speak to this dilemma: the broken God without a home."[17] While the challenge remains, I suggest a greater burden exists for those who wish to reduce the symbolic nature of language found in literature to explanation, rather than treat them as experiential.

Brown has challenged the flattening of analogy and metaphor in literature characterized by "the resultant tendency to think of metaphors as redundant," adding, "while of course some eventually do die, with many there remains [. . .] an inexhaustibility that makes it worth our while to return to them again and again, not only for intellectual stimulation but also as a way into experiencing God."[18] Following Ricoeur, T. R. Wright also argued: "The deeper meaning to which the symbol points remains inexhaustible and ultimately inexpressible. In theology as in literature symbolism involves a rejection of the positivist belief that reality can be dis-covered, laid bare by language. No-one, for example, not even Melville himself, can say precisely what Moby Dick 'stands for.'"[19]

Similarly, as in theology, philosophy has become further awakened to literature's role for mediating truth. For example, in response to a question concerning the role of literature in philosophy, John Caputo comments:

> Philosophy should turn to literature for instruction, not illustration. Philosophers often "use" literature as an "example," to "illustrate" a point that has been independently established by philosophy. That is dabbling with literature. I think philosophy must submit to literature, be humbled by it, and allow itself to be taken by it to a place that left to its own resources it cannot go. That is also how I feel about biblical texts, and what Levinas was saying to the philosophers: here is a voice you have not heard before. Incline your head, hear it well.[20]

---

17. Hass, "The Future of Literature and Theology," 856.

18. Brown, *God & Mystery in Words*, 7. Following Jacques Derrida, Jeffery Russell alludes to the idea of resurrecting metaphors commenting, "Derrida argued that some metaphors that die can come alive again when we enter into the worldview that produces them. Although Christian metaphor and poetics had become stale by the 1960s and so crumbled easily in the 1970s, they only need a revival of the imagination." See Russell, *Paradise Mislaid*, 156.

19. Wright, *Theology and Literature*, 140. For issues surrounding those stressing a reconstructuralist model of reading and those that focus on reception theory see Jauss, *Toward an Aesthetic of Reception*, 140–41.

20. Cole, "Emmet Cole Interviews John D. Caputo" (2005).

A long poetic tradition exists that seeks to move beyond theology or philosophy "dabbling" with literature.[21] Where poets such as, Dante and Milton sought to open up possibilities, doctrinal constructions tend to be more concerned with closure.[22] Fiddes makes the case:

> There are alternative ways of formulating doctrine, even when the theologian is aiming at consistency with past development in the tradition. Creative literature enables theologians to make decisions about the coherence of Christian doctrine, within itself and in connection with the world outside the Christian community.[23]

Fiddes' appeal envisions an approach where "the enclosure of a certain body of material by a community should not result in reading it to the *exclusion* of other texts, but always in reading it in *relation* to others."[24] Far from being a new strategy, examples abound in the early centuries of Christianity where theologians wrestled with the best way to read the pagan poets in relation to the Hebrew and Christian scriptures. For example, although arguably carrying out different approaches, Basil the Great and John Chrysostom argue for reasons why literature is essential for theological education.[25]

Fiddes provides three areas where literature can impact systematic theology: "First, there are artworks which hold traditional Christian images and stories in tension with new images and stories, without any explicit commitment to the religious tradition (I am referring here to what is characteristic of the text, not to what may be supposed about the beliefs or intentions of the author)."[26] Fiddes provides an example of "the image and the stories of the risen Christ . . . brought into conjunction with the story of Ann Cavidge in Murdoch's novel, *Nuns and Soldiers*."[27] A second literary resource are those works that utilize tradition and engage doctrine with new stories and images, with a clear intention to struggle with a tradition's doctrine. Here, Fiddes gives the instance of "the eighth-century Anglo-Saxon poem usually

---

21. See Markos, *Heaven and Hell*.
22. Fiddes, "Concept, Image and Story in Systematic Theology," 9.
23. Ibid., 17.
24. Ibid., 16.
25. Stenger set Chrysostom's *On Vainglory* in conversation with Basil's *Address to the Young* in Stenger, "Athens and/or Jerusalem?" (2013). Where Chrysostom was more negative towards the pagan poets, Basil was much more open to a synthesis according to Stenger.
26. Fiddes, "Concept, Image and Story in Systematic Theology," 13.
27. Ibid., 13–14.

titled "Dream of the Rood."[28] Finally, there remain texts completely outside a tradition that do not "explicitly enter into dialogue with Christian images, but where image and story indicate a transcendence towards mystery and the 'infinitely other' which can be correlated with Christian symbols."[29] He argues that such images can be found in the novels of Virginia Woolf, more particularly, *Mrs. Dalloway*.[30]

Fiddes' third resource is most relevant to my examples in this chapter, but my examples also connect with the first two areas of Fiddes' taxonomy. As Abraham Kuyper highlights, and as I emphasized in the first part of this book, there is arguably not place in all creation untouched by the Holy Spirit, so it is not farfetched to suggest that artistic articulations of doctrine will find traces in all three areas.[31] Fiddes' third point is of special interest because it points to the Spirit's work in all creation. As accounted for in his biography, Hollenweger's pneumatological approach, "from life to theology" included alternative ways of articulating doctrine; in particular for Hollenweger, narrative exegesis as "using narrative forms for theologizing.[32] His warrant was, as we have seen, the model of Scripture."[33] For Hollenweger, the theological task is unending, where "we are offered no conceptual closures."[34] Recent commentators of ancient texts have derived similar connections by observing changing attitudes within the literary traditions.

Although his interests are more poetic than theological, Louis Markos finds within the Western poetic tradition texts that express (beyond knowledge, order, and justice) "things we most desperately want to be assured of: 1) that we will see our dead family and friends again; 2) that love is eternal and community everlasting; 3) that nothing is finally lost, for all will be redeemed."[35] In humanity's search for home and wholeness, Markos draws attention to humanity's fear of the living or the "undead":

> In one sense, the ubiquitous human fear of ghosts is ridiculous, for how can a mere ghost, a diaphanous shade do us any harm? But then, it is not the fear of physical harm that gives us the

28. Ibid., 14–15.

29. Ibid., 15.

30. Ibid.

31. See Kuyper's fifth lecture in, *Lectures on Calvinism*. Kuyper argued, "the world of sounds, the world of forms, the world of tints, and the world of poetic ideas, can have no other source than God and it is our privilege as bearers of His image, to have a perception of this beautiful world, artistically to reproduce, and humanly to enjoy it" (118).

32. Price, *Theology Out of Place*, 151.

33. Ibid., 79.

34. Ibid., 150–51.

35. Markos, *Heaven and Hell*, 16.

gooseflesh and makes our hair stand on end. We fear, rather, the prospect of a soul cut off from its body, a mode of existence that lies outside our experience but which we can nevertheless conceive. The psychiatrists tell us that no human being can imagine his own death: that is to say, we cannot imagine the extinction or annihilation of our personhood. Every part of our being tells us that we—the inner we, the real we—will persist. The fear of ghosts, I believe, comes from the fear that our soul will be trapped in between this world and the next, forced to wander homeless and displaced.[36]

"Fear" of remaining in a state of non-resolution can be witnessed in a second Markos observation: "the monsters that haunt the nightmares of every nation and tribe are trapped in a living death, animated corpses that can find neither hope nor rest in this world or the next."[37] By beginning with Homer's *Odyssey*, Markos illustrates how the Greeks finally arrive at a human afterlife in "the Elysian Fields (or Elysium or the Blessed Groves)."[38] Markos adds, "though this description [referring to Elysium] sounds a bit like Homer's Olympus, Elysium is finally a human place; the ideal of man and God dwelling together that is hinted at in the Old Testament is not part of the ancient Greek soul."[39]

Christian eschatologies that are more earth-bound (whether emphasizing Jewish concepts or not) continue to relegate God's realm to heaven and humanity's place on earth and, though most would emphasize the broken veil between heaven and earth, the separation still remains. As McDannell and Lang have observed, attitudes towards heaven as a human place is outside the mainstream of systematic theology.[40] Millennial discussions, rapture theologies, new earths, and mapping the end-times seem to dominate the discussions regarding last things. The area of theology and aesthetics, especially phenomenological analyses which pay more attention to how people experience life and how they construct meaning, must be given more importance if one is to move towards Hollenweger's, "life to theology" rather than "from theology to life."[41] Interestingly, McDannell and Lang compare the fate of heaven in contemporary theology to the fate of the Greek gods described in Markos' work. Referencing the poetry of Schiller,

36. Ibid., 4.
37. Ibid., 16.
38. Ibid., 14.
39. Ibid.
40. Lang, *Heaven*, 351.
41. Price, *Theology out of Place*, 125.

heaven in contemporary theology is arguably comparable to the fate of the Greek gods of Olympus, now only shades.[42]

While Markos aptly shows the extent to which the poetic literary tradition has served to enliven the imaginations of successive generations, new forms of media have taken this literary tradition and produced films to once again consider epic questions of humanity in popular culture, including one's journey from displacement to home.[43] Not to overlook the uneasy relationship between literary and cinematic forms of theology, literature has always provided film creators with opportunities to imaginatively explore the areas in-between. Although critique from the literary direction acknowledges this type of innovation in film production, it is not always kind and gentle in reply.[44] The relationship between narrative and film has been reevaluated in recent years by those writing in the field:

> It is not the story per se but the reduction of film interpretation to literary techniques that is the problem. After all, the vast majority of commercial film is narrative in structure, rooted in storytelling. But how that story is to be understood needs redefinition and expansion in many of the present descriptions of movies by theology and film critics. For movies are both "pictured" and "heard," not just described. Thus, there needs to be an expansion of method to include the visual and the aural, if theology and film is to escape its literary captivity.[45]

One way forward is to observe the ways in which films take up literary devices, yet move beyond the words to image (thus, not leaving language completely behind, but moving words to an aural/visual dimension), as suggested.[46] Of course, this is not suggestive of forgetting the importance of reading the classic texts in relation to images. Both literature and film must seek to provide a way into the question: "why do we demand some kind

---

42. Lang, *Heaven*, 351.

43. Markos observes: "Homer's aesthetic decision to send his epic hero to Hades established a convention that all future epic writers (from Virgil to Dante to Milton to Tolkien) would feel obliged to imitate? The convention came to be known as the *nekuia* (*nekros* in Greek means corpse), a word used to refer both to the descent itself and to the questioning of the dead souls by the hero. Though Virgil, Dante, and Milton all had their own theological philosophical reasons for including a *nekuia* in their epic, they also felt a strong aesthetic need to fulfill the epic convention laid down by Homer. Indeed, after the *Odyssey*, no hero can truly qualify as an *epic* hero without enduring the awe and terror of the land of the dead." Ibid., 17.

44. Jasper, "On Systematizing the Unsystematic," 244.

45. Johnston, "Reframing the Discussion," 19.

46. Theodorakopoulos, *Ancient Rome at the Cinema*, 121.

of ending to a story, and why does an end seem more difficult to achieve today than before?"[47] This is no less true in theology. For Fiddes, a "balance between openness and closure is, fundamental to a truly religious view of the end of all things."[48] He argues: "there has to be a certainty about the overcoming of evil and the triumph of God's purposes, but the freedom of God and the freedom of human beings to contribute to God's project in creation also demands an openness in the future."[49]

In making the distinction between "afterlife and apocalypse," Alice Bennett points to the work of Frank Kermode who considered "immanent endings" or "personal last things" as only a mere "diluted modern microdrama" of the larger issue of apocalypse.[50] Bennett observes how "Kermode finds that it is the apocalyptic model of imagined but deferred endings that gives meaning to the present, and allows for ways of thinking about time that turn it from a simple succession into a patterned and meaningful shape."[51] Bennett, on the other hand, is mostly interested in the afterlife's place within Kermode's "apocalyptic model."[52] She suggests:

> Making sense is something which is much more a part of death and the afterlife than of apocalypse, perhaps precisely because of the afterlife's supplementary quality. The "after" of apocalypse is totally different and separate from what has gone before: it is the end of time and the end of everything. An afterlife beyond death provides a provisional kind of closure, with a life that continues after the end. Taking a model of fiction from this leaves a sense of an ending which retains the revelatory qualities of apocalypse, but without its total annihilatory potential: an afterlife is partial and supplementary, making sense of an ending but undermining any claims to finality or unproblematic closure. If another life can be added to an apparently completed existence, why shouldn't endings multiply indefinitely.[53]

The difficulty for the apocalyptic model, as described by Bennett, is not only found within literature, but also within film (chapter seven more explicitly comments on the challenges films face in attempting to provide narratives of post-apocalypse). As human experience testifies, "microdramas" are

47. Fiddes, *The Promised End*, 5.
48. Ibid., 23.
49. Ibid.
50. Bennett, *Afterlife and Narrative in Contemporary Fiction*, 31.
51. Ibid., 23.
52. Ibid.
53. Ibid.

performed daily, once and for all in the lives of those we love, which in turn represents a hermeneutical challenge to navigate the finality of death, while also affirming the hope of resurrection.[54]

A Christological perspective, indeed, places all hope of the resurrection in the post-resurrected/ascended Jesus, who carries immediate implications for how humans imagine bodily and relational continuity/discontinuity in heaven. As I have argued in chapter four, heaven must be interpreted in relation to bodies and relationships. Death has been destroyed (1 Tim 1:10), which means that the finality of death (not just in a post-*eschaton* sense) resists postponing the hope of resurrection into a later future. By describing literature's role in providing the imagination with the narrative devices for theological development, I now turn towards a specific example of film's use of narrative, which is an example of the visual/aural aspect of narrative. In what follows, I will argue that films that take individual death and judgment more seriously can challenge contemporary theologies of postponement by focusing on what happens immediately after death.

HEAVENLY CONTINUITY/DISCONTINUITY IN THEOLOGY AND POPULAR CULTURE

Ridley Scott's film *Gladiator* (2000) opens with a dramatic scene featuring Maximus (played by actor Russell Crowe), the highly decorated Roman general, giving his soldiers one last devotional talk before entering the battle. Set in a wood in late second-century *Germania*, Maximus implores his soldiers to use their imaginations, to consider this coherent, war ridden world yet, "overlaid with otherness":[55]

> Three weeks from now, I will be harvesting my crops. Imagine where you will be, and it will be so. Hold the line! Stay with me! If you find yourself alone, riding in green fields with the sun on your face, do not be troubled. For you are in Elysium, and you're already dead. Brothers, what we do in life (pause) echoes in eternity.[56]

Death and afterlife themes follow throughout the film. Arguably an example from pagan literature (Elysium) is far from the Christian conception of heaven. In referring to the historical context, Elena Theodorakopoulos observes that "the anticipation of Christianity" in relation to Rome is

---

54. Ibid., 31.
55. Bauckham and Hart, *Hope against Hope*, 88.
56. *Gladiator,* DVD (2000).

"avoided" in the film and although she places the character Maximus within the common practices of ancestral worship, she acknowledges:

> One cannot help but suspect that his prayers are also intended to introduce a very modern kind of spirituality, more private than institutional, at the core of which is a notion of the stable family unit. In this way, Maximus is distanced from the more alien world of pagan Rome and its rituals and brought closer to the modern world.[57]

I would argue, furthermore, that there are a number of observations concerning the Christian tradition in the film that encourage us to think about heaven as fulfillment.

Adam Barkman has recently drawn attention to Scott's film, particularly in looking at gender survival and relationships. Barkman observes:

> Using the Christian language he was raised with, though correctly recognizing an enormous overlap between Roman polytheism and Christian monotheism, Scott says that "Heaven" (In the film, "Elysium") is the "central spiritual backbone to the movie." What is satisfying for many here is the curious but ancient idea that we, as gendered beings, endure in the next life, and moreover, that many of our relationships (including some of our marriages) might also subsequently endure.[58]

The "enormous overlap" that Barkman highlights is evident in an early scene where Maximus is praying before his impending execution.[59] He prays, "blessed Father (one immediately observes the monotheistic reference or at minimum a paternal reference), watch over my wife and son. Whisper to them that I live only to hold them again."[60] Barkman argues that a Christian philosophy is the most promising way to interpret the film:

> True Jesus said, "When the dead rise, they will neither marry nor be given in marriage: they will be like the angels," but what of this? Why think Jesus supposes angels and spirits in general—to be *genderless* or marriages unable to *continue*? Since Roman polytheism is no longer practiced, and since Scott clearly invokes Christianity in his commentary on the movie, Christian philosophy seems to be the best basis from which to

---

57. Theodorakopoulos, *Ancient Rome at the Cinema*, 98–99; 105.

58. Barkman, "*Gladiator*, Gender, and Marriage in Heaven," 275. Barkman cites "Documentary," *Gladiator*.

59. Ibid.

60. Scott, *Gladiator*.

explore the director's vision of gender and marriage in Heaven. Just as Scott's ethereal vision sends the imagination far above the film, so will a careful Christian understanding of the relations between spirit and gender, body and sex, and masculinity and femininity take us far from the particulars of the film. Such flight will ultimately have the concrete purpose of convincing readers that Maximus was right when he tells Juba, "My wife and son are waiting for me."[61]

Although Barkman's comments serve to highlight the importance of the longing for reunion, he needs to acknowledge the radical nature of Jesus' words in Matthew 22:30 to include matters of discontinuity. Practical theology must still address the question of multiple earthly marriages stemming from divorce or death of partners, and the implications for understanding what Jesus means by this radical discontinuity between earthly and heavenly existence. Nevertheless, Barkman is correct to allow for more considerations. Where I want to affirm degrees of bodily and relational continuity, I am also aware that discontinuity is an important factor. In our finitude, and in our shared memories, we can imagine a heaven where broken relationships are reconciled or reunited. If earthly marriages are transformed into deeper friendships, where sexuality and production is no longer the focus, one can imagine the type of discontinuity Jesus envisioned. The intention is not to aim at a negative view of sexuality, nor to minimize the role that sexual desire plays in marriage, but to consider, then, possibilities for discontinuity.

The movement of the film's main character, Maximus, follows from the General's international conquests and victories for Rome, to enslavement by Caesar's son, Commodus (played by actor Joaquin Phoenix). Commodus assassinates his father Marcus Aurelius (played by Richard Harris), claiming his right to rule. Out of fear of his influence as a beloved general and loyal servant to Aurelius, Commodus orders Maximus' arrest. Commodus then orders the soldiers to execute Maximus but his command is not fulfilled, as Maximus skillfully escapes. Through a long and difficult journey, Maximus makes his way home to Spain where he last held his wife and child. A horrific scene ensues upon arrival home (the gut wrenching discovery of his murdered wife and son). This too was carried out under the command of Commodus. Wounded and exhausted from his escape, Maximus lies in the soil of his family's graves on the hillside of what was once a beautiful scene, now a charcoaled past consumed by earthly flame. Upon awaking, Maximus discovers he is now under the control of slave traders. He, along

---

61. Barkman, "*Gladiator,* Gender, and Marriage in Heaven," 276.

with several others, is subsequently purchased by Proximo (played by actor Oliver Reed) in a Roman Province known as Zucchabar. Proximo (once a slave and gladiator himself) is on a quest to revive the gladiator games. He won his freedom by becoming the greatest gladiator and now spends his time buying and trading slaves for the sake of sport and financial gain. Not until later does Proximo discover the renown of his gladiator, Maximus.

Throughout the film, Maximus is characterized not only as a fearless warrior, but as one carrying a burden and longing to rejoin his family in the afterlife. Although sorrowful for how they perished, he still believes that he will be reunited with them. A prayerful and pious man, he firmly believes in a human post-mortem existence where there is continuity between longing for reunion, memory and bodily continuity. The challenge for the theologian is to discern where degrees of continuity leave room for discontinuity. Scott's film provides a good example for exploring such questions of continuity/discontinuity, which naturally leads to further theological considerations.

Eschatology as Death or Judgment?

One of the important points of convergence for literature and film is found in the challenge to either open or close narrative endings. This is no less true in theology. For example, the quandary for Christian theology is always where the emphasis should rest in one's eschatology. Does one emphasize the finality of death or death followed by a waiting period prior to a later judgment, or both/and, rather than, either/or? Likewise, does one place the focus on personal judgment over against a general public judgment at a postponed date? Bennett has recently drawn attention to the oldness of such ambiguities:

> The four last things of death, judgment, heaven and hell . . . has been disturbed from its origins, as the addition of heaven, hell and judgment to death ought to undermine the finality and significance of death. How can it be a last thing if there is so much after it? Similarly, the fraught temporal gap between death and judgment—the judgment that occurs immediately post-mortem and at the end of all time—marks off different theological positions and, again, adds more time after these "last things".[62]

Arguably, Scott's *Gladiator* portrays an afterlife where death is final. Maximus dies in the arena and what comes next is the actualization of the

---

62. Bennett, *Afterlife and Narrative in Contemporary Fiction*, 3–4.

hope that sustained his earthly journey, a new life. Such a view disrupts and challenges much of contemporary theology's stress on a later judgment and later death and/or resurrection. Tugwell aptly shows the historical developments surrounding these debates and they are no less important in contemporary thought. For example, just as Pope John XXII in the fourteenth century wanted to lay stress on a general judgment to encourage a shift towards a bodily resurrection at the *eschaton*, he left entry into the presence of God until after the final judgment.[63] Similarly, Wright and others have captivated much of academic theology and church leadership in recent times by shifting the focus away from heaven and towards a general, earthly resurrection at the end of time. Tugwell argues that it was not that John XXII was wrong in drawing attention to the inconsistency in the Latin's church's acceptance of a final, public judgment while still trying to maintain an immediate residence of blessedness.[64] His problem laid in his focus on a postponed resurrection without much hope for the intermediate state.[65] According to Tugwell, the Avignon Pope paid too little attention to the way in which the "tradition had developed in the intervening centuries."[66] Tugwell argues that Bernard of Clairvaux, who followed Ambrose (both were "main sources" for John XXII), "could be read as teaching, not that the saints are deprived of beatitude until the judgment, but that there is either a progress in beatitude until the judgment or at least that there is an increase in beatitude at the judgment."[67]

Wright's position seems to face a similar dilemma to John XXII, by postponing hope into another future stage. Although he is determined to talk about the finality of death in one sense, he seems to deny even the slightest difficulty in a delayed hope as the most accurate interpretation of scripture.[68] Wright is correct in his assertion that within "the central New Testament belief: at last, death will be not simply redefined but defeated."[69] He wants to allow "that all the Christian departed are in substantially the same state, that of restful happiness," but while the corpse is dead, the "real person—however we want to describe him or her—continues."[70] I argued in chapter two, Wright still seems to be left with some type of dualism.

---

63. Tugwell, *Human Immortality and the Redemption of Death*, 137, 141.
64. Ibid., 141.
65. Ibid., 137.
66. Ibid., 141.
67. Ibid., 142.
68. Wright, *Surprised by Hope*, 15.
69. Ibid.
70. Ibid., 171.

Geddes MacGregor observed that "belief in the resurrection of the dead is not incompatible with the concept of the immortality of the soul that Plato expounds, but the latter doctrine is not what Paul teaches."[71] Geddes goes on to argue:

> What is proclaimed in the New Testament and the Christian creeds and celebrated in Christian worship is not any particular form of "rising from the dead" but, rather, the conquest of death. Death has "lost its sting," having been conquered by the power of Christ. The Risen Christ has indeed a body: one far more powerful than the one made of flesh and bone that had been his embodiment during his life on earth.[72] This body is what Paul describes as *pneumatikos*, a "glorious" or "spiritual" body [1 Cor 15:39–53].[73]

Juxtaposed to the view that death is a mere entry into a waiting place where one is still hoping for a distant resurrection is the position tied to Scott's depiction of death as a final judgment. Although Scott does not portray a negative side of judgment, the viewer is left with Commodus' story ending in the arena where hope does not arise. Admittedly, the variations between these positions are numerous and serve to point out that any attempt to lock down a final interpretation is wisely avoided. Part of the problem for many, including Aquinas and Lombard before him, is to understand how death can be defeated as Paul declares and judgment still remain a distant future occurrence.[74] Although "death cannot be finally escaped," it seems for some, death can remain open ended for a later event.[75]

Although I will return to the issue concerning resurrection bodies, it is important to highlight at this stage the question of delayed hope. It is not farfetched to imagine what happens when theology continues to delay hope. Even more popular forms of American evangelicalism expressed in periodicals like *Christianity Today* find an important disjunction between minimizing heaven and elevating universal resurrection. Consider Mark Galli's cover article comments: "in general, when life-after-the afterlife folks talk about this future state, the language gets global and the vision abstract. There is a lot of talk about how 'justice will reign,' and 'evil will be defeated.' There are sweeping statements about 'the culmination of history' and 'the

---

71. MacGregor, *Images of Afterlife*, 154.
72. Ibid., 156.
73. Ibid., 155.
74. Ibid., 164.
75. Fiddes, *The Promised End*, 67.

coming reign of God' and 'the renewal of the whole earth.'"[76] Even in light of all the truth that he finds in such statements, Galli draws attention to the blatant disconnect that "life-after-the-afterlife" talk elicits:

> It doesn't always connect with the widow whose husband was struck by a fatal heart attack. It doesn't always speak to the 10-year-old whose mother just died of cancer. It doesn't necessarily help those who wrestle with a question that troubles millions: "What happens when I die?" Some of us (usually the highly educated among us) may be most interested in life after the afterlife, but most people in the pews are deeply concerned simply with the afterlife—the one that comes right after this one. Their highest existential priority is not that justice will reign in all the earth, but to hear some good news about "what will happen to me next."[77]

Galli's point also raises a question concerning whether or not the theological imprecision of an "uneducated" church may discover the richness of life in the Spirit not considered by more elitist perspectives. Jesus seemed to stress this point in emphasizing the relationship between his kingdom and children (Luke 18:15–17), not to mention examples within early Christianity such as the visions preceding the martyrdom of Perpetua and Felicity.[78]

Within the numerous configurations within Christian eschatology, most will agree upon MacGregor's observation: "that death is what must be expected to issue from our sinful nature; nevertheless God has given us, as pure gift, through the resurrection of Christ, the capacity to be resurrected with him (Romans 6.20–23)."[79] MacGregor also reemphasizes, "resurrection of the person is a consequence of the resurrection of Christ rather than a condition of the human soul."[80] Therefore, we can be clear that "there is no doubt at all that resurrection is at the very heart of the Christian hope."[81] In light of such consensus, the centrality of the resurrection "gave rise to intolerable problems . . . about what happens to the individual between death and resurrection."[82] He adds:

> Did the dead sleep to be awakened by the Last Trumpet, as was generally supposed in the first century C.E.? Such a notion

---

76. Galli, "Incredible Journeys," 30.
77. Ibid.
78. Zaleski, ed., *The Book of Heaven*, 116–18.
79. Ibid., 154.
80. Ibid., 159.
81. Ibid., 123.
82. Ibid., 165.

would seem highly plausible when the Last Day was so imminently expected; when it seemed indefinitely postponed, difficulties proliferated. Was there a particular judgment for each individual at death and a temporary resurrection body to serve till the Last Day, whenever that might be, when it would be exchanged for the permanent resurrected body?[83]

Again, Scott's character Maximus is an example of popular art that leans into the problem of postponement theory by allowing bodily existence to rise immediately upon death. This is not to imply that all doctrinal questions are resolved but, rather, to draw attention to a tradition that is clearly found within the long Christian tradition. My principal concern here is, then, to see how popular culture breaks in and reopens the theological question, which addresses humanity's first concern, the hereafter or the "immediate impact for Christ's resurrection" that was so prominent among martyrs in the early church.[84] Reopening a question, apparently closed in theological discussion by postponement theorists, also reopens the question concerning resurrection bodies: If humanity, by the grace of God, is gifted this *pneumatikos* of which Paul describes (1 Cor 15:44), what kind of body are we talking about since "we find ourselves in possession of corpses?"[85]

Heaven and Resurrection Bodies

Scott's depiction does not eliminate the question of the human corpse, and neither does Maximus transition into the hereafter without a body. In chapter four, I established the view following the work of H. H. Price that a recognizable *re-embodiment* (i.e., not the same physical body) in post-mortem is philosophically viable and also carries the warrant of scripture, most importantly giving accounts of the resurrected and ascended body of Jesus. As Pannenberg concedes, "it is incontestable that this view finds support in the NT."[86] Still, some may argue concerning Jesus' resurrection and ascension that unlike our common situation, his corpse was raised with him and the tomb is empty (Luke 24:3). Admittedly, at first glance this seems to serve into the interpretation that human resurrection should come much later, since (as the logic implies) a person is not fulfilled in a state of disembodiment. Paul seems to add weight to a future general resurrection in 1 Corinthians 15:50–58, although this should not overshadow

---

83. Ibid.
84. Brown, *Discipleship & Imagination*, 112.
85. Tugwell, *Human Immortality and the Redemption of Death*, 165.
86. Pannenberg, *Systematic Theology*, vol. 3, 578.

Paul's statements in Philippians 1:23–26, as well as in Colossians 3:1–4 and 1 Thessalonians 5:10, not to mention 2 Corinthians 5:8.[87] As Pannenberg makes explicitly clear:

> Already in 1336 [following John XXII] the decision of Benedict XII had opened a door for the concept of full participation in salvation for individuals immediately at death by stating that the soul of those perfected in faith, inasmuch as they are not in need of purgatory, attain to the beatific vision of God directly after death (DS 1000).[88]

Corpses remind us that we are not alone in our stories, but they do not prevent us from imagining a life of participation that is far greater than the present situation.[89] The uniqueness of Christ's resurrection to inaugurate a new experience of his presence should not be underestimated; neither should it detract from Christ's humanity in the resurrection.[90]

In *Gladiator*, the viewer is left with the reality of Maximus' corpse in the arena, while at the same time presented with Maximus' movement through the door into the afterlife. The viewer is relieved of any interpretive doubt between the continuity of Maximus' earthly personhood and heavenly existence. Of course, the film's special effects used to create the sense of transition help make this movement from death to heavenly life conceivable, but achieving clarity to satisfy such visual developments within the narrative must still account for the corpse. The perspective Wright represents seems to leave a person with a type of dualism where the "real person" is alive, but waiting for the realization that the body is "no longer left behind."[91] Jerry Walls argues that it is difficult to think about a surviving person without holding to some type of dualism, but as I have argued, it is possible to imagine a different type of body, such as Jesus' post-resurrected body.[92] Tugwell suggests that "the essential tradition is a two-stage doctrine . . . ," but it is important to note his (Tugwell's) cinematic visual analogy to understanding the hereafter. He asserts that the hereafter requires of us a "sort of split-screen, just as the Homeric eschatology did. Homer's dead heroes are both in Hades and lying on the battlefield and the Christian eschatology similarly

---

87. Ibid.
88. Ibid., 577.
89. Tugwell, *Human Immortality and the Redemption of Death*, 165.
90. Brown, *Discipleship & Imagination*, 111.
91. Tugwell, *Human Immortality and the Redemption of Death*, 165.
92. Walls, *Heaven: The Logic of Eternal Joy*, 99.

supports the propriety of saying both that the dead are in heaven and that they are in their tombs."[93]

Tugwell does not stop here, however, but further takes into account the perspectives of those in heaven. For much of contemporary theology, the afterlife perspective is of little use for earthly consideration. On the other hand, from the perspective of contemporary fiction (and film for that matter), as Bennett so aptly examines, imagining meaning-making from the point of the afterlife is one way to explore how time lapses function differently according to perspective without relying too heavily on an eternity with bodies that no longer have time or purpose.[94] As Tugwell observes, Aquinas worked with the concept of "*aevum*, which allows for successiveness but is not measured by the movement of the heavenly bodies. The bodies of the resurrected saints, on this basis, could be allowed to move in their own kind of time, even while the soul was, in itself, beyond time."[95] As Tugwell noted, "it is hard to imagine bodies existing timelessly."[96] Tugwell provides the example of Aquinas who posited a future resurrection, which was necessary from our point of view, but not from the perspective of those in heaven.[97] Tugwell explains:

> From our point of view, the life of the saints is hidden in God. What we have is, so to speak, what they have left behind in time, their bones and their influence and so on. In that sense they are still part of *our* story, part of the temporal story of the world. According to St. Thomas it is from this point of view that the dead are judged at the last judgment. As far as they [the blessed dead] are concerned, their story came to its conclusion and was judged at the time of their death.[98]

One could ask whether this is an adequate solution or not? If the resurrection holds significance for the whole of our humanity, then, sharing time is not necessarily problematic. Admittedly, the question of time certainly raises questions of bodily finitude and infinitude. Although human finitude and God's infinitude have at points in modern history tended to unite Creator and humanity in post-mortem without leaving any distinction between the two, Scott's film displays a clarity concerning how human beings remain

---

93. Tugwell, *Human Immortality and the Redemption of Death*, 164–65.
94. Bennett, *Afterlife and Narrative in Contemporary Fiction*, 32.
95. Tugwell, *Human Immortality and the Redemption of Death*, 167.
96. Ibid.
97. Ibid., 165.
98. Ibid.

distinct from God by presenting a very human Maximus in a resurrected body.

Having discussed human finitude in chapter one, it is pertinent to note how Pannenberg stressed the need to "distinguish between finitude and mortality."[99] He later adds, "if we know our finitude only as we know that death is ahead of us, this is because we live our lives independently of God in the way that characterizes human sin," which connects for Pannenberg, earlier understandings of participation in how one can describe the church's rejection of Monophysitism and chose to confess "that even the risen Christ, too, remained a man, and therefore a finite being distinct from God, even though he will never die again."[100] It follows, for Pannenberg, that believers will also share in this hope.[101] Pannenberg is drawing from the argument over the comparison between our bodies and Christ's body in early controversies surrounding questions of the Trinity, between the Monophysite movement and those representative of Chalcedon (the Fourth Ecumenical Council in 451 AD). The supporters of Chalcedon claimed that Christ has two natures, both human and divine in one nature. Eutchyes and the Monophysites argued that Christ's body was not the same in that he was both divine and human in one nature.[102] To Pannenberg's point, the church was correct in rejecting Monophysitism, which in turn allowed for the sameness between Christ's body and our bodies. Upon further consideration, not only does the subject of resurrected bodies raise questions of unity of person, but also as mentioned above, questions of bodily movement and perfection come into play.

Heavenly Perfection Re-Imagined

Virtuous perfection, as depicted in Scott's film constitutes a type of inspired courage to continue on one's journey. The movement in the film follows from Maximus' sacrifice in service of Rome, to faithfulness towards family, to the descent into slavery, to the sacrifice of plotting against injustice, to the final act of heroism in death. Although the metaphor weakens, Maximus' stamp of courage and vocational valor is illustrated as he continues on to the next world wearing his gladiator armor. Juxtaposed to the understanding of an intermediate waiting period that lacks mobility and participation in the fullness of God's creation, Scott's portrayal makes room for a body

---

99. Pannenberg, *Systematic Theology*, 560.
100. Ibid.
101. Ibid.
102. Pelikan, *The Emergence of the Catholic Tradition (100–600)*, vol. 1, 270–71.

that enters into the afterlife with a sense of purpose and participation. This aspect of heavenly perfection has a long trail within the Christian tradition. As Lang observes in considering the more anthropocentric heaven, "movement, progress, and productive work" are all important "despite its lack of sin, estrangement, disappointment, war, and death."[103] Included among Lang's examples is the American philosophical theologian Jonathan Edwards as one who advocated "eternal progress in all these things."[104] Lang quoting from Edwards' *Miscellanies*, "we shall forever increase in beauty ourselves; where we shall be made capable of finding out and giving, and shall receive, more and more endearing expressions of love forever: our union will become more close, and communion more intimate."[105] Edwards' view of God as "beauty itself" is observed in Sherry's work:

> For Edwards, God's beauty or "lovely majesty" is pre-eminent among his attributes: God is beautiful, indeed beauty itself, and the source and foundation of all beauty in the world. He says that the Father created the world with his Son (he cites John 1.3, Col. 1.16, and Heb. 1.10 on this point), and that the Holy Spirit, being the harmony, excellence, and beauty of the deity, has the particular function of communicating beauty and harmony in the world.[106]

According to Sherry, Edwards "describes the spiritual beauty of Christ's human nature in terms of his many virtues and his holiness, and says that it is the image and reflection of the beauty of his divine nature."[107] In this context, we can understand Lang's use of Edwards to allow for movement, progression, and activity in heaven.

As I argued in chapter five, memories of suffering are not the same as living in a sin riddled eternity, but this line of thought naturally leads to questions of fulfillment in heaven. How can one be truly fulfilled if perfection as we imagine it is simply an overestimated venture into a timeless, fixed state of leisure? Maximus is portrayed returning to his farm where he will once again perform work. For some, the thought of work in heaven is profoundly distorted. Imagining heaven with too many high expectations would be for some a reality full of anxiety and unrest—an extended Weberian narrative of labor efforts among ascetic Protestants.[108] On the

103. Ibid.
104. Ibid., 20.
105. Ibid.
106. Sherry, *Spirit and Beauty*, 12.
107. Ibid., 73.
108. Weber, *The Sociology of Religion*, 182–83.

other hand, Lang documents some European theologians such as Hans Urs von Balthasar, Ladislaus Boros, and Jürgen Moltmann who, from Lang's perspective, "discovered that everlasting progress was rooted in tradition, philosophically defensible, and humanly attractive."[109] In his dissertation, MacEwan asks the following questions:

> What are we to make of a creation which has been granted the freedom to glorify God, for example in conscious decision, through the living of life, moral action, art, prayer and praise, yet which glorifies God in the consummation by being known and loved by God? Why should we not think that God would be glorified by creaturely action beyond death as much as before it?[110]

Fulfillment is that area of human longing where hope waits to burst forth upon an existence lacking nothing in terms of one's wellbeing, while at the same time leaving room for growth. What about rest? One does not need to contradict Augustine's view of the Sabbath rest where God is at "rest in us" compared to his "work in us."[111] Even as God rests, he "never cease[s] to do good" and even as we experience "the great holiness," his presence is "forever at rest" in his unique relationship with humanity.[112] Granted, Augustine did not have to place work and rest into time and timelessness. For Thiselton, a "*somatic* existence" includes, "bodiliness, purpose, narrative, and temporality."[113] Following Pannenberg and Moltmann, Thiselton suggests: "A timeless existence would be a *reduced* mode of existence, devoid of all adventure, of new purposes, of memory and hope, of anticipation, development, excitement, and surprises." He adds, "Can this be what the *living* God has prepared for his people and for his creation, which is '*raised in power, raised in glory*' (1 Cor. 15:44)?"[114]

"Heavenly" perfection is a term highly charged with theological implications. Interlinked with ideas of sanctification, glorification and deification, theories of perfection have attempted to elevate the work of the Spirit in humanity which describes a completed goal or *telos*. Perfection does not necessarily entail, then, an extreme polarization or "opposition" between eternity and time, as much of twentieth-century Protestant theology

---

109. Lang, *Meeting in Heaven*, 21.
110. MacEwan, "Missing Persons," 262–63.
111. Augustine, *Confessions*, 346.
112. Ibid., 346–47.
113. Thiselton, *The Hermeneutics of Doctrine*, 577.
114. Ibid.

envisioned.[115] The term "fulfillment" embodies a wider breadth of purpose and tradition, as well as how artists have been able to explore the narrative of heaven. Neither does the idea of fulfillment reduce notions of movement and progress. For example, Gregory of Nyssa gleaned from the writings of the Apostle Paul (Phil 3:13) in matters of virtue, "its one limit of perfection is the fact that it has no limit."[116] Gregory deduced, "certainly whoever pursues true virtue participates in nothing other than God, because he is himself absolute nature. Since, then, those who know what is good by nature desire participation in it, and since this good has no limit, the participant's desire itself necessarily has no stopping place, but stretches out with the limitless."[117]

Gregory's point is important for considering how relational development in heaven can be achieved in differing degrees, but still within the realm of perfection. Contrary to the notion that all change is negative, one can certainly imagine new relational depths through understanding the capacities of those relationships shaping us, as well as experiencing new relationships in heaven. For example, it is not difficult for a husband to imagine growing in mutual participation with his wife and children. It seems implausible that we can relate to everyone to the same degree, but in different ways. This in no way limits perfection. God is not limited, in that he can relate to everyone, but humanity can only relate in our finitude and this perspective allows us to imagine development in heaven. Although Scott's film points us in the direction of further consideration of heavenly progress and mobility, noticeable weaknesses arise, which require discernment of the critic in how far one can venture down this interpretative path.

For example, arguably a part of Scott's limitation is in presenting a visual depiction of the afterlife that looks more like a historical flashback than a glorious present or future. *Gladiator* does depict a way in which

---

115. MacEwan observes this extreme separation between eternity and time in twentieth century Protestant thought. He writes: "the human being in common with all other creatures enjoys a finite existence, whose limits are the temporal events of birth and death. Human mortality is, for these theologians, a function of human finitude, and so is an essentially natural event (no matter how sudden or violent). As temporal, human life has a span, which has a beginning-point and an end-point." See MacEwan, "Missing Persons," 261–62. MacEwan finds in Pannenberg the possibility of a transformation of time in eternity (266).

116. Gregory of Nyssa, *The Life of Moses*, 4. Eighteenth-century developments of the doctrine can be observed in the writings of John Wesley. For Wesley, the idea of perfection was "not absolute. Absolute perfection belongs not to man, nor to angels, but to God alone" as well as defined as "perfect love" (1 John 4:18). See Hollenweger, *Pentecostalism*, 148–49.

117. Ibid., 5.

transformation is in fact imaginably possible by displaying Maximus' wife and child, both hung from crosses, as healed in body and appearance while at the same time lacking the precision of the biblical witnesses which describe Jesus with bodily scars. We have no evidence that facial scarring from the beating he endured caused any part in Jesus' initial non-recognizability, but nonetheless, part of Scott's limitation is presenting a visual depiction of the afterlife that tries to restore a sense of normality that predates moments which surely shaped the characters' identity. For Scott the idyllic state of the heavenly body includes the healing of physical wounds, but it is as if the viewer is taken back to a time before wounds occurred. Healing does not entail a return to a previous way of life. Bodily wholeness is a key sign of the Kingdom of God for many Christians in that healing is the kingdom now, signaling the 'not yet' to come. Before explaining how "healing in the liturgy [for the majority world] is a matter of course," Hollenweger observes: "in all cases healing is not automatic. Neither a reasonable lifestyle nor prayer nor operations guarantee healing. It is therefore important that the topic of illness and health becomes part of our liturgies."[118]

Christian theology must understand what it means by healing and wholeness. Especially in his chapter, "Resurrecting Down Syndrome and Disability: Heaven and the Healing of the World," Amos Yong traces examples from Augustine's *Enchiridion*, as well as in the *City of God* to illustrate how attitudes within the tradition have sought to make a case for the continuity of personal identity in heaven by stressing the healing of disabilities or abnormalities, but at the expense of creating a false picture of a person's narrative.[119] Augustine is only one example, including much earlier Hebrew sources in the Old Testament into the New Testament where Yong argues for a needed theological renewal in considering the resurrection body. Yong argues, "in some ways Jesus' healing narratives served to perpetuate, at least implicitly the ancient Hebraic beliefs regarding the connections between 'disability' and sin, impurity, and disorder."[120] While answering in the affirmative, Yong asks:

> Is it possible to conceive that the glory and power of the resurrection body will derive not from some able-bodied ideal of perfection but from its being the site of the gracious activity of God's Spirit? In this case, might not the unending journey of the

---

118. Hollenweger, *Pentecostalism*, 234.

119. Yong, *Theology and Down Syndrome*, 262–63.

120. Ibid., 25–26. Using (John 9), Yong shows where Jesus challenges some unhealthy connections between disability and sin.

resurrection body also be from glory to glory and from perfection to perfection?"[121]

Here, Yong turns back to Gregory of Nyssa's category of *epectasis* to show the continuance and continuity between body and soul throughout eternity.[122] Yong is after what he calls, "a pneumatological and dynamic eschatology."[123] He provides a number of instances of individuals who experience either degenerative diseases, cerebral palsy, or his main concern, down syndrome to raise the important matter of whether or not these will remain with the identity of a person into eternity. In qualifying his thoughts, Yong stresses that these examples, "should not be read as a stubborn insistence on preferring disability to ability."[124] Rather, theology must reconsider the ways in which our identities are shaped. For Yong, "the Spirit who begins a good work in us in this life continues that work in life everlasting."[125] Contemporary examples provided by Yong seem to insist that not only will they retain some of those distinctive characteristics in their resurrected bodies, but that to imagine a pre-conditioned state would be unimaginable. They would not be who they have become.[126] For Yong:

> Of course, the ongoing work of the eschatological Spirit means that people with Down Syndrome will continually increase in goodness, knowledge, and love, vis-à-vis both the communion of saints and the triune God, all of which will have implications for their bodily and our corporate transformation as well.[127]

The view that an idyllic state of the body will appear constituting a transformation of the soul, knowledge, and virtue, seems to linger around the idea that crossing the finish line is the most important matter pertaining to life with God and may indeed be somewhat misleading. Yong mentions examples of the conflict between faith healers praying God will change a person's birth condition, rather than seeing how God is shaping that person.[128] Yong does not ignore the challenge of those who hope their physical condition will be completely altered, but this goes back to Jesus' challenge in healing the blind man (John 9). One of the central questions posed in

121. Ibid., 282.
122. Ibid.
123. Ibid., 281.
124. Ibid., 269.
125. Ibid., 280.
126. Ibid., 268.
127. Ibid., 283.
128. Ibid., 268.

the event is what does blindness entail.[129] Yong is right to challenge current attitudes to reconsider what values we place on the individual. In articulating his position, Yong writes:

> Set in this dynamic pneumatological perspective, might we be permitted the following speculations? Deceased infants—whether healthy, microencephalitic, or otherwise disabled, whether dead from natural or other causes—would have a glorious and powerful resurrection body not measured by Arnold Schwarzenegger or Miss U.S.A. in their prime but by their nestedness in the communion of saints and by the redemptive caregiving in the eschatological community. Hence, there is continuity and discontinuity with the resurrection body: on the one hand, infants are recognizably infants in the eschaton, although, on the other hand, their bodies are no longer subject to decay even as we are unable fully to anticipate the mysterious transformation of the resurrection body. But the work of the eschatological Spirit also means the infants do not stay infants eternally, but are unendingly transformed along with other members of the eschatological community in and toward the triune God.[130]

Certainly, Scott's work does not try to turn the heavenly Maximus or his family members into people they are not, but, I would suggest, his film also does not go far enough in navigating these important concerns for contemporary theology. For some, the desire to imagine a different "person" is indeed an escape from who we are becoming and Yong's suggestion is helpful in reasserting a challenge against that strange notion criticized by Tugwell:

> There would certainly be something very odd about a doctrine of resurrection ex nihilo, without any kind of continuity of existence between the person who died and the person who was resurrected. That would smack very much of the production of a replica of the dead person, rather than a genuine resurrection of the same person.[131]

Certainly, this does not disrupt the understanding of heaven as a place for painless existence.

One can easily imagine heaven as a place where those negative attributes that hinder personal development in the disabled, as well as in those

---

129. Ibid., 25.
130. Ibid., 282.
131. Tugwell, *Human Immortality and the Redemption of Death*, 163.

considered "enabled," to be remedied without significant identity modification. Here, the discontinuity between the frustrations of earthly disability and the freedom from such frustrations in our heavenly dwelling is important to highlight. Space will not allow for a description of attitudes prevalent at particular points of history that encouraged the way bodily change impacted entrance into the afterlife. Instead, I will briefly discuss two examples of popular films that depict such attitudes and beliefs in the footnotes below.[132] If Scott's bodily depiction does not take us far enough in addressing healing issues pertaining to our images of bodily and identity perfection, I have one final point of contention to highlight concerning Scott's image of the afterlife as "home".

Heaven as a Renovated History or a Glorious Present?

Maximus' entrance into the afterlife features a scene descriptive of a pre-destroyed homeland. Here, Scott takes a rather less than imaginative approach, although perhaps this is all the character desired. It is as if the postwar Maximus is replaying in the afterlife what he imagined would have occurred before having been arrested by Commodus. He merely wanted to return to his homeland to be with his family. The afterlife is depicted more

132. Two films for consideration are *The Eagle* and another Ridley Scott film, *Kingdom of Heaven*. In the 2011 film, *The Eagle*, General Marcus Aquila (played by Channing Tatum) and his slave Esca (played by Jamie Bell) are on a search to recover the Golden Eagle lost by the Roman, Ninth Legion to a Tribe in the Northern part of Britain, known as the Seal people. Marcus' father died in that battle as the General of the Ninth. Well into their journey past Hadrian's Wall, the two encounter a Roman named Lucius Caius Metellus or known by his tribe as Guern (played by Mark Strong), who had fought with the Ninth and had since made his home amongst another tribe. He leads Marcus and Esca to what he refers to as the "killing ground" and proceeds to describe the horrific details of the battle. Referring to the "painted warriors of the Seal people," Guern explains that, "they hacked the feet off of the dead so their souls couldn't walk into the afterlife." See *The Eagle*, DVD (2011). Of course, one might argue that the theology of the "Seal people" is a bit far from the Christian doctrine of entering the afterlife, but consider the latter film, *Kingdom of Heaven*. The context is set during the Crusades, where Muslims and Christians are fighting for control of Jerusalem. Balian (played by Orlando Bloom) is trying to find forgiveness of sin. Balian murdered the town priest, after the priest had the body of his dead wife beheaded due to her suicide. Prior to Balian's unleashed wrath, the priest urges him to go with his biological father to Jerusalem. The priest pounces on Balian's anxious nerve: "I tell you [Balian], God has abandoned you. I swear to you . . . you will have no peace so long as you stay here. No man ever needed a new world more. The village does not want you. If you take the crusade, you may relieve your wife's position in hell. I-I put it delicately—she was a suicide—she is in hell. Though what she does there without a head?" See *Kingdom of Heaven*, DVD (2005).

like a pre-suffering earthly life. This is also part of my critique of some restorationist theologies that want to imagine earth restored, as if all that had gone before doesn't matter, but simply erased. Such depictions make earth seem more real than heaven or picture death "as an absolute divider between the realm of the imperfect and the realm of the perfect," which simply hinders the imagination to consider a world that is quite different from this one, yet with continuity.[133] As Lewis prompted his readers, "all the things that have ever deeply possessed your soul have been but hints of it—tantalizing glimpses, promises never quite fulfilled, echoes that died away just as they caught your ear."[134] We must remember, "the desire—much more the satisfaction—has always refused to be fully present in any experience."[135] Heaven is not something nostalgic where we return to the "glory days", but rather as Lewis comments: "your place in heaven will seem to be made for you and you alone, because you were made for it—made for it stitch by stitch as a glove is made for a hand."[136]

For Maximus, the heavenly home is so human that you return or reverse back to an old state as can be found in some restorationist theologies, such as found in Wright, that only look back to resource the future. That would be more historical rather than eschatological. Maximus seems to be returning to an old life, not a new one. Heaven is not a return to an old way of life, but a new way of life, not devoid of our narratives, but characteristic of once again, "our willingness to reorder that past into a narrative in conformity with the story of Jesus."[137] I am not suggesting that the imagination should leave behind the possibilities of how a more realistic homeland could encourage one to think of a home, not spoiled by evil. At the same time, I am also not advocating a heaven where "the saints are free from labor" or where "they receive immediate wisdom" as "God's elect are even spared the troubles of research and study."[138] Rather, I am directing attention to the need to consider divine transcendence, which provides these glimpses of heavenly overlap. McGrath points to Psalm 137:1–4 and adds, "Christians are to see themselves as cut off from their homeland, and nourishing the hope of return from exile [in this case from Babylon to Jerusalem], often under difficult and discouraging circumstances."[139] By home, I intend not

---

133. Lang, *Heaven*, 180.
134. Lewis, *Problem of Pain*, 131.
135. Ibid., 133.
136. Ibid., 132.
137. Brown, *Continental Philosophy*, 209.
138. Lang, *Heaven*, 179–80.
139. McGrath, *A Brief History of Heaven*, 177.

the contents of geography, but more in terms of the relationships that shape us, especially our relationship in Christ. Juxtaposed to the "homeless" dead of contemporary life mentioned earlier by Markos, heavenly wondering is more essential to the Christian narrative than is eternally wandering.[140]

Yet, still, there remains a tension in eschatology that is not easily resolved as it pertains to the picture of heaven as home. For example, Randy Alcorn's popular work on heaven illustrates my point with his selections from the nineteenth-century Baptist preacher, Charles Spurgeon.[141] Without qualification, Spurgeon can be found in sermons offering a rather less than fulfilled view of heaven:

> Many believers make a mistake when they long to die and long for heaven. Those things may be desirable, but they are not the ultimate for the saints. The saints in heaven are perfectly free from sin and, so far as they are capable of it, are perfectly happy. But a disembodied spirit never can be perfect until it is reunited to its body. God made man not pure spirit but body and spirit, and the spirit alone will never be content until it sees its physical frame raised to its own condition of holiness and glory. Think not that our longings here below are not shared in by the saints in Heaven. They do not groan so far as any pain can be, but they long with greater intensity than you and I for the "adoption . . . the redemption of our bodies" (Romans 8:23). People have said there is no faith in heaven, and no hope. They know not what they say—in heaven faith and hope have their fullest swing and their brightest sphere, for glorified saints believe in God's promise and hope for the resurrection of the body.[142]

From Spurgeon's example (which may be very near to many Protestant versions of this difficult doctrinal articulation, including Wright's), one might deduce that the "not-yet" aspect of eschatology must continue beyond death. If heaven is "home", it seems once again merely temporary. Yet, Spurgeon can also be found in other sermons offering the following declaration: "dying is but going home. Indeed, there is no dying for the saints."[143] Expounding on this idea of fulfillment, he asserts, "Oh, brothers and sisters, we shall soon know more of heaven than all the Christian scholars tell us! Let us go home now to our own dwellings, but let us pledge ourselves that

---

140. Markos, *Heaven and Hell*, 16.
141. Alcorn, *We Shall See God*.
142. Ibid., 27.
143. Ibid., 3.

we will meet again. We will meet with Jesus, where he is, where we shall behold his glory."[144]

Contemporary eschatology seems to provide a picture that hope in heaven leads to escapism, but the opposite fear has also been witnessed in the Christian tradition. For example, McGrath points out that "Bernard of Clairvaux (1090–1153) and others discerned a similar danger in the Christian life—that Christians will come to prefer their place of exile to their homeland, and in effect choose to remain in exile."[145] Paul encourages the Philippians to remember their citizenship in heaven (Phil 3.20) or as McGrath notes, "the image of a 'colony (*politeuma*) of heaven.'"[146] McGrath expounds:

> This image thus lends dignity and new depths of meaning to the Christian life, especially the tension between the "now" and "not yet," and the bitter-sweet feeling of being outsiders to a culture—being in the world and yet not of that world. Christians are exiles in the world; citizens of heaven rather than of any earthly city.[147]

1 Peter 1:1 refers to those "foreigners" or "strangers" in the world. Even though I think the image Scott presents in the film of Maximus returning to his old setting has some obvious weaknesses, I also would suggest that his imaginative approach towards a home that is blessed and loving may be the hint of something more to come. The account in John 14:1–4 provides the metaphor of the Father's house where there is always another room, an abundance of rooms and the disciples will find their way to where Jesus is going. John is not simply describing renovation, but longing for reunion and reconciliation.

CONCLUSION

Clearly, film would be impoverished without the literary device of narrative to open up possibilities for the imagination as endings seem to be as vital, if not more so than beginnings, as well as the literary backdrop for cinematic engagements with history and the theological tradition. At the same time, the visual and aural dimensions of film allow a reader to imagine the historical drama in a new light. The intertextuality of literature, film, and theology

---

144. Ibid.
145. Ibid., 180.
146. Ibid., 178.
147. Ibid.

is observed in Theodorakopoulos' response to Scott's *Gladiator*: "Scott also shows a very sharp sense of what it might mean to present history in images rather than words."[148] Here, we find an appeal to the imagination as a way of not only knowing something about our past selves, but also possibly our future.

By interweaving history, literature, theology, philosophy, and film, I have argued that a contemporary theology of fulfillment in heaven should consider the immediate question of participation in heaven as vital to humanity's relationship in Christ. This includes the possibility for continued growth and development in relation to community and with God. I addressed implications for understanding death and judgment, resurrected bodies, and conceptions of bodily perfection, in relation to the idea of heaven as home. I analyzed and criticized what I see as weaknesses in some popular films concerning issues of healing of the whole person and home as renovation, rather than reconciliation. Scott's film, *Gladiator*, although not without weaknesses, serves as an important example for ways in which films wrestle to make sense of human endings and take up contemporary visions of heaven that can challenge dominant strands in contemporary Christian eschatology. By offering a vision that defamiliarizes contemporary theological considerations, my hope is that the imagination will be enlivened to consider the possibilities of heaven.

---

148. Theodorakopoulos, *Ancient Rome at the Cinema*, 121.

7

Why Can't We Imagine Creation beyond the End?

Thus far, I have argued that an imaginative approach towards the doctrine of heaven is a productive way forward. Nonetheless, I have yet to consider examples in popular culture that attempt to provide a narrative of post-apocalyptic life on a renewed earth. Such examples could lend support for this-worldly eschatologies of which I have criticized throughout the book. In this chapter, I aim to remedy this shortcoming by providing an analysis of a selection of films that portray life after the end. I will argue that contemporary cinematic modes of narrative show signs of difficulty imagining earth-bound eschatology.

A difficulty with some post-apocalyptic films is that they stop short of offering an image of fulfillment that is more than material. Films such as *The Road*, *The Book of Eli*, and *Wall-E* are all post-apocalyptic fictions that depict earthly life after the end. I focus on these three films for two main reasons. First, although these earthly fulfillment depictions are trying to point to something more, life after the end seems to turn towards improvement strategies for human beings to regain sustainability. The same types of human problems tend to arise in post-apocalyptic narratives, rather than pointing us towards different types of heavenly experiences. Secondly, different forms of cinematic art are represented in these films. *Wall-E*, for example, is animation and focuses on humanity's relationship to the natural environment. Where *The Road* focuses on familial aspects of drama, *The Book of Eli* emphasizes global justice.

Although I have chosen examples from post-apocalyptic fiction as representative, I am aware that different forms of narrative fiction abound in

WHY CAN'T WE IMAGINE CREATION BEYOND THE END? 189

dramatic film genres that could also raise important theological implications for consideration. For example, popular culture's emphasis on other-worldly possibilities should not be received as a neglect of history. Films depicting the nearness of heaven provide narratives that imply a shared or parallel history with concern for the earthly drama. For instance, Tom Shadyak's, *Dragonfly* portrays Kevin Costner's character, Joe, moving from a naturalistic conception of the cosmos to a more enchanted one.[1] In mourning his wife's death, Joe's beliefs come under contestation. He is a medical physician and approaches his vocation in an empirical manner, leaving little room for considering possibilities of afterlife, that is until Emily's tragic death. Emily is in some degree present in Joe's situation, leading him on a journey to discover their child. This image of the dead trying to serve on behalf of humanity can offer a critique or corrective for escapist narratives. Although such films, depicting the nearness of heaven, show concern for the wellbeing of the living, however, they do not take us all the way to imagine an earth-bound eschatology on a renewed earth. In a scientific-materialist culture that tends to emphasize the need to prolong and sustain creation through care and healthy cultivation, I do not think this is in any way conditioned by a simplistic escapist mentality, which has sometimes been attributed to the popular arts as being Platonic or even gnostic.[2] Rather, this shows the difficulty for the post-apocalyptic to imagine the type of eschaton proposed by scholars such as N. T. Wright.

The evidence that contemporary culture has very little problem (in theory) imagining the end of the world is beyond dispute. For example, Slavoj Žižek used forms of popular culture in a speech given in New York City to a crowd of protesters in front of Wall Street to lift the imaginations of his hearers to alternative, political/economic possibilities:

> Carnivals come cheap, he [Žižek] admonished. What matters is the day after, when we will have to return to normal life. Will there be any changes then? I don't want you to remember these days, you know like, "Oh, we were young, it was beautiful." Remember that our basic message is: We are allowed to think about alternatives. The rule is broken. We do not live in the best possible way. But there is a long road ahead. There are truly difficult questions that confront us. We know what we do not want. But what do we want?[3]

---

1. *Dragonfly*, DVD (2002). Further examples may include such films as *Hereafter*, DVD (2010) or *Charlie St. Cloud*, DVD (2010).
2. Wright, *Surprised By Hope*, 90.
3. Lee, "Slavoj Žižek Joins Occupy Wall Street," 2011.

Žižek uses popular forms of art such as film and literature to describe how humans have imagined and still imagine the end of the world, but asks why do people have difficulty imagining the end of an economic method with "better alternatives" or possibilities?

This type of question not only points to the difficulty of imagining the socio-economic and political realities of life that emerge in popular culture, difficulties concerning theological accounts beyond the end present no less a challenge for humanity to imagine a utopian post-apocalyptic environment free from depravity. Why is it so difficult to imagine a post-apocalyptic renewed earth, where the kingdom of God is established? Helping provide a way into the previous question, I will use three further guiding questions with the aid of popular film selections illustrating the challenges for the post-apocalyptic to imagine the type of eschaton proposed by scholars such as Wright: *How do we imagine living between the death or end of the world, while waiting for a second death, a personal death? What does it mean to live faithfully after the end of the world? How do we imagine what it is like to live on a renewed earth?* These guiding questions will be analyzed through the following popular films: *The Road, The Book of Eli,* and *Wall-E.* Before attempting such an analysis, I will offer some brief comments of clarification regarding the genre of apocalyptic and what I mean by post-apocalyptic.

WHAT COMES AFTER THE END?

Conrad Ostwalt suggests one way to understand what is going on in apocalyptic films is to make a distinction between traditional apocalyptic portrayals and secular apocalyptic portrayals.[4] According to Ostwalt, traditional apocalyptic narratives separate themselves from secular counterparts by involving a supernatural agent initiating the end; whereas secular apocalyptic portrayals rely heavily upon human agency and collectively self-inflicted demise, which brings about the end of the world.[5] Ostwalt elaborates:

> With no divine agency to rely upon, stories about the end of time turn to a variety of means to the end: aliens, disease, chance, natural disasters, and the like. What normally occurs in these disaster films is that humankind replaces God in the apocalyptic drama in that humanity becomes responsible either for the destruction of the earth or the salvation of it or both. This anthropocentric element is the key feature of the secular apocalyptic

---

4. See Conrad Ostwalt's article, "Apocalyptic," 379.

5. Ibid.

drama, yet most critical attempts at categorization focus on the origin of the threat or on the setting after destruction.[6]

Among other examples, Ostwalt provides the *Left Behind* films as a form of the traditional apocalypse and *Waterworld* as a secular example.[7] Whereas the *Left Behind* films, based on the Jerry Jenkins and Tim LaHaye novels, present "a particular way of reading biblical apocalyptic texts and include tribulations for those left behind after the rapture, the rise to power of the Antichrist, and the ultimate battle between good and evil, Armageddon," secular narratives exemplified by films such as *Waterworld* present a worldview of "searching for and finding paradise beyond the world of water—a new heaven, dry land."[8] Ostwalt observes: "when dry land is found, humans are clearly at home in this new heaven and earth, the remnant of what human beings had nearly destroyed."[9]

Ostwalt includes the *Left Behind* films within the traditional apocalyptic genre, "not because they are biblical, since they take liberties in providing the biblical texts with contemporary settings," but because they include "the apocalypse unfolding as part of a divine plan with supernatural causes and effects."[10] If we are to "preserve what we value," Ostwalt argues that a distinction between the traditional side, which can "devalue the environment or the world by a focus on a heavenly kingdom" and "secular worldviews [which] might overvalue human effort and science," can bring about a mutually corrective dialogue.[11]

While I find Ostwalt's distinction helpful in his encouragement to discover points of dialogue for worldview modification, I am not convinced that some recent films, primarily focused upon a post-apocalyptic life, fit easily into his two categories. Rather, such films persist in creating an "uncertainty of categories, blurred boundaries and the undecidability of present or meaning [which] is the antithesis of the apocalyptic model for a narrative's sense of an ending."[12] That is not to deny that others, such as Richard Walsh, have interpreted films like *The Road* as "a wholly secular post-apocalypse," but, even in this case, the category breaks down as Walsh goes on to establish a case for rereading the film as an innovation on the

---

6. Ibid.
7. Ibid., 378–79.
8. Ibid., 378–81.
9. Ibid., 381.
10. Ibid.
11. Ibid., 382.
12. Bennett, *Afterlife and Narrative in Contemporary Fiction*, 194.

OT Job narrative.[13] Nor am I suggesting, in the words of Tillich, that, "the religious should be swallowed by the secular, as secularism desires, nor that the secular should be swallowed by the religious, as ecclesiastic imperialism desires."[14] Rather, I would draw attention to examples which resist simple categorization into either of these camps. By taking more seriously the social implications of theology, and Robin Gill has encouraged us in this direction, the demarcations between traditional and secular will become less pronounced because the sociology of knowledge has informed our understanding of how theology so easily crosses such demarcations and distinctions, as witnessed through the medium of film.[15] Ostwalt does include "the setting after the destruction" within his definition of apocalyptic, but for my purpose here, I will refer to the *after* setting as post-apocalyptic.[16]

Although Ostwalt may still consider such films portraying a *secular* version of the apocalyptic narrative, I want to suggest that certain films, although not focusing on the events and agency leading up to the end of the world, do portray a continued relationship between God and humanity in post-apocalyptic life, even if only vaguely hinting at such possibilities. I am interested, then, in understanding the challenges for popular culture to imagine life on a renewed earth as proposed by NT scholars, such as Wright. I am well aware that some theologians may insist on further degrees of difference between more traditional forms of depicting biblical and doctrinal interpretations for what it means to live after the end, but such degrees of differentiation only serve to strengthen my thesis that the search for a culturally unconditioned interpretation of the *eschaton* is unwarranted, and a more effective way forward is to seek understanding of the ways in which humanity imagines life after death in heaven. Some may be tempted to dismiss the argument too quickly, suggesting that utopian models are quite different from Christian "kingdom of God" models. Yet, many will agree that Christian "kingdom of God" models do not come in uniform constructions. At the same time, all anticipate a universal impact on humanity. Surely, learning where society has difficulty imagining particular nuances of doctrine is worth further investigation. In what follows, I will argue that contemporary culture has great difficulty in imaging the type of postponement theories supported by some trends in contemporary theology, which insist that heaven is, at best, a waiting place.

---

13. Walsh, "(Carrying the Fire on) No Road for Old Horses."
14. Tillich, *Theology of Culture*, 42.
15. Gill, ed., *Theology and Sociology*, 146.
16. Ostwalt, "Apocalyptic," 379.

Difficulty Imagining Life After the End

The Road, based on Cormac McCarthy's novel, provides a grueling cinematic example portraying family life on a dead earth.[17] The earth is dry, barren, and cruel—beyond a state capable of bringing forth life. No sign of a renewed creation sits waiting on the horizon. All systems, including government, economics, justice, education are completely void. The only remaining social structure still fighting for survival is the family. Imagining a post-apocalyptic context, the narrative follows a father and son through their journey to survive in a world characterized by horrific depravity. As Walsh observes, this is a place where "stories are slipping away. Even names are a thing of the past," he observes, referring to the main family unit, "Papa" and "Boy" no longer are called by their given names.[18] In citing the film, Walsh considers that for Papa, the Boy "is God's word, the last god, or 'God never spoke.'"[19] One of the central markers dividing those who have descended below human standards and those who are still *carrying the fire* (a phrase the father uses with his son to spark their imagination of a post-apocalyptic hope for a better existence and for some, a reminder of a nostalgic existence) is the practice of cannibalism. Within the film, the practice carries absolutely no trace of religious associations and is limited to those who have succumbed to the passions for survival, engaging in horrific acts of murder in order to postpone their death beyond apocalypse.

This division between the others who eat their children and the ones *carrying the fire* (the good guys) provides the narrative with a significant amount of conflict theory. Part of imagining life in a post-apocalyptic context entails trying to imagine an earth where values do not default into a depraved state. The will to survive without succumbing to deviant behavior becomes more difficult, as pressure mounts in an increasingly dangerous environment. Walsh finds one of the dominant themes that of loss running through the entire narrative.[20] Not only is the loss of trust in neighbor clear, but a loss of rest, as a Darwinian paradigm for survival for daily basics, "food, water, and shelter," becomes central.[21] Papa's insistence that his Boy be prepared to commit suicide with their final bullet, avoiding a fate of being consciously destroyed and devoured by cannibals, is a telling image of loss, including loss of value and purpose in the mayhem of survival. After

---

17. *The Road*, DVD (2009).
18. Walsh, "(Carrying the Fire on) No Road for Old Horses."
19. Ibid.
20. Ibid.
21. Ibid.

Boy experiences a bad dream while sleeping, Papa replies, "when you dream about bad things—you are still fighting?"[22]

Where Walsh considers a loss of God in the narrative, I, on the other hand, find the characters attempting to understand God's dealings, even after the end of the world. "The movie's Papa still claims to believe in God, but he prays only to thank people who have left provisions behind."[23] The phenomena of gratitude within a context from antagonism to joy and thankfulness, appears symptomatic of humanity's struggle to tell a story of complete loss without some type of residual hope, but is there an alternative image?

Mark Fisher seems to have located the crucial variable in this type of post-apocalypse: "we are not in a new world so much as a bombed-out space, strewn with debris of failed political-economic systems."[24] According to Fisher, earlier post-apocalyptic films have often been "pretexts for imagining utopia," but in films such as *The Road*, we witness "a symptom of the inability to imagine alternatives to capitalism's entropic, eternal present."[25] The film "by no means clears a space for imagining something different."[26] Not only is imagining a renewed earth found difficult, but imagining closure becomes nearly futile. Bennett observes: "Without revelation or closural meaning, the afterlife often offers an ending that repeats itself in a loop between life and afterlife."[27] It is precisely at this point that one can identify a tension of being at once able to imagine the end, and a struggle to imagine a renewed earth after the end. A simple reductionist interpretation might be to identify the nihilistic dimensions of popular culture concluding such failings as symptomatic of culture's inability to read scriptural texts rightly. Of course, a number of variables can contribute to imaginative impediments for reflecting on the tension of living on a post-apocalyptic earth or a dead earth, while awaiting a second, personal death, but the difficulty is a real one and should not be dismissed too easily.

DIFFICULTY IN IMAGINING FAITHFULNESS AFTER THE END

If loss seems to be one of the dominant themes for imagining characters who hinge the old earth and the new earth or post-apocalyptic earth, then

22. Hillcoat, "The Road."
23. Walsh, "(Carrying the Fire on) No Road for Old Horses."
24. Fisher, "The Lonely Road," 17.
25. Ibid., 15.
26. Ibid., 16.
27. Bennett, *Afterlife and Narrative in Contemporary Fiction*, 194.

perhaps living faithfully still holds some purpose for existing. Here, *new* in the post-apocalyptic sense is clearly not better, but worse. To use Ostwalt's categories for a moment, oddly, neither traditional nor secular images find the *new* existence as a better way of being. Many theologians might argue that the scriptures use *new* to describe a beautiful and perfected creation, yet still within the limits of this world. It seems strange that both slants have great difficulty imagining the *new* as beautifully wonderful, rather than darkly depraved. Even more recent films, such as Darren Aronofsky's *Noah*, feature characters deeply troubled, trying to imagine living in a post-flood creation.[28] This early apocalypse has remained an important symbol of the end to the present day. Ulrich Simon observes, "just as Noah hinges the two worlds—before and after the Flood—so Christian Baptism hinges the world of condemnation and death on the one hand, and that of forgiveness and life on the other."[29]

Aronofsky's Noah is portrayed with a haunted imagination concerning the question of how the new world can be new, if humanity takes up residence. Interestingly, the struggle is not to imagine a beautified creation in a sense, but to imagine a vision of creation including humanity in it. Interestingly, the image usually runs in the opposite direction with humans surviving, while the rest of creation is lifeless—a clear reduction of creation to mere matter. As Hans Boersma observes: "according to Maximus [the Confessor], this harmonious relationship was torn through Adam's fall: Adam, he explained, had failed to regard creation spiritually so as to discover the divine *logoi* in it. Instead, he had looked at nature in line with his passions, thereby reducing creation to a purely material reality."[30] Either way, popular culture struggles to imagine life on a renewed earth post-apocalypse, bringing humanity and the rest of creation into harmony.

The Book of Eli is a post-apocalyptic film featuring another *hinge* figure, Eli.[31] Like Noah, Eli connects the world as it was and how it is becoming. He lives pre and post cataclysm. His purpose is wrapped up in justice, which for Eli is heavily weighted on obedience to God. Eli sees his mission as divinely providential carrying with him transformative religious experiences, where God promised to protect him in his calling. His purpose is to keep moving west, as he is in possession of the last Bible and as such, he is a truth bearer. Near the conclusion, one learns that he literally carries the *Word of God* in his heart and memory, as he dictates the whole Bible to a scribe at the place

28. *Noah*, DVD (2014).
29. Simon, *The End Is Not Yet*, 174.
30. Boersma, *Heavenly Participation*, 32.
31. *The Book of Eli*, DVD (2010).

of new beginnings (what was once Alcatraz Island, housing the infamous prison in the San Francisco Bay Area). After encountering numerous crises and near death events, he arrives at his goal. He is the prime archetype for self-control and focused determination, as he makes his way among others. Cannibalism, sexual deviance, and murder characterize this post-apocalyptic context. Again, although post-apocalyptic in Ostwalt's secular sense, *The Book of Eli* is not easily categorized. Eli interprets his experience as being personally directed by God and the Bible is the prime object of power. Although critics have offered a much more comprehensive summary of the film, I aim simply to draw attention to the fact that the only image of restoration which appears on the horizon is Eli's arrival to the Island where a large effort has been undertaken to restore and rescue knowledge through an onsite library housing important books having been lost in the apocalypse. Remembering life before apocalypse allows Eli to trace the development in value theory before and after the end. Now, the most valuable object is the Bible, next only to water. In a sense, one could make the case that a reconstructive effort at new creation was on the way, but nowhere near have the images claimed to be found within scripture made an appearance here. An important aspect of the film imagines that *purpose* survives beyond daily basic needs. Denzel Washington's character, Eli, is driven by a divine purpose. Once again, the lines between traditional and secular intertwine. In a context dominated by deviant appetites, Eli is not without purpose. Purpose is a critical component for humanity and although post-apocalyptic images fail to imagine a new creation, at least we are given glimpses of the continuance of divine purpose. I turn to a final question relating to the way popular culture imagines living on a renewed earth.

DIFFICULTY IN IMAGINING "NEWNESS" AFTER THE END

If contemporary society struggles to imagine life on a post-apocalyptic renewed earth, as well as consistently showing signs of strain imagining how humanity and the rest of creation can perfectly coincide in a new creation, the evidence points in the direction of other- worldly possibilities. Before considering this, however, we should first, draw attention to one of the few examples in popular culture that places emphasis on an earth transformation derived, not from divine intervention, but by a recolonization and global clean-up initiative. The animated film *WALL-E* describes a post-apocalyptic context where the ecological priority is explored at great length.[32]

32. *Wall-E*, DVD (2008).

In *WALL-E*, humans are required to board a space cruise for an extended time with the incentives appealing to the appetites for relaxation, recreation, and rest. The assignment of a hover chair provides comfort ensuring that each person is free from work, including the effort to walk. Everything is mass produced on this cruise, including robots to accomplish the cleaning and daily tasks. Although not widely communicated by world leaders, the ecological conditions are creating an unliveable earth in *WALL-E*. Recolonization is the only hope but, first, a global cleanup is delegated to robots who can collect, compact, and organize all rubbish and artifacts left behind. WALL-E is the last artificial intelligence to survive the clean-up initiative. All other robots are unable to sustain productivity in an environment lacking sufficient machine maintenance. Sandstorms also pose a major threat to the robots' survival. WALL-E continues in what appears to be a failed project. Earth has been reduced to a giant trash heap, left for robots to oversee. One of the important differences, in light of other post-apocalyptic films, is that memory of a different world is only artificial. Approximately seven hundred years expire, while humans live comfortably on the space cruise. Through a number of circumstances, the captain of the space cruise undergoes a significant crisis as he discovers recorded moving pictures of a once beautified earth in decay. After receiving information and a plant specimen from a robot scout, the captain comes to the conclusion that the reason the project failed was not that earth could no longer sustain life, but that people had failed to care for the earth. Generations passed with no hope of returning. Life was easier in the hover chair. Through a valiant effort, the captain engages the return functions of the ship. The story concludes with the people deboarding the ship to begin a great recolonization experiment. The failure was one of stewardship for creation.

The story does not go further in elaborating how one can imagine a renewed earth. Overturning excessive eating habits, the inability to care for selfand for, the rest of creation are themes left underdeveloped. Social problems relating to over rest and lack of physical conditioning are not explored further, except for people being forced to leave the comfort of their cruise hover chair, and literally, to learn to walk again. The death and restoration of earth is explored in this film, but not the death and resurrection of human beings, only a return from space.

CONCLUSION

A significant portion of popular post-apocalyptic films do not venture to imagine a new heaven, new earth, or utopian-like this-worldly existence beyond the End. Interpretations of this phenomenon will surely vary, but what I hope I have offered here is a convincing analysis of the difficulty for popular culture to imagine what a much later, renewed earth entails. Popular culture's lack of offering later utopian visions, while at the same time providing a plethora of images giving priority to other-worldly realities, should awaken contemporary theology to important shifts with implications for reflections on heaven. Also, remarkably missing from post-apocalyptic films is a category for the dead—whether in terms of re-embodiment or resurrection. Indeed, death still happens in the post-apocalypse context, as well illustrated in *The Road* and *The Book of Eli*, but in an overly material world, it is difficult to maintain a better future, even for the dead. This could be a symptom of these fictions trying too hard to offer ideological interpretations of current problems, but regardless, the larger questions concerning what happens after a person dies still transcends various ideologies. The majority of post-apocalyptic films do not even entertain popular undead imaginings, such as zombies or vampires, which are common "archetypal monsters."[33] Again, perhaps this is in large part due to missing other-worldly possibilities for these appear to be "trapped in a living death."[34]

Also problematic are fairly consistent themes running through post-apocalyptic images, such as the stoppage of time, limited purpose, minimal existence and ecological aspects illustrated in *WALL-E*. According to Boersma, "we sometimes tend to think that the 'other-worldly' view of the church fathers lies at the root of our ecological problems. In actual fact, the opposite is the case. Their participatory or sacramental ontology allowed them to treat the material creation as a sacred Eucharistic offering to God."[35]

After defining post-apocalyptic, as well as asking three guiding questions concerning the imagination and a renewed earth through a selection of post-apocalyptic films, it seems quite evident that contemporary culture has great difficulty imagining what some contemporary theology maintains is the only valid interpretation. While I am aware that different historical situations perceived a necessary shift in attitude towards postponement theories of the *eschaton*, theological priority for understanding how popular culture imagines life after death is critical for Christian eschatology.

Some may want to level the critique that my argument regarding a Christian understanding of heaven suffers from the same indictment of stopping too short. Where I argue that narratives continue to develop in relation to Christ, one may ask how the *eschaton* fits into my account. Does

---

33. Markos, *Heaven and Hell*, 16.
34. Ibid.
35. Hans Boersma, *Heavenly Participation*, 32.

my account of heaven suggest denying a major strand of Christian thought concerning the new heaven and new earth? Early on in my book, I implicitly suggested that there may be more in the divine plan. Here, I will state more explicitly that it is very plausible to read John's Apocalypse in the NT as suggesting that the union of a new heaven and new earth is that of God valuing material aspects of creation, which is then taken up into the life of heaven. I have argued that post-apocalyptic films tend to stress disaster, but often lack an adequate depiction of a this-worldy fulfillment. An other-worldly heaven allows for a wider range of possibilities for experience, where this-worldly narratives end up with similar types of experiences, and these are often very negative ones.

Conclusion

Why are other-worldly possibilities so prevalent in popular culture while, at the same time, minimized by areas of contemporary biblical and theological studies? This book set out to theologically engage popular forms of art by exploring the ways in which the creative imagination can both challenge and keep alive aspects of the Christian doctrine of heaven as an other-worldly possibility. The research has emphasized popular forms of art, such as film (including its relation to popular music and literature), which can bring to light dormant aspects of teaching that have been close to the roots of the gospel story.

Ulrich Simon wrote extensively in the area of eschatology and more specifically on heaven.[1] He made the following observation regarding other-worldly possibilities in the parables found within the gospels:

> Even stories which appear to move on an earthly level involve the hearer in other-worldly concerns: for example, the penitent decides to turn not for moral reform but in order to gain the eternal Kingdom; or again, the creditor forgives in order to obtain a higher recompense. Every virtue—such as generosity and diligent justice—is portrayed as going beyond itself and feeding on the Perfection which does not belong to this world, just as every vice—such as laziness and hardness of heart—receives its real condemnation only at the End when Evil is fully exposed in the glare of the divine assizes.[2]

These images that Jesus used in his parables also draw attention to humanity's need for imaginative understanding. As has been argued throughout this book, the writers of scripture observed the multiple traces of truth within the wider culture in which they were located. Where, however, are

---

1. See Simon's works, *Heaven in the Christian Tradition*; *The Ascent to Heaven*; and *The End is Not Yet*.

2. Simon, *The End Is Not Yet*, 29.

these traces, these images to be found today if theologians are reticent to interpret "popular" scriptures as valid imaginings for other-worldly possibilities? I have argued that the evidence points not only to the fact that popular art, such as film, music, and literature can keep dormant aspects of teaching alive, but that it can also provide theologians with imaginative possibilities for thinking theologically about heaven. By recognizing the ongoing action of the Holy Spirit in the world of culture, as well as the continuing hermeneutic task of reception within history, contemporary narratives play a vital role in helping us consider human endings and heavenly possibilities.

Although not limited to the following points, I would like to conclude by drawing attention towards some of the major contributions of this study, and to some of the possible implications for further research.

Part 1 (chapters one to three) contributed new developments in method by providing new apparatus for theologically engaging a range of popular forms of art with the imagining of heaven. At the same time, after creatively engaging and interpreting the selected examples, the research pointed towards an unfamiliarizing impact concerning aspects of Christian teaching and belief on heaven. These unfamiliar images provoked fresh insights as they were placed in a conversation not merely with popular forms of art, but also with the Christian scriptures, traditions, and contemporary theology. The research stands on the borderlands of the theology and popular culture dialogue, and thus allows for a deeper level of hermeneutical listening. By pursuing a hermeneutic of popular imaginings of heaven that can both challenge and aid the theological task, these images contribute by opening up possibilities for seeing the development of doctrine and the activity of God in fresh ways.

As heaven is a part of Christianity's narrative, Rush observes how this narrative is "traditioned into the future by a process in which tradition and reception, tradition and innovation, reception and effect enable rejuvenating receptions to be concretized as new questions arise."[3] Specifically, Christianity has understood the Spirit of God as being of central importance to God's continued activity in this culturally conditioned situation. Theologian Clark Pinnock once suggested that Barth sensed a "felt need of a more satisfactory theology of the Spirit" and that Barth's theology "would have been stronger, and it might even have permitted him to have issued a kinder judgment on liberal theologians and their appreciation of the role of experience."[4] As the research set forth, both Moltmann and Hollenweger indicate that by emphasizing the experience of the Spirit in revelation, "there are truths to

---

3. Rush, *The Reception of Doctrine*, 362.
4. Pinnock, *Flame of Love*, 10.

recover and possibilities to explore."[5] Far from neglecting a trinitarian focus, the emphasis has been, then, on how humanity experiences the divine, through the action of the Holy Spirit before constructing doctrine.

This book has sought to combine interlocutors representing varied backgrounds of theological, philosophical, and cultural understandings. Conversing with theologians, philosophers, and artists from Roman Catholic, Protestant, and non-confessional backgrounds has encouraged an ecumenical approach to a more robust Christian constructive theology of the popular imagining of heaven. Also, a hermeneutical approach to narrative in theology and popular culture can widen the path for new directions by furthering our understanding of the human imagination. As Hedley so aptly observes: "the imagination is needed in art to reconcile the eternal with the characteristics of one's own age."[6]

How does an engagement with these popular imaginings open up new possibilities concerning an other-worldly heaven? In his introduction to Paul Ricoeur's collected essays on religion, Mark Wallace offers some observations regarding the imagination and hermeneutics that directly relate to my attempts at providing a hermeneutic of popular imagery towards a constructive theology of heaven:

> The metaphorical imagination is an ally for the understanding and articulation of faith. In its essence, faith is a living out of the figures of hope unleashed by the imagination. Glossing Kant, Ricoeur argues for the power of the productive imagination to "schematize" novel relationships between the data of experience and the figures of the imagination even though both realms of understanding seem initially unrelated to one another. The imagination generates new metaphors for synthesizing disparate aspects of reality that burst conventional assumptions about the nature of things. Figurative discourses *suspend* first-order references to literal objects and events in order to *liberate* second-order references to a more basic and nonliteral world of unimagined possibilities. The role of the living metaphor is to juxtapose two dissimilar forms of articulation in order to bring to language dimensions and values of reality that have been previously hidden by straightforward, descriptive discourse. "Metaphor is the rhetorical process by which discourse unleashes the power that certain fictions have to redescribe reality." "Lamb" and "God," for example, are two distinct terms that resist combination. But the union of both terms in the metaphor "lamb of

5. Ibid.
6. Hedley, *The Iconic Imagination*, 260.

God" sets free a new understanding of the divine life—as bloody and innocent salvation-bringer—hitherto unavailable to the interpreter apart from this metaphorical innovation.[7]

Although it was necessary to limit the number of works examined, this has enabled me to focus on how specific examples of popular art may contribute to major areas of theological enquiry concerning the afterlife: namely, questions of appearance recognition in a heavenly context (chapter four), memory in heaven associated with earthly experiences (chapter five), and continuity/discontinuity regarding the question of fulfillment in heaven (chapter six). As Wallace affirms, "the power of the text to disclose new possibilities offers the reader [or viewer; or listener] an expanded view of the world and a deeper capacity for selfhood."[8]

Chapter four raised questions about the self in relation to others. The examples selected for investigation provided enriching perspectives on questions of appearance and reality. Partly, this is due to the different artistic forms and genres represented by the examples. For instance, *What Dreams May Come* is a dramatic fantasy, featuring the historical question between appearance and reality for the sake of magnifying the even more significant question concerning how one might relationally recognize the other in heaven. This example also draws attention towards possible questions concerning the continuity between earthly and heavenly bodies, not to mention the ways in which the visual arts reconfigure long standing theological questions concerning appearance and reality. Also, by looking at an example of animation in *Toy Story 3*, possibilities for the creative imagination to aid theology in thinking about the body, personal identity, and recognition, can also challenge more conventional strategies of understanding the self, such as materiality and soul, potentially impacting both philosophy and theology.

A further implication of the research and a potentially fruitful path to pursue in terms of the self and reunion with others could be found in examples that represent the nearness of heaven. For instance, although the book did not consider near-death narratives in particular, the critical apparatus set forth in Part I could nonetheless be applied equally to an analysis of such narratives.

For example, an analysis of Clint Eastwood's film *Hereafter* might disclose further possibilities regarding the hope of reunion and memory in heaven. The film clearly depicts the theological concept of survival in the afterlife, but focuses on three narratives describing the tension of living with other-worldly prospects and the historical realities of relational tragedies.

7. Wallace, "Introduction," in Paul Ricoeur's *Figuring the Sacred*, 8.
8. Ibid.

Again, this might also widen the range of film genre under consideration. The film describes humanity's quest to understand the veil between the physical and spiritual in vivid detail. Marie, a French television journalist (played by actress Cecile De France) illustrates the desire to understand her near-death experience and throughout the film, Marie's decisions describe a situation where more of the answers are to be found in the spiritual realm and more of the questions reside in her earthly existence. Eastwood's film would broaden, therefore, the scope of research by including near-death experiences but such research could build fruitfully on the critical apparatus set forth in Part I of the book.

Chapter five concentrates on the identity of self and memory related to a theology of heaven. By focusing on memory of earthly existence as a divine gift in heaven, the research allowed for ways to understand how art forms in popular culture, such as music, help contribute to shaping our biographies in ways that encourage us to imagine how suffering and the memory of suffering can be interpreted as redemptive in a heavenly context. This allows for a greater emphasis upon remembrance as love for the other. Admittedly, this wide field of inquiry only serves, again, to accentuate the possibilities for further research. The range of popular musical examples, from the Rusted Root's "Heaven" to Alpha Rev's "Heaven" are only two of a host of songs among different styles and genres that reflect interest in heaven.[9] Also, theological questions concerning guilt, blame, reward and punishment provide critical areas for investigating how we understand memory and identity, or lack thereof, in heaven. These would be of particular interest to pursue further on the popular imaginings of heaven.

In considering the way that different forms and genres of popular films work in chapter four, one could also consider the question of memory through further animated cinematic examples such as the film *Inside Out* where the emotions are working with memories on a journey to discover how joy and sadness might relate in the self without tainting a person's overall narrative.[10] In analyzing further how different musical styles shape biographies, yet come to coexist in a loving relationship, one might also consider the film *If I Stay*.[11] This near-death story features a classically trained cello artist who falls in love with a rock artist. Here, one witnesses two musical sub-genres being drawn together by love. The intertextuality of music and ultimate life questions focused on loving relationships might produce some helpful interpretations of music, film, and memory in heaven.

9. Rusted Root, "Heaven," in *Remember*, 2004.
10. *Inside Out*, DVD (2015).
11. *If I Stay*, DVD (2014).

Chapter six stimulates further theological questions surrounding more traditional categories, such as the interim state in discussions of eschatology and conceptions of perfection of the self. There are a range of implications from this research, including the need for further emphasis, in biblical studies, on the representation in popular art of the resurrection, particularly as it relates to personal and/or collective eschatologies, along with other-worldly possibilities. The question of physical and mental modification of the self in heaven holds implications, also, for studies in Christian spiritual formation and theological ethics, especially in how we value and imagine the degrees of the transformation of a person in the afterlife, including the change in physical and mental conditions that can play significant roles in shaping our personal identities.

In a similar way, chapter seven opens up questions concerning popular film and imaging the *eschaton*. One of the interesting discoveries of the research was the lack of popular examples that actually represent some type of this-worldly resurrection. This significant lacuna, nonetheless, supports my wider argument that other-worldly possibilities should be taken more seriously in biblical and theological studies. It is interesting to note how this-worldly resurrection narratives in popular culture tend to focus on partial living forms, such as in the case of zombies. Again, this only serves to show popular culture's challenge to imagine a this-worldly eschaton that includes fulfillment and perfection.

Admittedly, heaven is a doctrine reliant on the imagination and does not offer up a single vision for interpretation. The examples I have navigated serve as theological possibilities. They indicate more generally, moreover, how the popular arts, such as film, may also lead to a type of "productive" failure in theological terms.[12] According to Ricoeur: "What is important is the way in which this challenge, or this failure, is received: Do we find an invitation to think less about the problem [or question] or a provocation to think more, or to think differently about it?"[13] My hope is that this research not only encourages more constructive eschatology about heaven, but will also contribute towards further work on the imagination, hermeneutics and the self in relation to God. Historical questions arise, as I have shown, in new forms of art. Innovation in different artistic medias contribute, moreover, to the cultivation of theological reflections on heaven that may fail and surpass, while preserving aspects of the Christian tradition.[14]

---

12. Ricoeur, "Evil, a Challenge to Philosophy and Theology," 256.
13. Ibid., 249.
14. Ibid., 256.

Throughout the book, then, I have advocated reception as a more promising metaphor than suspicion; not a passive reception, but an actively engaging one. For Christian theology, it seems advantageous in our time to rediscover the many ways that the creative imagination, as revealed through popular culture, can help point in the direction of heaven. My hope, moreover, is that the critical apparatus that I have brought to bear on Christian eschatology might also be useful in future scholarly analyses of other aspects of Christian doctrine. As my engagement with a large number of scholars currently working in the field suggests, the theological engagement with popular culture is a burgeoning critical discourse. This book models a way, then, of approaching this discourse, and enabling the hermeneutic richness of popular culture to speak to, and challenge, contemporary theology.

Bibliography

Adler, Mortimer J. *The Angels and Us*. New York: MacMillan, 1982.
Alcorn, Randy. *We Shall See God: Charles Spurgeon's Classic Devotional Thoughts on Heaven*. Carol Stream, IL: Tyndale House, 2011.
Alpha Rev. "Heaven." On *New Morning*. Hollywood Records, Inc., 2010. http://itunes.com.
Augustine, Saint. *Confessions*. Translated by R. S. Pine-Coffin. New York: Penguin, 1961.
Bakker, Freek L. "Reincarnation in Western Cinema." In *Blick über den Tod hinaus: Bilder vom Leben nach dem Tod in Theologie und Film/Seeing Beyond Death: Images of the Afterlife in Theology and Film*, edited by Christopher Deacy and Ulrike Vollmer, 83–94. Marburg: Schuren, 2012.
Balthasar, Hans Urs von. *The Glory of the Lord: A Theological Aesthetics. Volume 1: Seeing the Form*. Translated by Erasmo Leiva-Merikakis. Edited by John Riches. Edinburgh: T. & T. Clark, 1982.
———. *Prayer*. Translated by Graham Harrison. San Francisco: Ignatius, 1986.
Barkman, Adam. "*Gladiator*, Gender, and Marriage in Heaven: A Christian Exploration." In *The Culture and Philosophy of Ridley Scott*, edited by Adam Barkman, Ashley Barkman, and Nancy Kang, 275–90. Lanham, MD: Lexington, 2013.
Barth, Karl. *Church Dogmatics*. Vol. III.3. Translated by G. W. Bromiley and T. F. Torrance. Peabody, MA: Hendrickson, 2010.
Beastly. Directed by Daniel Barnz. USA: CBS Films, 2011. DVD.
Beaudoin, Tom. "Foreword." In Clive Marsh and Vaughan S. Roberts, *Personal Jesus: How Popular Music Shapes Our Souls*. Grand Rapids: Baker Academic, 2012.
———. "Popular Culture Scholarship as a Spiritual Exercise: Thinking Ethically with(out) Christianity." In *Between Sacred and Profane: Researching Religion and Popular Culture*, edited by Gordon Lynch, 94–110. New York: Palgrave Macmillan, 2007.
———. *Witness to Dispossession: The Vocation of a Post-Modern Theologian*. New York: Orbis, 2008.
Beetlejuice. Directed by Tim Burton. USA: Warner Bros., 1988. DVD.
Begbie, Jeremy. "Beauty, Sentimentality and the Arts." In *The Beauty of God: Theology and the Arts*, edited by Daniel J. Treier, Mark Husbands, and Roger Lundin, 45–69. Downers Grove, IL: IVP Academic, 2007.
Bennett, Alice. *Afterlife and Narrative in Contemporary Fiction*. London: Palgrave Macmillan, 2012.

Bethge, Eberhard, ed. *Dietrich Bonhoeffer: Letters and Papers from Prison*. Reprint. London: SCM, 1967.

Bockmeuhl, Markus. "Did St. Paul Go to Heaven When He Died." In *Jesus, Paul and the People of God: A Theological Dialogue with N. T. Wright*, edited by Nicholas Perrin and Richard B. Hays, 211–31. Downers Grove, IL: IVP Academic, 2011.

Boersma, Hans. *Heavenly Participation: The Weaving of a Sacramental Tapestry*. Grand Rapids: Eerdmans, 2011.

The Book of Eli. Directed by The Hughes Brothers. USA: Warner Bros. Pictures, 2010. DVD.

Brant, Jonathan. *Paul Tillich and the Possibility of Revelation through Film*. Oxford Theological Monographs. Oxford: Oxford University Press, 2012.

Brown, David. *Continental Philosophy and Modern Theology: An Engagement*. Reprint. Eugene, OR: Wipf & Stock, 2012.

———. *Discipleship & Imagination: Christian Tradition & Truth*. Oxford: Oxford University Press, 2004.

———. *God & Mystery in Words: Experience through Metaphor and Drama*. New York: Oxford University Press, 2008.

———. *Tradition & Imagination: Revelation & Change*. Oxford: Oxford University Press, 1999.

Brown, Frank Burch. *Good Taste, Bad Taste, & Christian Taste: Aesthetics in Religious Life*. Oxford: Oxford University Press, 2000.

———. *Religious Aesthetics: A Theological Study of Making and Meaning*. Princeton, NJ: Princeton University Press, 1989.

Bruce Almighty. Directed by Tom Shadyak. USA: Universal Pictures Buena Vista International, 2003. DVD.

Brueggeman, Walter. "A First Retrospect on the Consultation." In *Renewing Biblical Interpretation*, edited by Colin Greene, Craig Bartholomew, and Karl Moller, 342–47. Carlisle, UK: Paternoster, 2000.

Callaway, Kutter. *Scoring Transcendence: Contemporary Film Music as Religious Experience*. Waco, TX: Baylor University Press, 2013.

Cameron, J. M., ed. *John Henry Newman's an Essay on the Development of Christian Doctrine*. The Edition of 1845 ed. Middlesex, UK: Penguin, 1973.

Caputo, John D. *What Would Jesus Deconstruct: The Good News of Post-Modernism for the Church*. Grand Rapids: Baker Academic, 2007.

Casselberry, Judith. "Were We Ever Secular? Interrogating David Brown on Gospel Blues, and Pop Music." In *Theology, Aesthetics, & Culture: Responses to the Work of David Brown*, edited by Robert MacSwain and Taylor Worley, 169–83. Oxford: Oxford University Press, 2012.

Chances Are. Directed by Emile Ardolino. United States: Sony Pictures, 1989. DVD.

Charlie St. Cloud. Directed by Bur Steers. USA: Universal Pictures, 2010. DVD.

Cheetham, David. *Ways of Meeting and the Theology of Religions*. Farnham, UK: Ashgate, 2013.

Clapp, Rodney. *Johnny Cash and the Great American Contradiction*. Louisville, KY: Westminster John Knox, 2008.

Clark, Lynn Schofield. "Why Study Popular Culture? Or, How to Build a Case for Your Thesis in a Religious Studies or Theology Department." In *Between Sacred and Profane: Researching Religion and Popular Culture*, edited by Gordon Lynch, 5–20. New York: Palgrave Macmillan, 2007.

Cobb, Kelton. *The Blackwell Guide to Theology and Popular Culture*. Malden: Blackwell, 2005.
Cole, Emmet. "Emmet Cole Interviews John D. Caputo." The Modern Word, 2005. http://www.themodernword.com/features/interview_caputo.html.
Cox, Harvey. *Fire from Heaven: The Rise of Pentecostal Spirituality and the Reshaping of Religion in the Twenty-First Century*. London: Cassell, 1996.
Cupitt, Don. "Free Christianity." In *God and Reality: Essays on Christian Non-Realism*, edited by Colin Crowder, 14–25. London: Mowbray, 1997.
Danielou, Jean. *The Angels and Their Mission: According to the Fathers of the Church*. Translated by David Heimann. Allen, TX: Christian Classics, 1957.
Danielson, Dennis R. "God's Other Book." In *Imagination and Interpretation: Christian Perspectives*, edited by Hans Boersma, 37–55. Vancouver, BC: Regent College, 2005.
Davies, Douglas. *The Theology of Death*. London: T. & T. Clark, 2008.
Davies, Eryl W. *Numbers*. New Century Bible Commentary. Grand Rapids: Eerdmans, 1995.
Deacy, Christopher. *Screening the Afterlife: Theology, Eschatology, and Film*. New York: Routledge, 2012.
———. "Heaven, Hell, and the Sweet Hereafter: Theological Perspectives on Eschatology and Film." In *Theology and Film: Challenging the Sacred/Secular Divide*, edited by Christopher Deacy and Gaye Williams Ortiz, 178–99. Malden: Blackwell, 2008.
———. "Theology and Film." In *Theology and Film: Challenging the Sacred/Secular Divide*, edited by Christopher Deacy and Gaye Williams Ortiz, 3–75. Malden: Blackwell, 2008.
DeCou, Jessica. *Playful, Glad, and Free: Karl Barth and a Theology of Popular Culture*. Minneapolis: Fortress, 2013.
Dragonfly. Directed by Tom Shadyak. USA: Universal Studios, 2002. DVD.
Dyrness, William A. *Senses of Devotion: Interfaith Aesthetics in Buddhist and Muslim Communities*. Art for Faith's Sake. Eugene, OR: Cascade, 2013.
———. *Visual Faith: Art, Theology, and Worship in Dialogue*. Grand Rapids: Baker Academic, 2001.
The Eagle. Directed by Kevin Macdonald. USA and Canada: Focus Features, 2011. DVD.
Ephrem the Syrian. *Hymns on Paradise*. Translated by Sebastian Brock. New York: St. Vladimir's Seminary Press, 1998.
Erickson, Millard J. *Christian Theology*. 3rd ed. Grand Rapids: Baker Academic, 2013.
Evans, C. Stephen. "Wisdom as Conceptual Understanding: A Christian Platonist Perspective." *Faith and Philosphy*, 27 (2010) 369–81.
Farrer, Austin. *The Glass of Vision*. Bampton Lectures. Glasgow: MacLehose/Glasgow University Press, 1948.
Fiddes, Paul. "Concept, Image and Story in Systematic Theology." *International Journal of Systematic Theology* 11, no. 1 (2009) 3–23.
———. *Participating in God: A Pastoral Doctrine of the Trinity*. London: Darton, Longman, and Todd, 2000.
———. *The Promised End: Eschatology in Theology and Literature*. Oxford: Blackwell, 2000.
The Fire Theft. "Heaven." On *The Fire Theft*. Rykodisk, 2003.

Fisher, Mark. "The Lonely Road." *Film Quarterly* 63, no. 3 (2010) 14–17.
Ford, David F. *Self and Salvation: Being Transformed*. Cambridge: Cambridge University Press, 1999.
Francis, D., L. Kellaher, and G. Neophytou. *The Secret Cemetery*. Oxford: Oxford University Press, 2005.
Galli, Mark. "Incredible Journeys." *Christianity Today*, December 21, 2012, 24–30.
Gardiner, Eileen, ed. *Visions of Heaven and Hell before Dante*. New York: Italica, 1989.
Garrett, Greg. *Entertaining Judgment: The Afterlife in Popular Imagination*. Oxford: Oxford University Press, 2015.
George, Timothy, ed. *Pilgrims on the Sawdust Trail: Evangelical Ecumenism and the Quest for Christian Identity*. Grand Rapids: Baker Academic, 2004.
Gill, Robin, ed. *Theology and Sociology: A Reader*. London: Chapman, 1987.
Gladiator. Directed by Ridley Scott. USA and Canada: Dreamworks Video, 2000. DVD.
Gooder, Paula. *Heaven*. London: SPCK, 2011.
Green, Garrett. *Theology, Hermeneutics, and Imagination: The Crisis of Interpretation at the End of Modernity*. Cambridge: Cambridge University Press, 2000.
Green, Joel B. *The Gospel of Luke*. The New International Commentary on the New Testament. Grand Rapids: Eerdmans, 1997.
Gregory of Nyssa. *The Life of Moses*. Translated by Abraham J. Malherbe and Everett Ferguson. New York: HarperOne, 2006.
Grenz, Stanley J. *Theology for the Community of God*. Grand Rapids: Eerdmans, 1994.
Guthri, Steven R. *Creator Spirit: The Holy Spirit and the Art of Becoming Human*. Grand Rapids: Baker Academic, 2011.
Hart, Trevor. *Between the Image and the Word*. Farnham, UK: Ashgate, 2013.
Hart, Trevor, and Richard Bauckham. *Hope against Hope: Christian Eschatology at the Turn of the Millennium*. Grand Rapids: Eerdmans, 1999.
Hass, Andrew. "The Future of Literature and Theology." In *The Oxford Handbook of English Literature and Theology*, edited by David Jasper Andrew W. Hass, and Elisabeth Jay, 841–58. Oxford: Oxford University Press, 2009.
Heart and Souls. Directed by Ron Underwood. USA and Canada: Universal Studio, 1998. DVD.
Heaven Is for Real. Directed by Randall Wallace. United States: TriStar, 2014. DVD.
Heaven: Where Is It? How Do We Get There? Directed by George Paul, 2005; United States: Mpi Home Video, 2006. DVD.
Hereafter. Directed by Clint Eastwood. USA and Canada: Warner Bros., 2010. DVD.
Hedley, Douglas. *Living Forms of the Imagination*. London: T. & T. Clark, 2008.
———. *The Iconic Imagination*. London: Bloomsbury Academic, 2016.
Hick, John. *Death and Eternal Life*. London: Collins, 1976.
Hoffman, Lawerance A. "Does God Remember? A Liturgical Theology of Memory." In *Memory and History in Christianity and Judaism*, edited by Michael A. Signer, 41–72. Notre Dame, IN: University of Notre Dame Press, 2001.
Hollenweger, Walter J. "All Creatures Great and Small: Towards a Pneumatology of Life." In *Strange Gifts? A Guide to Charismatic Renewal*, edited by David Martin and Peter Mullen, 42–53. Oxford: Blackwell, 1984.
———. *Pentecostalism: Origins and Developments Worldwide*. Peabody, MA: Hendrickson, 1997.

Hopps, Gavin. "Infinite Hospitality and the Redemption of Kitsch." In *Theology, Aesthetics, & Culture: Responses to the Work of David Brown*, edited by Robert MacSwain and Taylor Worley, 157–68. Oxford: Oxford University Press, 2012.
If I Stay. Directed by R. J. Cutler. USA: DiNovi Pictures, 2014. DVD.
Inside Out. Directed by Pete Docter and Ronnie Del Carmen. USA: Disney Pixar, 2015. DVD.
Janzen, J. Gerald. *Job*. Interpretation. Atlanta: John Knox, 1985.
Jasper, David. "On Systematizing the Unsystematic: A Response." In *Explorations in Theology and Film*, edited by Clive Marsh and Gaye Ortiz, 235–44. Oxford: Blackwell, 1997.
———. *A Short Introduction to Hermeneutics*. Louisville: Westminster John Knox, 2004.
———. "The Study of Literature and Theology." In *The Oxford Handbook of English Literature and Theology*, edited by David Jasper Andrew W. Hass, and Elisabeth Jay, 15–32. Oxford: Oxford University Press, 2009.
Jasper, David, and Robert Detweiler, eds. *Religion and Literature: A Reader*. Louisville: Westminster John Knox, 2000.
Jauss, Hans Robert. *Toward an Aesthetic of Reception*. Translated by Timothy Bahti. Brighton, UK: Harvester, 1982.
Johnston, Robert K. *God's Wider Presence: Reconsidering General Revelation*. Grand Rapids: Baker Academic, 2014.
———. "Introduction: Reframing the Discussion." In *Reframing Theology and Film: New Focus for an Emerging Discipline*, edited by Robert K. Johnston, 15–26. Grand Rapids: Baker Academic, 2007.
Karkkainen, Veli-Matti. *Christ and Reconciliation. Vol. 1. A Constructive Christian Theology for the Pluralistic World*. Grand Rapids: Eerdmans, 2013.
Kaufman, Gordon D. *The Theological Imagination: Constructing the Concept of God*. Philadelphia: Westminster, 1981.
Kearney, Richard. "Imagination's Truth: An Interview with Richard Kearney." Filmed October 2012. Youtube video, 17:26. Posted October 2012. https://www.youtube.com/watch?v=V1hmmdoAons.
———. *Poetics of Imagining*. New York: Fordham University Press, 1998.
———. *The Wake of Imagination*. London: Routledge, 1998.
Kelly, Hubert Dreyfus, and Sean Dorrance. *All Things Shining: Reading the Western Classics to Find Meaning in a Secular Age*. New York: Free, 2011.
Kenney, Randy. "National Academy Sells Two Hudson River School Paintings to Bolster Its Finances." In *Art and Design: New York Times*, December 5, 2008.
Kerr, Fergus. "What's Wrong with Realism Anyway?" In *God and Reality: Essays on Christian Non-Realism*, edited by Colin Crowder, 128–43. London: Mowbray, 1997.
Keuss, Jeffrey F. *Your Neighbor's Hymnal: What Popular Music Teaches Us about Faith, Hope, and Love*. Eugene, OR: Cascade, 2011.
Kierkegaard, Søren. *Fear and Trembling*. Translated by Alastair Hannay. Reprint. New York: Penguin, 2006.
Kingdom of Heaven. Directed by Ridley Scott. USA and Canada: 20th Century Fox, 2005. DVD.
Kreeft, Peter. *Before I Go: Letters to Our Children about What Really Matters*. New York: Sheed & Ward, 2007.

———. *Everything You Ever Wanted to Know about Heaven: But Never Dreamed of Asking*. San Francisco: Ignatius, 1990.

Küng, Hans. "Art and the Question of Meaning." In *Theological Aesthetics: A Reader*, edited by Gesa Elsbeth Thiessen, 256–59. Grand Rapids: Eerdmans, 2004.

Kuyper, Abraham. *Lectures on Calvinism: Six Lectures from the Stone Foundation Lectures Delivered at Princeton University*. Reprint. No loc: ReadaClassic.com, 2010.

Lang, Bernhard. *Meeting in Heaven*. Oxford: Lang, 2011.

Lang, Bernhard, and Colleen McDannell. *Heaven: A History*. 2nd ed. New Haven: Yale University Press, 2001.

Larsen, Timothy. "The Evangelical Reception of Dietrich Bonhoeffer." In *Bonhoeffer, Christ and Culture*, edited by Keith L. Johnson and Timothy Larsen, 39–57. Downers Grove, IL: IVP Academic, 2013.

Lawler, Steph. *Identity: Sociological Perspectives*. Cambridge: Polity, 2008.

Lawrence, Joel. *Bonhoeffer: A Guide for the Perplexed*. London: T. & T. Clark, 2010.

Lee, Amy. "Slavoj Zizek Joins Occupy Wall Street." *The Huffington Post*. 2011. http://www.huffingtonpost.com/2011/10/10/slavoj-zizek-occupy-wall-street_n_1003566.html.

Levinas, Emmanuel. *An Essay on Exteriority*. Translated by Alphonso Lingis. Reprint. Pittsburgh: Duquesne University Press, 2011.

Lewis, C. S. *An Experiment in Criticism*. Cambridge: Cambridge University Press, 1961.

———. *Mere Christianity*. Reprint. New York: Touchstone, 1996.

———. *Problem of Pain*. Reprint. New York: Touchstone, 1996.

Locke, John. *An Essay Concerning Human Understanding*. Oxford: Oxford University Press, 2008.

The Lovely Bones. Directed by Peter Jackson. USA: Dreamworks Pictures, 2009. DVD.

Lyden, John, ed. *The Routledge Companion to Religion and Film*. New York: Routledge, 2011.

Lynch, Gordon. "Some Concluding Reflections." In *Between Sacred and Profane: Researching Religion and Popular Culture*, edited by Gordon Lynch, 157–63. New York: Palgrave Macmillan, 2007.

Lynch, Gordon. *Understanding Theology and Popular Culture*. Oxford: Blackwell, 2005.

MacEwan, Donald G. "Missing Persons: Individual Eschatology in Twentieth Century Protestant Theology." PhD diss., University of Dublin, 2000.

MacGregor, Geddes. *Images of Afterlife: Beliefs from Antiquity to Modern Times*. New York: Paragon House, 1992.

Markos, Louis. *Heaven and Hell: Visions of the Afterlife in the Western Poetic Tradition*. Eugene, OR: Cascade, 2013.

Marsden, George M. *Fundamentalism and American Culture: The Shaping of Twentieth-Century Evangelicalism 1870–1925*. Oxford: Oxford University Press, 1980.

Marsh, Clive. "Audience Reception." In *The Routledge Companion to Religion and Film*, edited by John Lyden, 255–74. New York: Routledge, 2011.

———. "Blick über den Tod hinaus: Bilder vom Leben nach dem Tod in Theologie und Film/Seeing Beyond Death: Images of the Afterlife in Theology and Film." *The Journal of Religion and Popular Culture* 25, no. 2 (2013) 310–11.

———. *Cinema & Sentiment: Film's Challenge to Theology*. Milton Keynes, UK: Paternoster, 2004.

———, with Vaughan S. Roberts. *Personal Jesus: How Popular Music Shapes Our Souls*. Grand Rapids: Baker Academic, 2012.

———. "Theology beyond the Modern and the Postmodern: A Future Agenda for Theology and Film." In *Explorations in Theology and Film*, edited by Clive Marsh and Gaye Ortiz, 245–55. Oxford: Blackwell, 1997.

———. *Theology Goes to the Movies: An Introduction to Critical Christian Thinking*. New York: Routledge, 2007.

———. "What If David Brown Had Owned a Television?" In *Theology, Aesthetics, & Culture: Responses to the Work of David Brown*, edited by Robert MacSwain and Taylor Worley, 184–96. Oxford: Oxford University Press, 2012.

Martin, David. *Christian Language and Its Mutations: Essays in Sociological Understanding*. Edited by Douglas Davies and Richard Fenn. Theology and Religion in Interdisciplinary Perspective. Farnham, UK: Ashgate, 2002.

McArthur, M. Jane. "Memory in the New Creation: A Critical Response to Miroslav Volf's Eschatological Forgetting." PhD diss., University of St. Andrews, 2004.

McClendon, James W. *Biography as Theology: How Life Stories Can Remake Today's Theology*. Nashville: Abingdon, 1980.

———. *Systematic Theology: Witness*. Vol. 3. Nashville: Abingdon, 2000.

McClintock, Pamela. "Box Office: 'Heaven Is for Real' Crushes Johnny Depp's Latest Bomb 'Trancendence'." *The Hollywood Reporter*, 2014. https://www.hollywoodreporter.com/news/box-office-heaven-is-real-697764.

McGrath, Alister. *A Brief History of Heaven*. Oxford: Blackwell, 2003.

———. *The Genesis of Doctrine: A Study in the Foundations of Doctrinal Criticism*. Oxford: Blackwell, 1990.

———. *The Open Secret: A New Vision for Natural Theology*. Oxford: Blackwell, 2008.

McKinney, George D. "The Azusa Street Revival Revisited." In *Pilgrims on the Sawdust Trail: Evangelical Ecumenism and the Quest for Christian Identity*, edited by Timothy George, 71–82. Grand Rapids: Baker Academic, 2004.

McLachlan, Sarah. "I Will Remember You." On *Mirrorball*. Sony Music CMG. 2002. http://itunes.com.

Meacham, Jon. "Heaven Can't Wait: Why Rethinking the Hereafter Could Make the World a Better Place." *TIME*, April 16, 2012.

Meister, Chad, and Charles Taliaferro, eds. *The Cambridge Companion to Christian Philosophical Theology*. Cambridge Companions to Religion. New York: Cambridge University Press, 2009.

Miller, Lisa. *Heaven: Our Enduring Fascination with the Afterlife*. New York: Harper, 2010.

Miller, Matthew "Eerdmans 100 Interview Series: Hans Boersma" Eerdmans 100 Interview Series, 2011. http://blogs.christianbook.com/blogs/academic/2011/08/29/eerdmans-100-hans-boersma/.

Moltmann, Jürgen. *The Source of Life: The Holy Spirit and the Theology of Life*. Translated by Margaret Kohl. London: SCM, 1997.

———. *The Spirit of Life: A Universal Affirmation*. Translated by Margaret Kohl. Minneapolis: Fortress, 1992.

———. *Theology & Joy*. London: SCM, 1973.

Morgan, David. "Studying Religion and Popular Culture: Prospects, Presuppositions, Procedures." In *Between Sacred and Profane: Researching Religion and Popular Culture*, edited by Gordon Lynch, 21–33. New York: Palgrave Macmillan, 2007.

Morris, Thomas V., ed. *God and the Philosophers: The Reconciliation of Faith and Reason*. New York: Oxford University Press, 1994.

Morse, Christopher. *The Difference Heaven Makes: Rehearing the Gospel as News*. London: T. & T. Clark, 2010.
Newlands, George. *The Transformative Imagination: Rethinking Intercultural Theology*. Farnham, UK: Ashgate, 2004.
Niebuhr, H. Richard. *Christ and Culture*. Reprint. San Francisco: Harper, 2001.
Noah. Directed by Darren Aronofsky. USA Paramount Pictures, 2014. DVD.
Noll, Mark A. *A History of Christianity in the United States and Canada*. Grand Rapids: Eerdmans, 1992.
Olthuis, James. "Taking the Wager of/on Love." In *Gazing through a Prism Darkly: Reflections on Merold Westphal's Hermeneutical Epistemology*, edited by B. Keith Putt, 150–62. New York: Fordham University Press, 2009.
Ortiz, Gaye, and Clive Marsh, eds. *Explorations in Theology and Film*. Oxford: Blackwell, 1997.
———. "Theology beyond the Modern and the Postmodern: A Future Agenda for Theology and Film." In *Explorations in Theology and Film*, edited by Clive Marsh and Gaye Ortiz, 245–55. Oxford: Blackwell, 1997.
Ostwalt, Conrad. "Apocalyptic." In *The Routledge Companion to Religion and Film*, edited by John Lyden, 368–83. New York: Routledge, 2011.
———. *Secular Steeples: Popular Culture and Religious Imagination*. New York: Trinity, 2003.
Pannenberg, Wolfhart. *Systematic Theology*. Vol. 1. Translated by Geoffrey W. Bromiley. Grand Rapid: Eerdmans, 1991.
———. *Systematic Theology*. Vol. 3. Translated by Geoffrey W. Bromiley. Grand Rapids: Eerdmans, 1998.
———, ed. *Revelation as History*. London: Sheed and Ward, 1969.
Pelikan, Jaroslav. *Acts*. Brazos Theological Commentary on the Bible. Grand Rapids: Brazos, 2005.
———. *The Christian Tradition: A History of the Development of Doctrine. Vol. 1. The Emergence of the Catholic Tradition (100–600)*. Chicago: The University of Chicago Press, 1971.
———. *Jesus through the Centuries*. New York: Harper & Row, 1985.
———. *The Vindication of Tradition*. New Haven: Yale University Press, 1984.
Pinnock, Clark H. *Flame of Love: A Theology of the Holy Spirit*. Downers Grove, IL: IVP Academic, 1996.
Plato. *The Republic*. Translated by Desmond Lee. 2nd ed. Baltimore: Penguin Classics, 1974.
Price, Henry H. *Essays in the Philosophy of Religion*. Based on the Sarum Lectures 1971. Oxford: Clarendon, 1972.
Price, Lynne. *Theology Out of Place: A Theological Biography of Walter J. Hollenweger*. London: Sheffield Academic Press, 2002.
Prickett, Stephen, and David Jasper, eds. *The Bible and Literature: A Reader*. Oxford: Blackwell, 1999.
Quash, Ben. *Found Theology: History, Imagination, and the Holy Spirit*. London: Bloomsbury, 2013.
Reimer, A. James. *Paul Tillich: Theologian of Nature, Culture, and Politics*. Münster: Lit Verlag, 2004.
Ricoeur, Paul. "Evil, a Challenge to Philosophy and Theology." In *Figuring The Sacred: Religion, Narrative, and Imagination*, translated by David Pellauer, edited by Mark Wallace, 249–61. Minneapolis: Fortress, 1995.

The Road. Directed by John Hillcoat. USA: Dimension Films The Weinstein Company, 2009. DVD.

Roth, Robert. *The Theater of God: Story in Christian Doctrines.* Philadelphia: Fortress, 1975.

Rush, Ormond. *The Reception of Doctrine: An Appropriation of Hans Robert Jauss' Reception Aesthetics and Literary Hermeneutics.* Rome: Gregorian University Press, 1996.

———. *Still Interpreting Vatican II: Some Hermeneutical Principles.* Mahwah, NJ: Paulist, 2004.

Russell, Jeffrey Burton. *A History of Heaven: The Singing Silence.* Princeton: Princeton University Press, 1997.

———. *Paradise Mislaid: How We Lost Heaven and How We Can Regain It.* Oxford: Oxford University Press, 2006.

Rusted Root. "Heaven." On *Remember*. DKE Records under license from Touchy Pegg, 2004.

Saliers, Don E. *Music and Theology.* Horizons in Theology. Nashville: Abingdon, 2007.

Scharen, Christian. *Broken Hallelujahs: Why Popular Music Matters to Those Seeking God.* Grand Rapids: Brazos, 2011.

Schleiermacher, Friedrich. *The Christian Faith.* Edited by H. R. Mackintosh and J. S. Stewart. Berkeley, CA: Apocraphile, 2011.

Schrader, Paul. *Transcendental Style in Film: Ozu, Bresson, Dreyer.* 1946. Reprint. Berkeley, CA: Da Capo, 1972.

Schwarz, Hans. *Theology in a Global Context: The Last Two Hundred Years.* Grand Rapids: Eerdmans, 2005.

Scott, Robert, and Henry George Liddell. *A Greek–English Lexicon.* Oxford: Clarendon, 1958.

Sherry, Patrick. *Spirit and Beauty: An Introduction to Theological Aesthetics.* Oxford: Clarendon, 1992.

———. *Spirit, Saints, and Immortality.* Albany, NY: State University of New York Press, 1984.

Simon, Ulrich. *The Ascent to Heaven.* London: Barrie and Rockliff, 1961.

———. *The End Is Not Yet: A Study in Christian Eschatology.* Digswell Place, UK: Nisbet, 1964.

———. *Heaven in the Christian Tradition.* London: Wyman, 1958.

Smith, Gary Scott. *Heaven in the American Imagination.* Oxford: Oxford University Press, 2011.

Smith, James K. A. *Desiring the Kingdom: Worship, Worldview, and Cultural Formation.* Cultural Liturgies Vol. 1. Grand Rapids: Baker Academic, 2009.

———. "Faith in American Beauty: Christian Reflections on Film." In *Imagination and Interpretation: Christian Perspectives*, edited by Hans Boersma, 179–89. Vancouver, BC: Regent College, 2005.

———. *The Fall of Interpretation: Philosophical Foundations for a Creational Hermeneutic.* 2nd ed. Grand Rapids: Baker Academic, 2012.

———. *Imagining the Kingdom: How Worship Works.* Cultural Liturgies Vol. 2. Grand Rapids: Baker Academic, 2013.

———. *Who's Afraid of Postmodernism: Taking Derrida, Lyotard, and Foucault to Church.* Grand Rapids: Zondervan, 2006.

Snyder, Bob. "Music and Memory: An Introduction." Cambridge: MIT Press, 2000.

Solomon, Robert C. *In Defense of Sentimentality*. Oxford: Oxford University Press, 2004.

Staiger, Janet. *Interpreting Films: Studies in the Historical Reception of American Cinema*. Princeton: Princeton University Press, 1992.

Steffler, Alva William. *Symbols of the Christian Faith*. Grand Rapids: Eerdmans, 2002.

Stenger, Jan R. "Athens and/or Jerusalem? Basil the Great and Chrysostom on Religious Education." Paper given in the Friday Seminar Series in the Classics Department, University of St. Andrews, 2013.

Taliaferro, Charles. *Aesthetics*. Oxford: Oneworld, 2011.

Taves, Ann. *Fits, Trances, and Visions: Experiencing Religion and Explaining Experience from Wesley to James*. Princeton: Princeton University Press, 1999.

Taylor, Barry, and Craig Detweiler. *A Matrix of Meanings: Finding God in Pop Culture*. Grand Rapids: Baker Academic, 2003.

Taylor, Barry. "The Colors of Sound: Music and Meaning Making in Film." In *Reframing Theology and Film: New Focus for an Emerging Discipline*, edited by Robert K. Johnston, 51–69. Grand Rapids: Baker Academic, 2007.

Taylor, Charles. *Varieties of Religion Today: William James Revisited*. Cambridge: Harvard University Press, 2000.

Taylor, Greg. "Top Ten Movies on the Afterlife." *Daily Grail*, October 22, 2010. https://www.dailygrail.com/2010/10/top-ten-afterlife-movies/.

Theodorakopoulos, Elena. *Ancient Rome at the Cinema: Story and Spectacle in Hollywood and Rome*. Greece and Rome Live. Exeter, UK: Bristol Phoenix, 2010.

Thiel, John E. "For What May We Hope? Thoughts on the Eschatological Imagination." *Theological Studies* 67 (2006) 517–41.

———. *Icons of Hope: The "Last Things" in Catholic Imagination*. Notre Dame, IN: University of Notre Dame Press, 2013.

Thiessen, Gesa Elsbeth, ed. *Theological Aesthetics: A Reader*. Grand Rapids: Eerdmans, 2004.

Thiselton, Anthony C. *Hermeneutics: An Introduction*. Grand Rapids: Eerdmans, 2009.

———. *The Hermeneutics of Doctrine*. Grand Rapids: Eerdmans, 2007.

———. *Life after Death: A New Approach to the Last Things*. Grand Rapids: Eerdmans 2012.

———. *New Horizons in Hermeneutics: The Theory and Practice of Transforming Biblical Reading*. Grand Rapids: Zondervan, 1992.

Thorsen, Donald A. D. *The Wesleyan Quadrilateral: Scripture, Tradition, Reason, & Experience as a Model of Evangelical Theology*. Grand Rapids: Zondervan, 1990.

Tillich, Paul. *On the Boundary: An Autobiographical Sketch*. London: Collins, 1967.

———. *Systematic Theology*. Vol. 3. Chicago: University of Chicago Press, 1963.

———. *Theology of Culture*. Edited by Robert C. Kimball. Reprint. Oxford: Oxford University Press, 1975.

Toy Story 3. Directed by Lee Undrich. USA: Disney Pixar, 2010. DVD.

Tracy, David. *Plurality and Ambiguity: Hermeneutics, Religion, Hope*. San Francisco: Harper and Row, 1987.

The Tree of Life. Directed by Terrance Malick. United Kingdom: Cottonwood Pictures, 2011. DVD.

Treier, Daniel J., Mark Husbands, and Roger Lundin, eds. *The Beauty of God: Theology and the Arts*. Downers Grove, IL: IVP Academic, 2007.

Tugwell, Simon. *Human Immortality and the Redemption of Death*. Springfield, IL: Templegate, 1991.
Veith, Gene Edward. *Painters of Faith: The Spiritual Landscape in Nineteenth-Century America Featuring the Works of the Hudson River School*. Washington, DC: Regnery, 2001.
Viladesau, Richard. *Theological Aesthetics: God in Imagination, Beauty, and Art*. Oxford: Oxford University Press, 1999.
Volf, Miroslav. *The End of Memory: Remembering Rightly in a Violent World*. Grand Rapids: Eerdmans, 2006.
Wallace, Mark I. "Introduction." In Paul Ricoeur, *Figuring The Sacred: Religion, Narrative, and Imagination*, edited by Mark Wallace, 1–32. Minneapolis: Fortress, 1995.
Wall-E. Directed by Andrew Stanton. USA: Walt Disney Studios Motion Pictures, 2008. DVD.
Walls, Jerry L. *Heaven: The Logic of Eternal Joy*. New York: Oxford University Press, 2002.
———. "Heaven and Hell." In *The Cambridge Companion to Christian Philosophical Theology*, edited by Charles Taliaferro and Chad Meister, 238–52. Cambridge Companions to Religion. New York: Cambridge University Press, 2009.
Walsh, Richard. "(Carrying the Fire on) No Road for Old Horses: Cormac Mccarthy's Untold Biblical Stories." *Journal of Religion and Popular Culture* 24, no. 3 (2012) 339–57.
Ward, Graham, ed. *The Blackwell Companion to Postmodern Theology*. Oxford: Blackwell, 2005.
———. *Christ and Culture*. Oxford: Blackwell, 2005.
———. "Theological Materialism." In *God and Reality: Essays on Christian Non-Realism*, edited by Colin Crowder, 144–59. London: Mowbray, 1997.
Ward, Vincent. "What Dreams May Come: Concepts of an Afterlife." 2009. http://vincentwardfilms.com/concepts/wdmc/treatment/.
Weber, Max. *The Sociology of Religion*. Translated by Ephraim Fischoff. London: Methuen, 1965.
West, Cornell, with David Ritz. *Brother West: Living and Loving Out Loud, a Memoir*. New York: SmileyBooks, 2009.
Westphal, Merold. "Faith Seeking Understanding." In *God and the Philosophers: The Reconciliation of Faith and Reason*, edited by Thomas V. Morris, 215–26. New York: Oxford University Press, 1994.
———. *God, Guilt, and Death: An Existential Phenomenology of Religion*. Bloomington, IN: Indiana University Press, 1984.
———. *Whose Community? Which Interpretation?: Philosophical Hermeneutics for the Church*. Grand Rapids: Baker Academic, 2009.
What Dreams May Come. Directed by Vincent Ward. USA and Canada: Polygram Filmed Entertainment, 2003. DVD.
Wilken, Robert Louis. *The Spirit of Early Christian Thought*. New Haven: Yale University Press, 2003.
Wood, Ralph C. *Literature and Theology*. Nashville: Abingdon, 2008.
Wright, Melanie J. *Religion and Film: An Introduction*. London: I. B. Tauris, 2007.
Wright, N. T. *For All the Saints: Remembering the Christian Departed*. Harrisburg, PA: Morehouse, 2003.

———. "Response to Markus Bockmeuhl." In *Jesus, Paul and the People of God: A Theological Dialogue with N. T. Wright*, edited by Nicholas Perrin and Richard B. Hays, 231–34. Downers Grove, IL: IVP Academic, 2011.

———. *The Resurrection of the Son of God*. Christian Origins and the Question of God, Vol. 3. London: SPCK, 2003.

———. *Surprised by Hope: Rethinking Heaven, the Resurrection, and the Mission of the Church*. New York: HarperOne, 2008.

Wright, T. R. *Theology and Literature*. Signposts in Theology. Oxford: Blackwell, 1988.

Yong, Amos. *Discerning the Spirit(s): A Pentecostal-Charismatic Contribution to Christian Theology of Religions*. Sheffield, UK: Sheffield Academic Press, 2000.

———. *Theology and Down Syndrome*. Waco, TX: Baylor University Press, 2007.

Zaleski, Carol. *The Life of the World to Come: Near-Death Experience and Christian Hope*. Oxford: Oxford University Press, 1996.

Zaleski, Carol, and Philip Zaleski, eds. *The Book of Heaven: An Anthology of Writings from Ancient to Modern Times*. Oxford: Oxford University Press, 2000.

Zijderveld, Anton, and Peter Berger. *In Praise of Doubt: How to Have Convictions without Becoming a Fanatic*. New York: HarperCollins, 2009.

Index

Adler, Mortimer, 108–9, 116
aesthetics, xvi, xvii, 61, 63, 72–73, 76, 84–85, 128–29, 153, 158–59, 164n43
afterlife, xv, xviii, 29, 37, 89, 105–6, 110, 115–17, 172, 183
Alcorn, Randy, 185
Alpha Rev., 204
Ambrose, 154, 170
Aquinas, Thomas, 9, 35, 42, 75, 154, 175
Augustine, 41, 112, 154, 178, 180

Badham, Paul, 104
Bal, Mieke, 50
Balthasar, Hans Urs von, 29, 63n59, 128–29, 178
baptism, 22, 25, 59
Barth, Karl, 14–21, 43, 71, 153–54, 201
Barkman, Adam, 167–68
Basil the Great, 161
Bauckham, Richard, 166
Beastly, 151–52, 155
Beaudoin, Tom, 59–60, 69, 76, 132
Beetlejuice, 120
Begbie, Jeremy, 3n1, 130, 138–39, 143
Bennett, Alice, 158n12, 165, 169, 175, 194
Berger, Peter, 43
Bernard of Clairvaux, 170, 186
Bernstein, Alan, 40
Bonhoeffer, Dietrich, 20, 42, 56, 70–71
Bockmuehl, Markus, 31–32

Boersma, Hans, 35–36, 38–39, 195
Bourdieu, Pierre, 47
Brandt, Jonathan, 56n17
Brown, David, xvi, 4–6, 22–23, 53, 59–60, 70–71, 73, 75, 77, 78n144, 82, 85, 119, 146–48, 156, 160
Brown, Frank Burch, 63n59, 84n178, 86n192, 87, 140, 144, 153
Browning, Don, 56
Bruce Almighty, xvi, 83
Brueggeman, Walter, 36
Brunner, Emil, 21
Bultmann, Rudolf, 20, 70

Callaway, Kutter, 101
Calvin, John, 154
Caputo, John, 131n43, 150, 160
Casselberry, Judith, 133, 146n125
Chalcedon, 176
Chances Are, 84
Charlie St. Cloud, 82
Cheetham, David, 61
Christ/Christology, 5, 7, 12–15, 18, 29–32, 55–56, 63, 69, 71, 78, 83, 103, 111–14, 150, 152, 155, 161, 166–67, 171–74, 176, 180, 200
Chrysostom, John, 161
Clapp, Rodney, 23, 134–36
Clapton, Eric, xv
Clark, Lynn Scholfield, 46–47, 49, 59n36
Cobb, Kelton, 45–46, 58, 76–77, 90, 117, 146
Cox, Harvey
Cullmann, Oscar, 30

Cuppitt, Don, 78
Cyprian, 32

Danielou, Jean, 35, 116
Danielson, Dennis, 8
Dante, xix, 43, 120, 161, 164n43
Davies, Douglas, 44
de Lubac, Henri, 35
Deacy, Christopher, xvii, 48, 55–57, 63, 75, 97, 104, 106, 108
DeCou, Jessica, 16, 17–19, 128
Delumeau, Jean, 40
Derrida, Jacque, 121, 160n18
Detweiler, Craig, 46, 50, 73, 76
Dewey, John, 73
Dragonfly, 82, 189
Dreyfus, Hubert, 120
Dyrness, William, 8, 43n100, 47n114, 48, 51, 59, 61, 98

Edwards, Jonathan, 177
emotions, xvii, 149, 204
Ephrem the Syrian, 127
Erickson, Millard, 19n95
ethics, 128–29, 205
eschatology, xiii, xix, 5, 19, 35, 53, 65, 91, 158, 163, 169, 174, 181, 186–88, 189, 198, 200, 205
Evans, C. Stephen, 100
experience, 7, 24, 51, 58, 63–64, 76, 85, 103, 106, 110, 113, 118, 120–21, 124–25, 127–28, 131–32, 142, 154–55, 174, 178, 183, 199, 201, 203

Farrer, Austin, xvi, 3–4, 10, 20–22, 25–27, 53, 77
Fiddes, Paul, xvi, 7, 118, 127, 161–62
filioque, 13
film, xiii, xvi, xvii, xix, 34, 58–59, 65, 75, 83, 88–91, 95, 97, 98–99, 100–101, 104, 106, 109, 116–17, 119, 124, 151, 155, 157, 164–65, 169, 175, 181, 183, 186, 189, 192–94, 198, 203–4
Ford, David F., 103, 113–14
Foucault, Michel, 77
Freud, Sigmund, 125

Gadamer, Hans-Georg, 5n13, 67, 74, 134
Galli, Mark, 171–72
Gardiner, Eileen, 118n94, 126n10
Garrett, Greg, 48n119
Gill, Robin, 192
Gladiator, 166–69, 174, 179, 186–87
Gooder, Paula, 100
Green, Garrett, 55
Green, Joel B., 13
Gregory of Nyssa, 86, 179, 181
Grenz, Stanley, 11n41
Guthri, Steven R., 10

Habermas, Jürgen, 5n13,
Harbison, E. Harris, xviii
Hart, Julian, 136
Hart, Trevor, 63n59
Hass, Andrew, 160n17
Heart and Souls, 84
Heaven, xiii, xv, xvi, xviii, xix, 7, 26, 28–31, 34, 36–39, 44, 48, 53–54, 58, 80, 91, 95–96, 98, 100, 105, 107, 109, 112–15, 117–23, 128, 130, 140, 143–44, 148–54, 156–59, 163, 166, 174, 177, 179, 181, 183–85, 188, 192, 199–205
Heaven is for Real, 90
Hell, 44, 104, 110, 115, 117, 150
Herder, Johann Gottfried von, 58
Hereafter, 203
hermeneutics, xiv, xvii, xviii, 3, 7, 19n95, 23, 27, 36, 51, 53–54, 64–66, 70, 75, 83–84, 86–88, 95, 98–100, 123–24, 128, 136, 145, 148–49, 201–2
Hedley, Douglas, xvi, 4, 202
Hegel, G.W., 33
Heidegger, Martin, 74
Hick, John, 104n38
Hoffman, Lawerance, 127
Hollenweger, Walter J., xvi, 9–10, 12–16, 18, 68–69, 162–63, 179n116, 180, 201
Hopps, Gavin, 144
Homer, xix, 33, 163–64, 174
Hudson River School, 118–19, 121–22

INDEX

immanence, 19, 119
Incarnation, 6,
interpretation, xiv, 22, 36, 39, 51, 52, 64, 66–67, 74, 88, 95–96, 100, 111, 112, 117, 121, 123–24, 132, 136, 155, 192, 194, 198
imagination, xiii, xv, xvii, xviii, xix, 4–5, 7, 12, 19–21, 25–27, 29–30, 34, 42, 44, 55–56, 61, 78–80, 82, 87, 90, 98, 100–101, 105, 107–11, 120–24, 126, 143–44, 149, 152–53, 157, 159, 166, 169, 186, 189, 201–2, 206
Israel, xiv

Jackson, Peter, 109
James, William, 64
Jasper, David, 74, 97–98, 159
Jauss, Hans Robert, 97
Jefferson, Thomas, 68
Jenkins, David, 130
Jerome, 86
John XXII, Pope, 170
Johnson, Elizabeth, 6
Johnston, Robert K., 7n23, 33n28, 58–59, 76, 97

Kant, Immanuel, 78, 143
Kärkkäinen, Veli-Matti, 17n82, 61–62
Kaufman, Gordon D., 34
Kearney, Richard, xiv, xv, xvi, 79–87, 129
Kelley, Sean, 120
Kermode, Frank, 165
Kerr, Fergus, 78, 81
Keuss, Jefferey F., 136–37, 139, 144
Kierkegaard, Søren, 125, 128–29, 150
King, Martin Luther, 24
Kreeft, Peter, 42, 80n158, 95, 116, 127, 158
Küng, Hans, 141
Kuyper, Abraham, 162

Lang, Bernhard, xv, 28–30, 36, 39–41, 43, 98, 118, 156–57, 163, 177–78
Larson, Timothy, 70n95
LaRue, Cleophus, 37
Lawler, Steph, 110, 117n92, 132

Levinas, Emmanuel
Lewis, C.S., xvi, 20, 37, 110–11, 145, 184
literature, 34, 91, 98, 157, 159–61, 164–66, 186
Locke, John, 131
Lovely Bones, 82, 109
Luther, Martin, 68
Lynch, Gordon, xvii, 45–47, 49–50, 55, 57–58, 63, 72–74, 76, 85, 97

MacEwan, Donald G., 20, 129, 178
MacGregor, Geddes, 171–72
Markos, Louis, 161n21, 162–64
Mardsen, George M., 8, 20
Marsh, Clive, xvii, 6, 19, 59–60, 72, 89, 91n216, 98n13, 98n17, 130, 132, 155
Martin, David, 141–42
Maximus the Confessor, 86, 195
McArthur, Jane M., 126, 128, 155
McClendon, James W., 132, 136
McDannell, Colleen, xv, 28–30, 36, 40–41, 43, 98, 118, 163
McGrath, Alister, 20, 21, 32, 44–45, 69, 184, 186
McKinney, George D., 23–24
Meachem, Jon, 36–37, 83n176
Merleau-Ponty, Maurice, 16n74
memory, xvii,, 104–5, 113, 121, 123–27, 130, 136–37, 139, 149–51, 154–55, 156, 178, 204
Miller, Lisa, 31, 38
Milton, John, xix, 161, 164n43
Mirandola, Pico della, 159
Moltmann, Jürgen, xvi, 6, 12–16, 20, 129, 178, 201
Morgan, David, 45, 48n119, 49, 72
Morse, Christopher, xiiin2
Mozart, Wolfgang Amadeus, 153–54
music, xix, 6, 19, 82, 91, 124, 126, 130–31, 133–34, 136–37, 140–42, 145–46, 148–49, 151, 154–55, 157, 159

New Testament studies, xvii, 12, 27, 39, 45, 53–54, 66
Newlands, George, 16, 62–63

Newman, John Henry, 67
Niebuhr, H. Richard, 34, 54–55, 63
Nietzsche, Friedrich, 125
Noah, 195
Noll, Mark A., 22–23

Olthuis, James, 90n213
Origen, 86
Ortiz, Gaye, 91n216
Ostwalt, Conrad, 64–65, 68–69, 145–48, 190–92, 195

panentheism, 15
Pannenberg, Wolhart, 4–5, 17, 173, 176, 178–79
Paul, St., 171–74, 179, 186
Pelikan, Jaroslav, xvi, 14, 24, 67–68, 69n92
Pentecostal(ism), 12, 16, 24–25, 142, 179n116
Pierce, C.S., 64
Pinnock, Clark, 201
Plato, 33, 35, 79–80, 84, 150, 171
pneumatology, 3–4, 6, 11, 14–17, 72, 162
Price, Henry H., 103–6, 116, 124, 173
Prometheus, xiv

Quash, Ben, 11, 87–88

Raboteau, Albert, 22
Rahner, Karl, 43, 98
religion, xviii, 12, 16, 45, 51, 57–58, 61, 76, 105, 141, 145, 147, 159
resurrection, xiv, xvii, 25, 28, 31, 33, 34, 91, 113, 158, 166, 170, 172–75, 180–81, 205
revelation, xvii, 3–5, 7–10, 14, 18–20, 25, 27, 29, 52, 60, 63, 100, 155, 194, 201
Ricoeur, Paul, 16n74, 67, 87, 134, 160, 202, 205
Roberts, Vaughn, 6, 19, 59–60, 130, 132, 155
Roth, Robert, xv, 42
Rush, Ormond, 67, 71–72, 201

Russell, Jeffrey Burton, 29, 40, 42–43, 112–13, 117–18, 121–22, 126n10, 146, 149–50, 160n18
Rusted Root, 204

sacramental(ism), 6, 19, 25, 35, 59–60
Saliers, Don, 130–31, 139–40, 152
Scharen, Christian, 149
Schleiermacher, Friedrich, 15–18, 100, 154
Scriptures, 3, 8, 10–11, 22–23, 45, 66
Schwarz, Hans, 70n95
Scott, Ridley, 166, 171, 173, 176, 179–82
Segal, Alan, xvi
sentimentality, 137–39, 142–44
Seymour, W.J., 23–24
Sherry, Patrick, xvi, 90, 153, 177
Simon, Ulrich, 195, 200
Smith, Gary Scott, 23n119, 40n66
Smith, James K.A., xvi, xvi, 5, 8n26, 17, 24–25, 47, 52, 59–60, 79, 97, 100, 109
Snyder, Bob, 131
Solomon, Robert C., 143–44
Soul, 109–10
South Park, 84
Spirit, Holy, xvii, xviii, 3, 6–8, 11–15, 18–20, 22, 24, 53, 65, 71–72, 146, 150, 162, 172, 181, 201–2
Spurgeon, Charles, 185
Steffler, Alva William, 83n173.
Stenger, Jon R., 161n25
Stephens, Mitchell, 48

Taliaferro, Charles, 51, 74n126
Taylor, Barry, 45n99–46, 50, 73, 76, 91n215, 97n4
Taylor, Charles, 64
television, xvi, 6n19, 59, 99, 148
The Book of Eli, 188, 195–96, 198
The Road, 188, 191–94, 198
The Tree of Life, 83
Theoderakopoulos, Elena, 166–67, 186
Thiel, John E., 113

Thiselton, Anthony C., xiv, xvi, 19n94, 29, 51, 52n141, 96n3, 97, 104, 178
Thorsen, Donald A.D., 12
Tillich, Paul, xiv, xv, 20, 56, 63, 77, 81, 116, 146–48, 192
Tolkien, J.R.R., 157
Toy Story 3, 96, 100–101, 121, 203
Tracy, David, 52, 56
transcendence 19, 25, 50, 58, 78, 98–99, 100–101, 118–19, 133, 142, 148, 152, 155, 162
trinitarian, xvii, 3–4, 15n65, 22, 109
The Simpsons, xvi
Tugwell, Simon, 30, 157, 170, 174, 175, 182

Vanhoozer, Kevin, 6
Veith, Gene Edward, 119
Viladesau, Richard, xvi, xvii, 63, 153
Virgil, xix, 164
Volf, Miroslav, xix, 124–28, 130

Wallace, Mark, 131n43, 202–3
Wall-E, 101, 188, 196–98
Walls, Jerry L., 91n214, 108–9, 124, 155, 174
Walters, Barbara, xv, xvi
Ward, Graham, 55, 58, 78n146, 81
Ward, Pete, 50
Ward, Vincent, 104–7, 110–11, 114–18, 120–21, 123
Weber, Max, 133, 177
Wesley, John, 12, 179n116
West, Cornel, 133–34
Westphal, Merold, 16n74, 67, 74–75, 104n37
What Dreams May Come, 89, 96, 98, 100, 104–7, 117, 121, 203
Wilberforce, William, 32
Wilken, Robert Louis, 33
Wood, Ralph, 99
Woolf, Virginia, 162
Wright, Melanie, 157
Wright, N.T., xiii, xviii, 28n1–29, 31–39, 53, 107–8, 170, 174, 184, 189
Wright, T.R., 158–60

Yong, Amos, 10n37, 11, 13, 61, 64, 180–82
Young, J.O., 74

Zaleski, Carol, 30, 34–37, 91n214, 106, 112–13
Zijderveld, Anton, 43
Žižek, Slavoj, 189–90
Zwingli, Ulrich, 140

www.ingramcontent.com/pod-product-compliance
Lightning Source LLC
Chambersburg PA
CBHW050441240426
43661CB00055B/2466